P9-CCW-714

THE BEAUTIFUL BERNESE MOUNTAIN DOGS

A Complete American Handbook

DIANE RUSS AND SHIRLE ROGERS

The Beautiful Bernese Mountain Dogs

Library of Congress Cataloging-in-Publication Data
Russ, Diane, 1931-
The beautiful Bernese mountain dogs: a complete American handbook / Diane Russ and Shirle Rogers.
p. cm.
Includes bibliographical references and index.
ISBN 0-931866-55-3
1. Bernese mountain dog. I. Rogers, Shirle, 1951- II. Title.
SF429.B47R87 1993
636.7'3—dc20 92-46693
CIP

Cover design by: *Dianne Borneman, Shadow Canyon Graphics, Evergreen, Colorado*
Text design and typography by: *Dianne Borneman, Shadow Canyon Graphics, Evergreen, Colorado*

Cover photograph: *Can. Am. Ch. Alpenblick's Alpine Alpenweide C.D., owned by P. and D. Harness, Brackendale, British Columbia. Photo copyright Linda Lindt Photography*

Back cover photographs: *Top, Friichnicht Barkley Sparkler CGC (Canine Good Citizen), TDI (certified Therapy Dog International), TT (temperament tested). "Barkley" also participates in carting, obedience, and agility. Photo copyright Faith A. Uridel. Bottom Left, Best in Show Am. Can. Ch. Gitana de Brye Am. Can. C.D., owned by Eve Ménégoz. Bottom Right, Raven Mountain Pandemonium v. Bev, CDX, clears the high jump. Photo copyright Melissa Bartlett.*

First Edition
3 4 5 6 7 8 9 0

Printed in the United States of America

CONTENTS

Dedicated to the
Decatur, Alabama Kennel Club
for their support,
and to
Zodiac's Fancy v. Sablemate,
who gave me twelve faithful and loving years.
Protector, top producer for her breed,
and giver of love.
January 1970-August 1981

ACKNOWLEDGEMENTS

Special thanks to all the members of the Decatur, Alabama Kennel Club for their unyielding support; to the Bernese Mountain Dog Club of America and the Bernese Mountain Dog Club of Canada for providing information and assistance; and to Alison Jaskiewicz, Records Chairperson for the BMDCA, and Annaliese Belknap, Historian, for supplying updates and checking facts.

Thanks also to Dianne Borneman for her excellent editorial assistance; and to Betty Jo McKinney and the staff at Alpine Publications for making this possible, for obtaining information and photographs during my husband's illness, and for providing guidance and support during the long and laborious process of putting a book together.

Ch. Halidom Davos v. Yodlerhof C.D., sire of forty-four champions, all-time top producer to date.
Breeder: Christina Ohlsen.

INTRODUCTION

This book brings together basic and specific knowledge about the Bernese Mountain Dog, including information on its history, development, personality, and training. You will learn what to look for when choosing a puppy, how to breed and whelp, how to groom and use grooming tools, and how to care for and feed this very special breed of dog. If you are a novice Bernese Mountain Dog owner, this book will help you grow in knowledge about the breed, and if you are an experienced breeder and exhibitor, you will find a depth of information to make this a valuable reference.

A lifetime of activity is open to you as the owner of a well-mannered Bernese Mountain Dog. In addition to conformation and obedience competition, you can participate in carting and therapy dog service. And, maybe the best of all, you can take a quiet walk in the woods or through the neighborhood with your friend for all seasons — the Bernese Mountain Dog.

FOREWORD

In February of 1970, an inquiry was received regarding the Sablemate "F" litter from a breeder of Labradors in Las Vegas. Some weeks later, following an exchange of several letters and more than a few telephone conversations, Zodiac's Fancy v. Sablemate flew to Nevada to become the foundation bitch for Diane Russ. I next saw Fancy in California at eleven years of age, still in good health and very much loved. From that beginning, the Buttonwillow line of Bernese was developed. Careful, thoughtful planning and true devotion to the breed have resulted in the production of many fine dogs.

Therefore, it was with real pleasure that I heard that Diane was preparing to write a book about the breed. There has long been a need for a book about Bernese and especially about their development in this country. Very little information has been available in the English language, other than what the Bernese Mountain Dog Club of America has generated through its very excellent periodicals. A British book published several years ago helped to fill the gap, but was focused on the development of the breed in the British Islands. Diane's insistence that this book should contain information gathered from a wide range of American breeders and fanciers serves to make it a particularly valuable tool, both in preserving our history and in acting as a guide for novice fanciers.

To be able to introduce to you Diane's great tribute to the breed and its breeders is a privilege I will long cherish.

— *Sylvia R. Howison*
"Sablemate"

Olympian's Rosebud Daphne CD. Owner, Lisa Allen; breeders, Eileen Brouck and Charles Kokenik.
Photo by Sandra Black.

ONE

Meet the Bernese Mountain Dog

Personality

One afternoon, some children were enjoying inner-tube rafting down a rocky offshoot of the Dungeneff River near Seattle, Washington. One nine-year-old girl was left behind as the other children arrived on shore, where a Bernese Mountain Dog named Bronson was waiting to greet them. Left alone on the water, the girl panicked and fell off of her inner tube into the roiling water. Her companions watched helplessly as she struggled in the water, but Bronson never hesitated. He leaped into the rough waters, swam to her, and grabbed hold of her clothes. Swimming strongly, he pulled the child to shore by the seat of her pants. But his Berner sense of duty was not yet satisfied. He also rescued a full-grown keeshond that was in the water. As a final victory, Bronson patrolled up and down the beach and would not allow any of the children to go back into the river.

The most amazing part of this story is that this Bernese Mountain Dog did not belong to any of the children whom he was protecting; in fact, none of the children knew him. He was just a big, friendly dog standing on the shore. But at least one family was very thankful that a big, tricolor dog was watching over a group of children that afternoon on the Dungeneff.

The Bernese Mountain Dog is one of the most widely enjoyable of the larger breeds. His personality combines devoted loyalty and affection with a wry sense of humor. The breed's temperament is rooted in its origins and duties as an all-purpose farmer's dog. He is versatile and capable of serving as a watchdog around the farm, as a cattle drover, as a companion for the alpine herdsman, and as an accomplished cart dog. This personality and attitude make him an excellent pet and companion for today as well. Although the Berner was used widely as a drover and draft dog in past decades in Switzerland, his main purpose today is as a companion. Many Bernese Mountain Dogs are shown in conformation and obedience competition. And, as in decades past, the Berner is still an excellent guard for home and family.

A true testament to his heritage as a farm dog, he lives easily and in harmony with other dogs and livestock. Dr. Scheidegger, one of the early promoters of the Berner in Switzerland, said of the breed:

> A "good dog" according to the farmer, is one that is watchful and alert without biting. He follows the master — at foot or between the rear wheels of the wagon — and does not run in freshly cultivated fields, defends his master if necessary, does not wander around and leaves the chickens and cats in peace.
>
> In mountainous regions [of Switzerland] the breed's qualities as a cattle guardian and cattle drover were valuable, but in the lowlands the Berner's ability to serve as a draft dog was more used. It is notable that many Berners performed all of these tasks often without special training.

The Bernese Mountain Dog is a loving, gracious member of the family. He is easygoing, quiet-natured, and affectionate. In fact, the Berner is a great "leaner." Males especially enjoy leaning against your legs in a warm, furry show of their love.

The breed is protective without being aggressive or shy. Some Berners tend to be aloof with strangers. Not to be confused with shyness, which is undesirable in any breed, aloof means that your Berner may not greet strangers warmly but will reserve his acceptance until he knows them better. He will lie quietly when company comes and watch them until he is comfortable with them. At that point, he may lean against them to show his approval. Away from home, the Berner is less reserved with strangers, but he still may not be wildly outgoing. Though not a common occurrence in Berners, any unwarranted aggression toward people, especially children or other dogs, is completely unacceptable. This tendency toward aloofness, however, does not pertain to every individual. Some Berners greet everyone with great flourish and a warm smile!

The Berner likes to be close to his family. He has a strong feeling for his territory and family. He is alert with guardian instincts and has an impressive voice but does not tend to be a barker. He possesses the rare combination of being sensible as well as protective.

The Bernese Mountain Dog is excellent with children. Even Berner puppies seem to recognize a child and generally will not rush, bump, or jump up; they approach and circle a child's feet, waiting for the child to make the first move. And when the Berner meets the occasional abusive child, he will walk away rather than be aggressive. This gentle, tolerant nature also makes him a prospective pet for the handicapped child or adult.

When one-year-old Tom Russ decided to explore the world of his Las Vegas neighborhood after the back gate was accidentally left open, no one knew it but the family dog — a six-month-old Bernese Mountain Dog named Fancy. Fancy followed him into a neighbor's yard and circled the toddler protectively. When Mom received a call from the neighbor, she was surprised to hear, "Your baby is in my front yard, and your dog is circling him and won't let me near him." Fancy was indeed circling Tom protectively. Fancy never growled or acted aggressively but nevertheless kept herself between Tom and the unfamiliar woman the entire time.

The Bernese Mountain Dog does not do well

Berners have a great sense of humor. *Art by Janet Wissman.*

Do I know you? A Berner is aloof and careful until he knows you. Ch. Yodler's Konig v. Bernerhof CD, owned by Suzanne Hostetter.

when isolated from people and activity. When left in a kennel for long periods, even the most even-tempered Berner may become shy. It is very important to get your Berner out and about and expose him to different sights, sounds, and people, because isolation intensifies any tendency toward shyness. Above all, he is a dog that thrives on being with his family and on taking part in anything that they do.

The Berner is a dog that nearly any family can enjoy. He is intelligent and quickly learns words and phrases. He will respond in ways that may surprise you, often replying with a soft, "purring" growl or yodel, almost seeming to talk to you. Because of his quiet nature, he can live comfortably in large yards or apartments. One Berner lives on a fifty-three-foot boat, except when he's on shore leave to answer nature's call!

The Berner's need to attach to humans, and his sensitivity and strong will to serve, make him one of the most enjoyable breeds to have. Perhaps the only sad note is that you will not be able to have your Berner friend with you as long as you would like. His average life expectancy is from six to eight years, although some live to ten or eleven. Even so, the years that you do share with your Bernese Mountain Dog will provide you with warm companionship, love, and great pleasure.

Physical Characteristics

The Berner is a rugged dog of good size and medium length. He possesses a very shiny coat of jet black, rich russet, and clear white. Males stand twenty-five to twenty-seven and one-half inches at the shoulder and may weigh 90 to 130 pounds; bitches are allowed twenty-three to twenty-six inches of height and may weigh 80 to 100 pounds. For his size, the Berner is nonetheless quiet and does not require extensive exercise; he is truly a town-and-country breed.

Could we share? Ch. Yodler's Konig v. Bernerhof CD tries to make a deal.

In this photo taken in 1948 near Bern, Switzerland, a Berner displays droving skill.

Although the Berner is a large dog, he should not be clumsy; he should possess the speed and alertness to be a good drover along with the strength to perform his carting duties. The Berner is a free-moving, balanced dog whose best gait is a jaunty, relaxed trot. He is not a long-winded galloper or a speed demon and requires only a moderate amount of exercise. He is happy to do whatever you do — a bicycle tour of the neighborhood, a jog in the park, or a quiet walk.

Because of his size, you might think that the Berner is suited only for the out-of-doors and a large backyard. However, he is less active than many popular indoor breeds and, given adequate opportunity for exercise to keep him fit, he can adapt to living as a house dog or in a small yard. His primary desire is to be where you are and to be part of your life.

The other outstanding feature of the Berner, his medium-length, straight or slightly wavy coat, would seem to suit him only to colder climates similar to that of his Swiss homeland. However, appearances to the contrary, the Bernese Mountain Dog is not an exclusively cool-climate dog. There are Berners living in all the hot-weather areas of the United States, where their owners take no special care other than to observe the hot-weather precautions required for any other breed — free access to cool, clean water and shade (although he might appreciate air-conditioning now and then on a very hot day).

The Berner does shed, as do most dogs. However, the Berner's coat stays reasonably free of tangles and requires minimal grooming. A bonus is that most dirt or mud that collects on the hair dries and slips free, usually without any grooming, making the Bernese Mountain Dog much easier to keep well-groomed than many other "coated" breeds.

The Bernese Mountain Dog is beautiful and quiet and is easy to groom and keep clean. The adult Berner enjoys relaxing with the grownups or roughhousing with kids. And does he drool? Unequivocally, he does *not*!

It herds! It carts! It hunts? Valleyvu's Kelah v. Neufundland, owned by Brent and Gaileen Marsh, retrieves grouse.

Left: A Berner and her boy. Zodiac's Fancy v. Sablemate poses with a young Tom Russ.

Below: Overseer v. Buttonwillow illustrates that Berners can move with energy.

Ch. Alpenrose Farms Brando with owner/breeder Susan Hostetter, all "Swissed out."

TWO

Early Origin of the Breed

It All Began in Switzerland

The Bernese Mountain Dog originated in Switzerland, where the breed is known as the Berner Sennenhund. "Berner" refers to the canton of Bern, Switzerland; "Sennen" is Swiss for alpine herdsman; and "hund" means dog. Thus, Berner Sennenhund means "Bernese alpine herdsman's dog." In America, however, following the British precedent, the breed became known as the Bernese Mountain Dog.

The origin of the breed is clouded in obscurity. Many sources suggest that the breed stems from dogs brought into Switzerland by invading Roman armies. These dogs, known as Molossers, are thought to have served as the origin for the Saint Bernard as well as for the four Swiss Mountain Dog breeds — the Bernese Mountain Dog, the Greater Swiss Mountain Dog, the Appenzeller Sennenhund, and the Entlebucher Sennenhund — of which the Berner is best known in the United States. The Romans used the Molosser breeds for herding livestock and pulling loads in carts. In the geographical isolation of Switzerland, the Molossers are said to have developed into the modern Swiss Farm Dog or Swiss Mountain Dog.

This theory is based on a clay lamp found in the excavation of the old Roman military camp of Vindonissa in Switzerland. The lamp shows a bas-relief of a long-haired dog with an upraised tail that resembles a Berner-like dog, but the origin of the dog stamp is unknown; nor is it known what the bas-relief is supposed to represent.

However, this theory is disputed by others who argue that the dogs brought to Switzerland by the Romans do not seem to have been of one certain breed. Skeletons of dogs found in excavations of other Roman settlements in Switzerland indicate that the Roman dogs ranged in size from that of a Dachshund to that of a modern-day German Shepherd. The only sure fact that can be gleaned from the conflicting evidence is that dogs have been in Switzerland since 4000 B.C., and dogs of the size of Bernese Mountain Dogs date to as early as 1000 B.C. to 600 B.C.

No one knows just how old the Berner may be. Many believe that the breed is very old and that it may have developed solely in and around the canton of Bern. Berner enthusiasts will have to be satisfied with knowing that the Bernese Mountain Dog has been bred in its present form at least from the end of the nineteenth century from Bernese farm dogs whose origin, age, and evolution have been lost in the course of history.

Area in Switzerland where the Bernese Mountain Dog originated.

No written records are available of the development of the Swiss Farm Dogs until the Middle Ages, and even then, little written record exists of the common farm dogs. However, through art and some writings, it is known that nobles in the thirteenth century treasured their hunting and lap dogs and allowed no breeding between the lowly farmers' dogs and their prized hunting dogs and pets.

Tracing the development of the Bernese Mountain Dog through art, Professor Albert Heim, champion of the breed, and later Hans Raber, editor of *Hundesport*, the official publication of the Swiss Kennel Club, found that most paintings were of lap dogs and hunting dogs. However, a painting by Dutch artist Paulus Potter in 1651 shows a large, tricolor dog that strongly resembles a Bernese Mountain Dog. Paintings done about 1773 by Swiss painter Freudenberg show farm scenes also containing large, Berner-like, tricolor dogs. According to an article by Mary R. Dawson in the *Alpenhorn*, the official publication of the Bernese MountainDog Club of America, the dogs in these paintings are probably related to the modern Berner. Though they were not a distinct breed at that time, these dogs did exhibit color-pattern variations — "Barris" (dogs with almost no white, or "bare") and 'Blassis" ("blazies," referring to the blazed face and white chest) — that are seen in Berners today. Some of these farm dogs were also known as "Ringgis" for the white collar or "ring" around their necks.

Some of the best descriptions, however, of the early Bernese farm dogs were written between 1836 and 1850 by the great portrayer of Swiss farm life, Jeremias Gotthelf. In *Michael's Search for a Wife,* he describes the splendid dog Bari with the "power of a lion" and the "power of human understanding." Ringgi, a great, black dog as big as a yearling calf, accompanies the cranky old hermit Hagelhannes at his daily chores, and the dog Blässen protects the farmer's daughter from the unwelcome advances of the itinerant tinker or pot fixer. These scenes of seventeenth-century farm life portrayed by Gotthelf depict dogs whose use and personality are also characteristic of the modern Berner. No breed names existed at the time, and there is no description of Bari, Ringgi, or Blässen; therefore, the appearance of these big dogs is not known.

In paintings of Swiss farm life of the last two

Albert Heim, one of the principal promoters of the Bernese Mountain Dog.

centuries, however, great mastiff-like dogs with sturdy limbs and large heads with triangular, hanging ears and strong, high-carried tails accompany their masters. Hair length and color, however, are not consistent. All types of color and coat are represented — nearly white dogs with a few colored patches, yellow-and-white or reddish dogs with small white markings, and black dogs. Frequently, the dogs are tricolored, but the "Gelbbackler" (yellow cheeks, probably actually tan) and the "Vieräugige" (four-eyes), as the tricolor dogs with tan spots above each eye were called, are not any more common than the red or yellow dogs. More significant than any consistency in color is the similarity in type stamped on these dogs through their uses in daily farm chores of droving, drafting, and protecting the farmstead.

Historical events also played an important role in shaping the Swiss Farm Dog that would become the Bernese Mountain Dog. German settlers arrived in Switzerland between the eighth and eleventh centuries and were assigned lands in the alpine foothills of the Schwarzenburg Mountains by the nobles and the monasteries. Small villages connected by isolated farmsteads grew up to form widespread communities. The farmers in that area prospered in stark contrast to the impoverished farm folk of other nearby regions, and that wealth enabled them to keep large farm dogs.

The need for these large dogs was probably also influenced by historical events. Bernese state archives of the sixteenth century describe the constant complaints of the erstwhile immigrants concerning the steady flow of disenfranchised soldiers, beggars, and tramps through their lands. Entire families would knock on doors, begging for alms, which one was obliged to give for fear of retribution by theft, arson, or even fear of disease. Because of this situation, people wanted to know who came and went around the farm. Over several centuries, traits would be selected in the farm dog that would help to create a breed of dog that suited the needs of the isolated farmer.

His dog had to be large enough to be respected and needed to be an attentive guard dog that took part in all farm work and got along well with the other animals on the farm. This dog had to be able to recognize the boundaries of his farmstead and not stray beyond them. While he must be ready and able to defend the farm and its people against ill-meaning intruders, he must not bite indiscriminately. Though he should not be a fighter, he had to be bold and fearless. These, then, were the attributes that the farmers selected in their dogs.

In addition to the well-to-do farmers, the cowherds of the rich middle land around Bern were also affluent enough to own large farm dogs. The forebears of the Bernese Mountain Dog were herding dogs that were clearly tied to an industry linking cattle, cowherds, and lowland farmers. During the Middle Ages, in areas higher than 3,000 feet in elevation where farming was impossible most of the year, the nobles and monks let their cattle graze in the alpine meadows. They employed men and boys as cowherds to care for the herds and move them between lowland villages, where the milk was sold, and the high meadows, where the herds grazed. Eventually, these cowherds became independent herd owners who leased the alpine meadows from the nobles and monasteries. The cowherds came to be considered experts in cattle husbandry and milk and cheese production.

Between the valley farms and the cowherds, a close cooperation developed that benefited both sides. The farmers bought milk from the cowherds to produce cheese while the cows grazed the meadows through the spring and summer. In the winter, the cowherds took their herds and dogs to the valley to work for the farmers. The farmers sold the cowherds hay, feed, and wood, which were paid for with cash from the sale of milk and cheese, and the cows provided the farmers manure to fertilize their fields.

Dogs were indispensable to the cowherds; a good droving dog was necessary to keep the herd together on the long march between the lowland towns of the Emmental and the Gurnigel Alps. Their dogs drove stragglers back to the herd, gathered the herd together for milking, and kept wild animals away. In the course of time and nature, the cowherds' dogs and the farmers' dogs probably mated; therefore, it is not surprising that the modern Bernese Mountain Dog still has a strong droving instinct. In fact, the herding dogs and the farm dogs were often the same type of dog. It is because of this that the Berner later came to be assigned a place among the other tricolor Swiss dogs as an alpine herding dog (Sennenhund), a designation that encompasses both herding and guarding.

Later, when lowland farmers discovered that ordinary "valley milk" made cheese just as delicious as the good "alpine milk," the obligatory cooperation between seminomadic alpine herdsmen and the sedentary farmers of the early nineteenth century came to an end. Between 1830 and 1860, farmers built cheese factories and enlarged their herds. The cowherds lost their winter quarters and had to find other occupations, and the farmer's dog got a new duty. He was hitched to a small wagon and had to deliver the milk from the herds in the upland pastures to the cheese factory each morning and evening. The events and needs of the Swiss farm and dairy industries thus played the first role in shaping the size, traits, and personality of the modern Bernese Mountain Dog.

Formation of the Modern Bernese Mountain Dog in Switzerland

Many types of early Swiss Farm Dogs were brought together to produce the modern Bernese Mountain Dog. At the end of the nineteenth century, several types of farm dogs existed throughout Switzerland. Known by the regions where they had been developed, the Entlebucher and the Dürrbächler were bred for their utility to the Swiss farmer. They were numerous but were not recognized as a particular breed. They were known as the "ganz gewöhnliche Hunde" — the common dog, or the farm dog or butcher's dog.

In 1860, rail lines from the rest of Europe connected Switzerland to the continent, opening the country to tourism. At this time, the world became fascinated with the Saint Bernard. It was the first Swiss breed to become well known outside the country. Until the founding of the Swiss Canine Association (Schweizerische Kynologische Gesellschaft [SKG], or Swiss Kennel Club, in 1883, no reliable description of the Saint Bernard had even existed. Now, the canton of Bern became an export region for this alpine breed. Thousands of red-white and yellow-white dogs acquired sudden worth and a name. Leonburger Mastiffs and Newfoundlands, recognized in Switzerland, were crossed with the "Bernhardiners" (Saint Bernards), but the tricolor, common cowherd's dog came to be considered worthless and largely disappeared to the outlying farms as other breeeds gained fame and popularity in Switzerland. As a result, the tricolor farm dogs without a name were largely forgotten.

The Farm Dog Gets a Name

The Schwarzenburg region south of Bern was one of the later areas to be connected by rail and road to the rest of Switzerland and to the world beyond. Into this rough land of raw climate and

Three of the four Swiss Sennenhunde. From left to right, Greater Swiss Mountain Dog, Bernese Mountain Dog, and Entlebucher. *Photo by Esther Muller.*

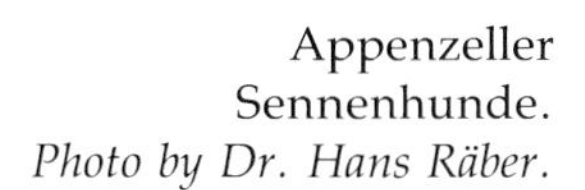

Appenzeller Sennenhunde. *Photo by Dr. Hans Räber.*

deep-cut watercourses, the beggars who had once plagued the affluent farmers had been driven. In time, they became makers and peddlers of home-made tools and baskets, and they became farmers. No dog dealers took the trouble to come here in search of dogs; therefore, the well-established, tricolor dog remained in isolation, preserving all the qualities that had made him the farmer's partner and helper. The farmer valued him as a strong draft dog, drover, and guardian of home, flock, and possessions. When they went to sell their wares, peddlers from the Ruschegg region even set the robust, tricolor dog to a cart in place of a horse. Not only were these big dogs kept for their practical ability but local superstition held that black dogs (especially those with the "split noses") kept evil spirits away.

Through this series of people and events, the Berner's ancestors came to be preserved in the isolated regions south of Bern. Unfortunately for the rest of Switzerland, and for the rest of the world, there was no prestige in owning a beggar's dog that didn't even have a name. But once again, events would change the fortunes of the breed that we know today as the Bernese Mountain Dog.

Also in the Schwarzenburg region lay the tiny community of Dürrbach, which would give its name to this breed of large, tricolor farm dogs. They would become known as Dürrbach dogs. Dürrbach at that time consisted of an inn and a farmhouse that had once been incorporated in the village Riggisberg. When a Saint Bernard breeder, Mr. Schumacher, wrote in 1860 of a "Riggisberg dog" of Saint Bernard stock and outstanding beauty and size, he was probably talking about a Berner-like dog. Over the next forty years, the Basel-Bern rail line passed through Dürrbach, and it became a regular mail station. Guests for a nearby spa at Gurnigelbad also traveled through Dürrbach, stopping to eat and exchange horses at the inn before continuing. Because the road through Dürrbach was the only good one in the area, any person thereabouts who dealt in cattle, cheese, or forest products spent time at the Dürrbach inn. Local farmers, cowherds, woodworkers, and peddlers for the outlying valleys gathered at the inn, accompanied by their dogs. The innkeeper, Mr. Hoffman, had similar dogs of his own that he used as house guardians and drovers. And so it came to be that the Berner butchers, milk dealers, crafts people, and gardeners came to that inn to get good draft dogs. They began calling them "Dürrbächler" or "Dürrbach" dogs, and the common farm dog that had been the anonymous mainstay of the Swiss agricultural community for centuries finally had a name.

The Dürrbächler Becomes a Breed

Around Bern, widely scattered breeders of purebred dogs came together relatively late. In 1899, a dog club called the Berna was founded. Finally, a forum was organized for breeders to discuss their thoughts and questions about breeding dogs. In 1902, the Berna sponsored a Swiss Dog Show at Ostermundigen. Three hundred and twenty dogs were exhibited, and in the "animal market" an article appeared about the Swiss "mountain" breeds by an editor named Tagmann. He wrote that the trial class for the Dürrbächler was well represented, and he characterized the Dürrbächler as playing a similar herding/guarding role in the canton of Bern as the Appenzeller Sennenhund did in its home canton of Appenzell. The difference, according to Tagmann, was that the Dürrbächler was larger and had long hair. Tagmann noted that the Dürrbächler was black and rust-red with reddish-yellow spots over the eyes like the Miniature Pinscher, and he mentioned that the breed took its name from Dürrbach, where it was still bred and valued. Tagmann believed that the Dürrbächler could be just as justified in its existence and as popular as any of the "blue-bloods" if an energetic breeder would take the time to promote the breed. There were three Dürrbächlers at the Ostermundigen show, all from the Bern area, but being shown did not automatically allow the breed to be placed in the Swiss stud books. Once again, the dog that would become the Bernese Mountain Dog was denied recognition in its native land.

Fritz Probst, coffeeshop owner and hunter, is recognized as the real initiator for recognition of the breed that until the early 1900s was unknown in Swiss dog circles. Living in Bern, he was an animal enthusiast, breeding hunting dogs; therefore, he joined the Berna and became acquainted with the issues of breeding purebred dogs discussed by that organization. Although he owned hunting dogs, he was also familiar with the tricolor Dürrbächler. Not only was he familiar with the breed from seeing individuals at their draft work along the paths in the Gurnigel and Gibellegge regions, but he met them often in the city doing their duty as cart dogs. In fact, he had liked the Dürrbächler since childhood.

In the Berna, Probst found the support to push for purebred status for the breed. At the International Dog Show held in Bern in 1904, the Berna sponsored a class for Swiss "shepherd dogs" (Schweizerishe Hirtenhunde), Appenzeller Sennenhunds, and Dürrbach dogs. This time, six Dürrbächlers were shown, all from Bern and the surrounding area except for Phylax, a Dürrbächler owned by a young veterinarian and German Shepherd breeder named Scheidegger from the town of Frutigen. Fritz Probst was the judge, and four prizes were awarded. The four winning dogs were placed in the 1907 Swiss stud book, signaling the breed's recognition by the Swiss Kennel Club.

This showing of the Dürrbächler gave the breed the impetus it needed to become recognized by dog enthusiasts as a pure breed. In Switzerland, not only did the Dürrbächlers attract the attention of the dog world, they were taken into the hearts of several dog enthusiasts who began breeding the dogs. These people were mainly well-acquainted manufacturers and businessmen from nearby Burgdorf and were already breeders of Saint Bernards, Fox Terriers, and Newfoundlands. They were familiar with breed clubs and ethical breeding practices and readily joined the Berna. They recognized the Dürrbächler as the dog that had earlier populated the area around Burgdorf and that had been highly prized by the local farmers, but that had become scarce, possibly due to mechanization and decline in use as well as to the sudden tremendous surge in the popularity of the Saint Bernard. They decided to purchase breeding stock and build the breed anew.

About 1904, Dr. Albert Heim, a dog-show judge, a professor of geology for the Swiss Federal Institute of Technology at Zürich, and an internationally known breeder of Newfoundlands, saw the Dürrbach dog for the first time. The Swiss Kennel Club had tried to push him to judge the "orphan" Appenzeller Sennenhund, but he warmed immediately to this other Swiss breed — the soon-to-be-named Berner Sennenhund. Heim was so impressed with the dogs that he offered a prize of ten francs for the best Dürrbächler at the next international show in Langenthal in 1905. However, no Dürrbach dogs appeared. Between 1905 and 1906, the "gentlemen of Burgdorf," manufacturers M. Schafroth, E. Heiniger, and E. Gunther, and businessman G. Mumenthaler bought their first breeding stock. Mumenthaler acquired his champion bitch Belline in Bern and through Tagmann found a suitable stud named Sultan. At Gerzensee, Schafroth found the bitch Prisca and in Reichenbach near Frutigen, the stud Bari, which Professor Heim would later characterize as one of the dogs truest to the type of the original Swiss Farm Dog.

At this same time, a breeder who would distinguish himself as an innovative collector of quality Dürrbach dogs entered the ranks of the first breeders of Dürrbächlers. He was Franz Schertenleib, wine dealer and builder of a spa called Rothohe. In 1892, Schertenleib had gone to Burgdorf to look for a type of dog that his father had described to him. In the Dürrbach region south of Bern, he found a dog that the old farmers in Burgdorf recognized fondly as a Gelbbackler (yellow cheeks — yellow actually meaning tan). Having found the type that he was seeking, Schertenleib bought more dogs from the Dürrbach area and then acquired individuals from the remote farm regions all around the canton of Bern.

In 1907, the Burgdorf breeders traveled with their Dürrbach dogs to a show in Lucerne, where Professor Heim had been assigned to judge the Sennenhunds. On the basis of what he learned from the exhibitors there, Heim published a detailed article about the Dürrbächler in the *Centralblatt für Jagd-und Hundliebhaber* (Central News for Hunting and Dog Lovers), the SKG's official publication at that time. There was only one opinion that Heim did not share with the new breeders, namely, that the true Dürrbach dog must have a split nose as he had seen on some of the exhibited dogs. The harelip gave the farmer's dog a truly fearsome appearance, which with his impressive voice was use-

Franz Schertenlieb, founder of the Bernese Mountain Dog in Switzerland.

ful for people who lived far from help and had to depend on their dog for warning and protection. However, Heim recognized that the fearsome appearance of the "spaltnase" or "split nose" would hinder acceptance of this gentle breed that was more aloof than fierce. The Dürrbächler breeders gave in to his arguments and renounced the breeding of dogs with split noses.

The Breed Becomes More Standardized

The Berner Sennenhund was lucky to have found in Albert Heim a promoter who, although he never bred the dogs himself, had a clear view of the breed and what it could be. From 1907 until his death, he judged Bernese Mountain Dogs and worked with the first breeders to define the essential character of the breed. It was a most inconsistent group that he found at the breed's beginnings as the Dürrbächler. From bitches only twenty-one inches tall, which appeared "too Appenzeller-like," to the twenty-eight-inch dog with a too-heavy head, all kinds of dogs appeared in the first Dürrbächler show classes. There were stocky, compact dogs and "Setter-like" dogs, and, most notably, there was great variation in color and markings. White collars, missing blazes, and pale yellow or generally washed-out colors were commonly seen in these first years.

With these inconsistencies to overcome, the first breeders of Dürrbächlers worked with fearless zeal to improve the breed, and they didn't hesitate to inbreed individuals with desired traits in order to firmly set those traits. Their success in standarizing the Dürrbächler could be seen from year to year. They worked to develop a sturdy dog of approximately twenty-five to twenty-seven inches in height for males and twenty-three to twenty-five and one-half inches for bitches, with great leniency in size in the beginning. The dog was to be rather stocky but not overdone in that respect. Heim always stressed that the Berner Sennenhund should not be "exaggerated," particularly the head.

Encouraged by positive opinion and pressure by Tagmann, the Burgdorf breeders drew together in November 1907 under the presidency of Fritz Probst to found the Swiss Dürrbach Club for the promotion of purebred Dürrbach dogs. In 1908, members of the Dürrbach Club were able to exhibit twenty-two Dürrbach dogs under Professor Heim at the International Jubilee Show celebrating the twenty-fifth anniversary of the founding of the Swiss Kennel Club. Half the dogs came from the breedings of the Burgdorf breeders, and the rest from other areas. With this event, the Dürrbach dog had found recognition and a place among the recognized breeds, and his continuation was assured.

The Name of the Breed Changes

At Langenthal, Heim suggested to the young Dürrbach Club that they name the breed as the other Swiss herdsman's dogs (Sennenhunde) were named — after the best-known geographic area where they were bred. Thus, the Dürrbach would be renamed "Berner Sennenhund" after the canton of Bern, the area where Burgdorf, Riggisberg, and Frutigen lay. This suggestion was met with vehement resistance by the Bernese and Burgdorf breeders. The name of their "darlings" was Dürrbach Dog, as it had been recognized at the "animal market" in 1902 when the breed had attended its first public showing. Finally, in 1913, they gave in to presure from the SKG. For the people of Bern, the breed is still known today as the Dürrbach Dog, but the dog that has made friends in Europe and elsewhere is known as the Berner Sennenhund, and in England, the United States, and Canada as the Bernese Mountain Dog.

The Breed Prospers Through Change

By 1911, the Swiss Bernese Sennenhund Club had forty members. In 1939, the SKG registered 129 dogs, and in 1948, the Schweizerische Klub für Berner Sennenhunde listed 336 Berner Sennenhunden (Bernese Mountain Dogs) in the registry. Dr. Heim lived to see the fruits of his labors ripen. In his book on the Berner, written about 1915, he had wished for the Berner to be protected, noticed, and increased in numbers. He was to live to see even more change in the Bernese Mountain Dog before his death in 1937.

The Berner began to lose vigor in the 1930s, and

Jerry Uhl's Priska vom Durrbach enjoys a quiet summer evening. Note the typical Berner sit. *Photo by Janet Wissman.*

by the early 1940s had, because of a small gene pool and incidental inbreeding, begun manifesting low fertility, inability of bitches to whelp naturally, and small litters that often had many stillborn puppies. Although the stud books had been closed for some time, some thought that new blood should be brought into the breed. An outcross to the Greater Swiss Mountain Dog had been done in the early 1900s but was apparently causing some puppies to be born with the short, harsh coat more reminiscent of the Greater Swiss than the longer, softer coat required in the Berner standard. Dr. Heim had much earlier agreed that admitting new blood in the form of the Newfoundland might restore vigor, size, and coat while maintaining the overall type of the Berner. The Newfoundland, a large, black water dog developed on the coast of Newfoundland, Canada, appeared to be of the same Mastiff stock as the Bernese Mountain Dog, namely, the Molosser. It was similar in body type and coat, although it was larger than the Berner.

Even though Dr. Heim was long deceased when the outcross occurred, a mating between a Berner bitch and a Newfoundland male did take place. According to Herta Janusevskis in her 1969 translation of the fiftieth anniversary book of the Schweizerische Klub für Sennenhunde, in 1948, the Newfoundland Pluto v. Erlengut, whether by accident or intent, leaped the hedge between himself and the Berner bitch Christine v. Lux, and in his "immense sympathy to the Berner Sennenhund" began the "new experiment." This mating produced Babette vom Schwarzwasserbachli, the dam of Christine v. Schwarzwasserbachli, who, in turn, produced the international champion Alex v. Angsdorf. Alex was the progenitor of the modern Bernese type.

Today, the goal of Swiss breeders is to produce

International Champion Alex v. Angstorf, progenitor of the modern Berner type.

Modern Swiss Berners at the 1979 Weltanstellung (World Exhibition) in Bern. S. Sollberger (middle) and Ch. Zwinger von Buchsischloessi with two progeny.

a robust, farm-type dog that is a lively, active, working dog. The most marked improvements since the early days have been in coat and color. Curly, short hair has almost disappeared. The modern Berner has a shining, medium-length coat of clear, well-defined colors without collars, "boots," or large neck spots, and the symmetry of the distinct broad blaze is generally present.

The Bernese Mountain Dog has kept many of the same qualities and behaviors that Jeremias Gotthelf observed and described in his time. Today, these dogs are suited to a larger community than the isolated farmsteads where they once lived, and a daily walk may replace the routes that they patrolled around the farm. While they may have a friendlier attitude toward strangers, they still keep each member of the family under their watch and follow attentively everything that happens at their modern "homestead."

The Bernese Mountain Dog has been exported to many countries since its official recognition in its native land. Currently in Switzerland, approximately 200 litters a year are produced, or about 800 puppies. Approximately 150 Berner puppies are exported yearly to European countries, the United States, Canada, South Africa, and South America.

AM/Can Ch. Deerpark Heartlight, 1988 National Specialty Winner.
Bred by Lisa Curtis and Denise Dean; owned by Denise Dean.

THREE

The Berner in the United States

Although the Bernese Mountain Dog was not recognized by the American Kennel Club until 1937, some Berners were brought into the country prior to that time. Arthur Hesser, a noted American judge and a German native, provided the information in this chapter in a 1977 letter to Berner fancier Dora Gruber.

In January 1926, farmer Isaac Shiess of Florence, Kansas, bought a bitch, Donna von der Rothohe, bred by Franz Schertenlieb, and a dog, Poincare von Sumiswald, bred by Herr Iseli. He wanted to register the dogs with the American Kennel Club (AKC) but was unable to do so because the breed was not recognized by the AKC. Even though Carl Wittwer, registrar of the Swiss stud book, made every effort to convince the American Kennel Club that the dogs were purebred, registry was still denied, and Shiess registered the dogs with the Swiss Kennel Club.

Poincare and Donna were bred and produced a litter of five puppies, born on May 26, 1926, which were also registered with the Swiss Kennel Club. Because the American Kennel Club would not register the Bernese Mountain Dog, no more Berners were bred in or imported into the United States until 1937, and there is no evidence that the breed was brought

Fridy v. Haslenbach, top bitch in Switzerland when purchased by Glen Shadow.

into the country prior to 1926 except for at least one picture of a farm boy in turn-of-the-century Nebraska with what appears to be a Berner puppy.

The Berner was recognized by the American Kennel Club on April 13, 1937, due to the efforts of Glen L. Shadow. The first two Berners registered were Fridy v. Haslenbach, a female, and Quell v. Tiergarten, a male, both owned by Glen L. Shadow. Shadow had wanted a Berner since the first grade, when he had seen an illustration in his reader of one pulling a milk cart. In an article in the January 1938 issue of *Western Kennel World*, Shadow wrote:

> In June, 1935 while recovering from an attack of influenza, I read an article published in the *American Kennel Gazette* written by Mrs. L. Egg-Leach of Winterthur, Switzerland about the Bernese Mountain Dog of the Swiss alps. I read this article some two or three times as this was a dog that I so much admired from the pictures showing the dogs drawing a milk cart in my first grade reader when I was a child.
>
> The childish desire to own some of these dogs was not completely abandoned, and while I was in France in 1918 and 1919, I had the opportunity of seeing some of these dogs, which rekindled this childhood fancy. Because financial circumstances did not permit me to buy or import these dogs at that time, it was necessary for me to abandon the idea as there were none to be had in the United States and no one had thought enough of this particular breed to import them.
>
> After reading Mrs. Egg-Leach's article, I took the liberty to write her and ask for further information regarding them, as well as some assistance in making a purchase. After some months of correspondence and untiring efforts on the part of Mrs. Egg-Leach, she succeeded in buying for me, on August 30, 1936, Fridy v. Haslenbach from Mr. Fritz Stalder, breeder. This was the best female dog in her breed in all of Europe. . . . On September 28, 1936, I forwarded draft to Mrs. Egg-Leach to purchase Quell v. Tiergarten (Felix, call name) from Mr. G. Walti. He was not the best to be had, as the owner of the best male refused to sell him at any price.

Therefore, in 1936, Glen Shadow was finally able to realize his dream of owning Bernese Mountain Dogs with the purchase of Fridy and Felix. The Shadows took the two grown Berners into their home in Rushton, Louisiana. The dogs were friendly but would not respond to any commands. Sometime later, Glen Shadow hired a man from Switzerland. The hiring was coincidence, but when the dogs heard him speak "their language" they were ecstatic. Within a year, however, the Swiss Berners had learned to respond to English as well.

The Berners withstood the heat of northwestern Louisiana and adapted themselves readily to their new home. They excited much interest in the public in general as Shadow exhibited them to an elementary school class studying Switzerland. The children and teachers were delighted with them and wanted to touch their beautiful, silky coats.

These two dogs were to be special to Glen Shadow in a significant way: in the fall of 1941, Fridy and Felix would save his life. On his farm in Rushton, Louisiana, while he was instructing farmhands, a ten-point buck that his younger brother, Hale, had raised from a fawn attacked him. He deflected the deer's first charge with a shovel that he was holding, but the second charge was straight on. He locked both arms around the great rack and was dashed to the ground repeatedly. One of the workers at the kennels saw the incident and released Fridy and Felix.

The Berners ran immediately to him, moving side by side. Just as they arrived at the scene, they looked at each other and, as if by plan and agreement, they parted, one taking the head, the other taking the flank of the angry buck. The deer broke off his attack and dragged the dogs to the lake, where they let go and returned to their master. The buck, later killed by the farmhands, dressed out at 160 pounds.

Shadow was taken to the hospital with a broken ankle, broken ribs, and a severely lacerated liver; he was not expected to live. But he recovered and lived another thirty years. Certainly, he owed those thirty years to Fridy and Felix as much as to the physician who treated him.

Glen Shadow later imported another male, Cedrico v. Allenluften, and for more than ten years, until 1949, he was the only breeder of AKC-registered Bernese Mountain Dogs.

During World War II, all importing of dogs into the United Statees ceased, but during 1949, 1950, and 1951, Bernese Mountian Dogs were imported from Switzerland by Robert M. Youngs, Stewart G. Mayse, and Yvonne Auer. After 1954, there was a moderate increase in the numbers of Berners in this country. A Swiss woman living in Vermont, Nelly Frey, bred a pair in 1959, and by 1962, AKC files listed Berners in widely differing areas of the United States. Dr. C. Mattingly of Louisiana and Dr. Judge M. Lyle of Texas owned them in the South. In the upper Midwest, Bishop W. W. Horstick and his daughter Mary Alice had been claimed by the handsome, tricolor dog. And in the Pacific Northwest, Mr. and Mrs. Charles Hutchins, Dr. and Mrs. Arthur Harberts, Mr. and Mrs. Harold Thompson, and Bea Knight were Berner enthusiasts. Bea Knight, already a well-known Saint Bernard breeder, appended her Sanctuary Woods Kennel name to Berners, and the breed began its rise to recognition in the show ring and in the hearts of everyone who met this easygoing working dog.

As Berners began to be shown, judges were unsure what to make of the rare breed, and reactions varied widely. Harold Howison was nearly thrown out of a dog show by George Foley of Foley Dog Shows; Foley thought that the Berner was a mutt. On the other end of the spectrum, one group judge approached the owner of Ultra v. Oberfeld and told him, "This is a beautiful dog, and I was very tempted to place him in group, but I have never seen one before and don't know what it should look like." This attitude on the part of judges, coupled with the lack of information on the breed, was frustrating for many early exhibitors. Bernese Mountain Dog owners were encouraged when Sanctuary Woods Black Knight placed fourth in the group at Riverside Kennel Club Show on November 6, 1966. Black Knight won the first three-point major in the breed and was later the first Bernese conformation champion in the United States. Berners began to make their mark in obedience competition, too, when Aya of Veralp, owned by W. W. and M. A. Horstick (later known as Shepherd's Patch Kennels), became the first Berner obedience title holder by completing a C. D. title.

Bea Knight established her Sanctuary Woods line of Berners with her imported bitch Gretel v. Langmoose and the Horsticks' Ultra v. Oberfeld. Out of this litter came Ch. Sanctuary Woods Black Lancer. Another important breeder of this time was Harold Thompson. He bred his imported bitch Bella v. Moosboden to Charles Hutchins's Bobi v. Bauernheim to begin the well-known Bella line. Bella's Clara (Bobi v. Bauernheim x Bella v. Moosboden), bred by the Thompsons, was the dam of Ch. Grand Yodeler of Teton Valley CDX, a dog that has greatly influenced the breed. As the beginning of Jim Brooks's Yodlerhof Kennels, "Yodel," together with Brooks's ardent desire to breed only the best Berners, produced foundation sires, such as Millicent Parliman's Ch. Halidom Davos v. Yodlerhof CD, who, in turn, produced more than fifty-four champions and left an indelible mark on the breed.

Another foundation breeder was Sylvia Howison of Sablemate Kennels. A longtime breeder of Dalmatians, she contributed much to the Berner breed by being the first to certify Berners clear of hip

Ch. Sanctuary Woods Copyright was well known in the early breeding programs. Breeder: Bea Knight.

Ch. Sanctuary Woods Landrover CD, an early Berner.

Sanctuary Woods Charm CD. Sire: Bella's Axel; dam: Gretel v. Langmoos. Breeder: Bea Knight.

Sanctuary Woods Black Lancer wins the first 3-point major in the breed, 1966. He was the first Bernese Mountain Dog conformation champion in the United States.

dysplasia with the Orthopedic Foundation for Animals (OFA), thereby bringing attention to the need for soundness as well as quality in the breed. Owned by Harold Howison, Sablemate's Ch. Wendy vd. Grasburg (OFA #1) was the first champion Berner to produce a champion in the United States. Sylvia produced many champions over the years, with a high percentage of dogs whose hips were certified by OFA. Not only a top breeder, Sylvia chaired the committee that developed the first revision of the Bernese Mountain Dog Standard.

Over the years, many dedicated people have come into the breed. Some, like Dr. Mary Dawson,

Ch. Grand Yodler of Teton Valley, CDX, owned by Jim Brooks, winning his first Group I in May 1974.

Ch. Sablemate Lancer of Vines, one of the early American Berners bred by Harold and Sylvia Howison.

Ch. Shelley von Muensterplatz, born in 1972 — quality even then. Breeder: Esther Mueller.

have served the breed by researching and writing about the Bernese Mountain Dog. The success of many in maintaining the breed is visible in the kennel names appearing in the winners' circles across the country and in the pages of the *Alpenhorn*.

Formation of the Bernese Mountain Dog Club of America

An organization devised to serve the interests of the breed, the Bernese Mountain Dog Club of America (BMDCA) came into existence in 1968, and its founding can be traced to the organizational skills and leadership of Carol Pyle of northern California. Introduced to the Bernese Mountain Dog by Bea Knight of Sanctuary Woods Kennels, Carol foresaw a need to bring together the still small number of widely scattered Berner owners and their dogs. She sent out letters to Bernese owners and received replies from thirty-three who were interested in membership. Those thirty-three also sent names of others who owned Berners or were interested in owning them. The thirty-three members owned approximately fifty Berners, most owning only one or two dogs, and those people and dogs were the beginning of today's BMDCA, which lists members in nearly every state and several foreign coutries.

The first elected officers of the club were Dr. Mary R. Dawson (president), Harold W. Howison (vice-president), F. M. Lockhart (treasurer), and Carol Pyle (secretary). The club established several objectives intended to promote and preserve the Bernese Mountain Dog in the United States.

Objective A as stated in the club's 1972 constitution, was to "do all possible to bring the natural qualities of the Bernese Mountain Dog (Berner Sennenhund) to perfection." The standard of perfection in structure and temperament was to be measured in the conformation and obedience rings, and members were exhorted further to maintain soundness in the breed by being aware of the occurrence of hip dysplasia in Berners. Members were encouraged to know the status of their dogs' hips and to plan breedings with that in mind.

Bella's Axel left his mark on the American breeding.

Gretel v. Langmoose, found in many early pedigrees. *Photo courtesy Carolyn Lockhart.*

Objective B called for the development of local Bernese Mountain Dog clubs, independent of the national club. The clubs must meet AKC's requirements for subsidiaries of a national breed club, and their role as required by the BMDCA was to organize events such as shows and matches and to serve as sponsor for a national specialty show if one was held in that area.

Objective C urged members to accept the AKC approved standard as the single standard for the breed and to abide by it. The next objective of the BMDCA was to protect and advance the interests of the breed while encouraging sportsmanlike com-

A very early gathering of northern California Berners (1968).

Above, right: Aya of Verlop CD, owned by W.W. and M.A. Horstick of Shepherd's Patch Kennel. She was the first Berner to earn an AKC obedience title, June 1962.

Right: A class is judged at Bernfest I.

Below: Diane Russ and five-month-old Zodiac's Fancy v. Sablemate at Bernfest I. It's Fancy's first show, and she's not impressed!

petition at dog shows and active participation in showing. At that time few Berners were being shown and no specialty shows were being held.

Objective D requested the club to protect and advance the interests of the breed and to encourage participation and sportsmanlike competition in dog shows.

The final objective was for clubs to conduct sanctioned matches, specialty shows, and obedience trials under AKC rules. These objectives continue to guide the BMDCA today.

The first club-sponsored event was Bernerfest I, held July 3, 1970, at Burgess Park Community Center in Menlo Park, California. Called the First All-West Fun Match, it was the largest gathering of Berners up to that time. Sixteen dogs were present. Most of the people attending had never seen more than one or two Berners at one time, and

Ch. Darius of Rutherford taking Winner's Dog and Best of Winners, 1978 National Specialty. Breeder: Mrs. Joe Pike. Owner: Gerald Kara.

Ch. Gerta v. Buttonwillow and Ch. Afterberner v. Buttonwillow. Breeder: Diane Russ.

everyone was excited to see so many of the dogs in one place. And if the people were excited, the Berners were joyfully peaceable.

By the end of 1970, membership in the club had risen to 97, and 103 Berners were registered with the AKC. Glen Shadow would have been pleased to see how far his beloved breed had come.

Today, the BMDCA lists more than 700 members, and 1,502 individual Berners, and 320 litters were registered with the AKC in 1991. The club now hosts an annual specialty show. The 1992 show was in Colorado Springs, Colorado.

The BMDCA publishes a monthly newsletter, *The Alpenhorn*, and sponsors educational and other activities devoted to the breed. It also has established an international database to collect health information and vital statistics on the breed (see the appendices for addresses).

		Carlo vd Grandfeybrucke
	CACIB Astor v Chaindon	
		Diana v Ruegsbach
CH. ZYTA V NESSELACKER		
		Carlo vd Grandfeybrucke
	Miggi v Nesselacker	
		Anette v Nesselacker

Ch. Yodler's Windsong v. Bernerhof, bred by Diane Russ and Harriet Rector; owned by Diane Russ. Shown here going Winner's Bitch at the 1980 National Specialty to finish her championship.

National Specialty Winners, BMDCA

Year	Dog		Owner/Breeder
1976	BOB	Ch. Zyta V Nesselacker	Mary Dawson
	BOS	Ch. Goliath V Zinggen	James Curtiss
	HIT	Mon Plaisir's Executive Touch	Alan & Karen Farkas
	BIS	Jacob VonHeller of Jamars	Linda J. McCogell
1977	BOB	Ch. Alphorn's Copyright of Echo	D. G. & Gretchen Johnson
	BOS	Ch. Car-Mar's A-Miss V Copyright CD	Marty Lockhart
	HIT	Mt. Chalet's Unique V Epic	Robert & Margarte Lentz
	BIS	Alphorns Honey	Gretchen Johnson
1978	BOB	Ch. Alphorn's Copyright of Echo	D. G. & Gretchen Johnson
	BOS	Ch. Gina V Zinggen	Esther Mueller
	HIT	Broken Oaks Arjana	Gale Werth
	BIS	Cassandra Vombreiterweg	Deborah Acord
1979	BOB	Ch. Halidom Davos V Yodlerhof CD	Millicent Buchanan
	BOS	Ch. Martha's Teddy Bear CD	Sam & Martha Decker
	HIT	Taliesin Copy V Meadowrock	Diane Currie
	BIS	Sunnyhill's Kilo of Halidom	Sharon Kullman
1980	BOB	Ch. Ashley V Bernerliebe	Christina & Joel Ohlsen
	BOS	Ch. Doska V Yodlerhof	Judge & Mrs. Robert Ranger
	HIT	Bernfield's Astraea V Car-Mar	April & Ervin Rifenburg
	BIS	Gunther von Vogel	Gail Vogel
1981	BOB	Ch. Marens Ajax	Lori Jodar/Marcus & Janice Ahrens
	BOS	Ch. Broken Oaks Bergita CD, TD	Andrew& Marjorie Reho
	HIT	Haylin's Brigette Bardot	Dorothy Lademann & Linda Williams
	BIS	Baron Tobler Vombreiterweg	John & Diana Chichester
1982	BOB	Ch. Ashley V Bernerliebe CD	Christina & Joel Ohlsen
	BOS	Tails 'N Hock Tasha of Black Mt.	Deborah Mulvey
	HIT	Andare Bere Bahi Nori	Leslie & Margaret Baird
	BIS	Madchen Von Baren Graben	Leon & Harriet Gehorsam
1983	BOB	Ch. Ashley V Bernerliebe	Christina & Joel Ohlsen
	BOS	Ch. Taunas Lady Silvertip	Beverly Search
	HIT	Bernfield's Astra V Car Mar CDX	April & Ervin Rifenburg
	BIS	Arak's Bittersweet Beau	B & L Petersen
1984	BOB	Ch. Broken Oaks Dieter V Arjana	Gale Werth
	BOS	Ch. Roundtop's Abigail	Mary Jo & Mary Beth Thomson
	HIT	Walchwil Robin Hood	Kathleen Rundquist
	BIS	Shersan's Advance Warning	Robert & Carolyn Kinley
1985	BOB	Bigpaws Yoda	Susan Quinn
	BOS	Broken Oaks I-Ching	Gale Werth
	HIT	Dallybeck's Andrea Bella	Marjorie Reho
	BIS	Olympians Tital	Eileen Brouck

(continued on next page)

Esther Mueller and Ch. Gina v. Zinggen going BOS from the Vereran's class at the 1978 National Specialty.

1986	BOB	Ch. Shersan Chang O'Pace V Halidom CD	Robert & Carolyn Kinley
	BOS	Gitana De Braye	Eve Menegoz
	HIT	Bernfield's Astrea V Car Mar CDT	April & Ervin Rifenburg
	BIS	Gitana De Braye	Eve Menegoz
1987	BOB	Ch. Harlaquin's Thor the Bear	Gina Wyss
	BOS	Ch. Bornedale Puffin V Ledgewood	Leon Kozikowski & Kim Behrens
	HIT	Ch. Gruezi Patty Melt V Reuben	K. M., A. S. & W. W. Getzel
	BIS	Kinderhof's Sweet Cider	Nora Ettinger
1988	BOB	Ch. Deerpark Heartlight	Denise Dean/Lisa Curtis, Denise Dean
	BOS	Gitana De Braye	Eve Menegoz
	HIT	Sandusky's Brighteye Abigail	Deborah Hotze
	BIS	Happiness' Diamond in the Ruff	Karen & Peter Ward
1989	BOB	Ch. Alpenblick's Alpine Alpenweide CD	Philip & Donna Harness
	BOS	Ch. De-Li's Chase the Clouds	Lilian Ostermiller
	HIT	Zeder Hugle's Raleigh V Rolo CD	Ruth Prenosil
	BIS	Lake Haus Count Jim In	Mary Alice Eschweiler
1990	BOB	Ch. Heartlight's Baby Grand	Gail Vogel
	BOS	Ch. Fraulein Abigale De Miacis CD	Michael & Nancy Kepsel
	HIT	Brighteye Nelle Belle TD	Deborah Hotze
	BIS	Bon Mead's Potter V Bernbrae	Mark & Ann Milligan

(continued on page 31)

Ultra von Oberfeld
Ch. Sanctuary Wood's Black Knight
Gretel von Langmoos
Ch. Tryarr Alphorn Knight Echo
Ch. Hektor v Nesselacker
Ch. Tryarr Conspiratress
Bella's Clara
Ch. Alphorns Copyright of Echo
Ch. Klaus von Kiesenthal
Ch. Clara's Christopher
Bella's Clara
Ch. Tryarr Alphorn Brio
Ch. Sanctuary Wood's Black Knight
Alpstein's Knight Dream
Bonne Amie

CH. MARENS AJAX

Ultra v Oberfeld
Ch. Sanctuary Wood's Black Lancer
Gretel v Langmoos
Ch. Argon v Wil-Lancer
Fairplay's Hannibal
Ch. Wilhelmina v Neugebauer CDX
Dorli vd Rehweid
Ch. Clara's Blass CD
Wachter v Konradshaus
Arno vd Grasburg
Rita vd Grasburg
Bella's Clara
Bobi v Bauernheim
Bella's Albertine
Bella v Moosboden

Dani v Senseboden
Flocki v Laupenacker
Kilian v Enggistein
Ch. Flora v Nesselacker
Arno vd Grasburg
Bella's Albertine
Galan v Mattendorf
Tilla v Quellbach
Arno vd Grasburg
Bella's Albertine
Ultra von Oberfeld
Gretel v Langmoos
Casar v Oberbottigen
Ch. Wendy vd Grasburg

Dani v Senseboden
Flocki v Laupenacker
Egon v Schwandelirain
Heidi v Altentorn
Goliath v Dursrutti
Anita v Burgholzli

CACIB Alex v Angstorf
Priska vd Grasburg

Ch. Maximilian v Nesselacker
Chlaus v Forst
Dina v Zielackerhof
Arlette v Zielackerhof
Ch. Wyemedes Luron Bruce
Ch. Sanctuary Wood's Black Lancer
Ch. Argon v Wil-Lancer
Ch. Wilhelmina v Neugebauer CDX
Wyemedes Sablemate Siren
Casar v Oberbottigen
Ch. Wyemedes Marta v Sablemate
Ch. Wendy vd Grasburg

CH. BROKEN OAKS DIETER V ARJANA

Ch. Sanctuary Wood's Black Knight
Ch. Tryarr Alphorn Knight Echo
Ch. Tryarr Conspiratress
Ch. Alphorns Copyright of Echo
Ch. Clara's Christopher
Ch. Tryarr Alphorn Brio
Alpsteins Knight Dream
Ch. Broken Oaks Arjana
Porthos La Vaux
Ch. Beatus vd Froburg
Era von Chaindon
Ch. Mon Plaisirs Shady Lady CDX
Ch. Sanctuary Wood's Gordo
Mon Plaisirs Enchantress
Mon Plaisirs La Reine Royale

Adam v Dahlihubel
Centa v Schneggenberg

Ultra v Oberfeld
Gretel v Langmoos
Fairplay's Hannibal
Dorli vd Rehweid
Chlaus v Forst
Zitta v Oberbottigen
Wachter v Konradhaus
Rita vd Grasburg
Ultra von Oberfeld
Gretel v Langmoos
Ch. Hektor v Nesselacker
Bella's Clara
Ch. Klaus v Kiesenthal
Bella's Clara
Ch. Sanctuary Wood's Black Knight
Bonne Amie
CACIB Astor v Chaindon
Anita v Blasenwald
Bari vd Taubenfluh
Bella v Chaindon

National Specialty Winners, BMDCA (continued from page 29)

Year	Dog	Owner/Breeder
1991	BOB Ch. Donar V Mutschen	Hans & JoDee Hauser
	BOS Ch. Shersan's Advanced Warning	Robert & Carolyn Kinley
	HIT Ch. Zeder Hugle's Raleigh V Rolo CDXTD	Ruth Prenosil
	BIS Cita V Sagispicher	Kim Behrens
1992	BOB Ch. Swiss Stars Blue Baron	Bin & Bobbie Hefner Michele Reed
	BOS Cita V. Sagespicher	Marianne Eiss & Kim Behrens
	HIT Ch. Swiss Star's Nitro Whatagas TD	Barbara Hefner & April Rifenburg
	BIS Ltng Ridge Ilsa of Lksedge	John & Nancy Miniter Mary & Walter Townson
	BIF Ledgewood's High Opinion	Kim & Kelley Behrens Kim Behrens

BOB: Best of Breed; BOS: Best of Opposite Sex; HIT: High in Trial; SW: Sweepstakes Winner; BIS: Best in Sweepstakes; BIF: Best in Futurity

Ch. Tauna's Lady Silvertip, top conformation bitch for 1983 and Best of Opposite Sex at the 1983 National Specialty. Owner: Bev Search. Breeder: Jim Smalley.

Iwil v Silvana

Can. Ch. Bari v Nydegghoger

Rosi v Nydegghoger

AM/CAN CH. BIGPAWS YODA

Bari vd Taubenfluh

Ch. Fino v Chaindon

Bella v Chaindon

Ch. Valleyvus Mutz

Ch. Argon v Wil-Lancer

Heidi v Gartenhugel

Blitzen

Ch. Kala Vombreiterweg

Ch. Clara's Christopher

Ch. Kusters Jocko of J'Bar

Alpsteins Knight Bell

Ch. Leisel Vombreiterweg

Ch. Sablemate Basko Vom

Ch. Ms Fireball Vombreiterweg

Ch. Wyemedes Heidi Vombreiterweg

Ch. Alex v Bauernheim
Eve vd Klosteralp
Carlo vd Grandfeybrucke
Diana v Ruegsbach
Ch. Sanctuary Wood's Black Lancer
Ch. Wilhelmina v Neugebauer CDX
Donar v Zielackerhof
Ch. Halidom Kela CD
Ch. Klaus v Kiesenthal
Bella's Clara
Ch. Sanctuary Wood's Black Night
Ch. Tabea of Altadena
Ch. Sablemate Machs Na
Ch. Sablemate Impossible Dream
Ch. Argon v Wil-Lancer
Ch. Caesars Legacy for Wyemede

Kilian v Enggistein

Ch. Hektor v Nesselacker

Ch. Flora v Nesselacker

Ch. Grand Yodler of Teton Valley CDX

Arno vd Grasburg

Bella's Clara

Bella's Albertine

Ch. Halidom Davos v Yodlerhof CD

Bari vd Taubenfluh

Sultan v Dursrutti

Kandi v Dursrutti

Ch. Ginger v Senseboden

Galan v Mättenhof

Diana v Moosseedorf

Kaya v Moosseedorf

Grey v Waldacker
Gunda v Nesselacker
Wachter v Konradshaus
Rita vd Grasburg
Bobi v Bauernheim
Bella v Moosboden
Ch. Alex v Bauernheim
Eve vd Klosteralp

Ch. York v Fluhwald
Cita v Balmhof
Ch. Alex v Bauernheim
Cilla v Ranfluh

CH. SHERSAN CHANG O PACE V HALIDOM CD

Chlaus v Forst

Donar v Zielackerhof

Arlette v Zielackerhof

Ch. Halidom Kelas Senn CDE

Dumpy v Tiefenhof

Ch. Halidom Kela CD

Zusi v Grunhag

Ch. Halidom Kali v Muensterplatz CD

Galen v Mättendorf

Ch. Klaus v Kiesenthal

Tilla v Quellbach

Vreni von Muensterplatz

Arno vd Grasburg

Bella's Clara

Bella's Albertine

Ch. York v Flühwald
Cita v Balmhof

Wachter v Konradshaus
Rita vd Grasburg
Bobi v Bauernheim
Bella v Moosboden

The 1985 BMDCA National Specialty Stud Dog Class Winners (left to right): Can. Ch. Bari v. Nydegghoger TT, Can. Am. Ch. Bigpaw's Yoda, and Can. Ch. Bigpaw's Beauregard.

					Ch. York v Flühwald
				Galan v Mättenhof	
					Cita v Balmhof
			Ch. Edo v Moosseedorf		
					Ch. Alex v Bauerheim
				Kaya v Moosseedorf	
					Cilla v Ranflüh
		Ch. Pikes Siegfried v Edo			
					CACIB Zorro v Mühlstein
				Bruno v Bauernheim	
					Madi v Mujnnenberg
			Christine vd Speichergasse		
					Dasso v Schurberg
				Bella v Barenhof	
					Setna v Stygli
	Ch. Pikes Harpo J Andrew				
				Wachter v Konradshaus	
			Arno vd Grasburg		
					CACIB Alex v Angstorf
				Rita vd Grasburg	
					Priska vd Grasburg
		Ch. Bellas Albertine Faymie			
				Bobi v Bauernheim	
			Bella's Albertine		
				Bella v Moosboden	
CH. ALPENBLICKS ALPINE ALPENWEIDE CD					
					Ch. Sablemate Basko Vom
				Ch. Sir Bruno Vombreiterweg	
					Ch. Wyemedes Heidi Vombreiterweg
			Valleyvus Bytown Barnabas		
					Ch. Argon v Wil-Lancer
				Valleyvus Heidi v Gartenhugel	
					Blitzen
		Valleyvus Beorn Baron Adalwin			
				Baron de la Baumez	
					Gittane de Chavannes
			Liesel de Chavannes		
					Marquis de Battassiaux
				Gittane de Chavannes	
					Kathe de Rappenfluh
	Ch. Alpenweides Alpha Heidi CDX				
					Casar v Oberbottigen
				Ch. Sablemate Machs Na	
					Ch. Wendy vd Grasburg
			Ch. Sablemate Basko Vom		
					Fairplays Hannibal
				Ch. Sablemate Impossible Dream	
					Bella's Angelique
		Vombreiterweg Lady Elsa			
					Ch. Sanctuary Wood's Malibu
				Noels v Raulph	
					Ch. Christines Noel
			Ch. Debonhofs Bisschen Gidget		
					Ch. Sablemate Basko Vom
				Ch. Heidis Gidget Vombreiterweg	
					Ch. Wyemedes Heidi Vombreiterweg

Ch. Donar v. Mutschen,
1991 National Specialty Winner.

Ch. Goliath v. Zinggen shown taking the working group in 1976. Owner: James Curtiss.

Ch. Marens Ajax, 1981 National Specialty Winner. Owner: Lori Jodar. Breeders: Marcus and Janice Ahrens.

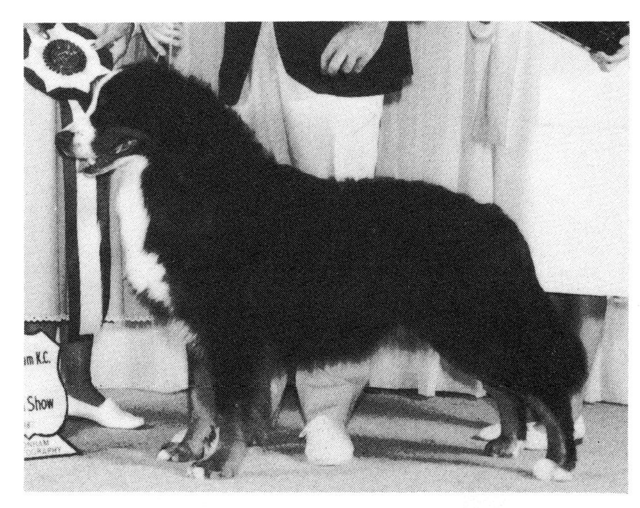

1987 National Specialty Winner Can/Am Ch. Harlaquins Thor the Bear. Breeder: Kim Kilroy. Owner: Ginna Wyss.

Right: Ch. Heartlights Baby Grand, 1990 National Specialty Winner. Owner: Gail Vogel.

International and German champion Berri Max von der Horlache, the first German Berner to pass the Swiss breeding test. Max is owned by Prof. Dr. Bernd Günter of Gaggenau-Freiolsheim, Germany.

Zodiac's Fancy v. Sablemate. *Photo by Pat Hatch*

Special delivery: A Deerpark puppy waits to give the postman a happy surprise.
Photo by Pat Hatch

Can. Ch. Donald vom Rotelbachtal, TT, HIC (top) and Can. Ch. Cliff vom Rotelbachtal HIC (below) in Jasper National Park. Owners: Dean and Tracy Ricard.

International Ch. Berri Max von der Horlache, the first German Berner to pass the Swiss breeding test. Sire: Brix v. Hochplateau; Dam: Asta v. Hofe Haub. Owner: Dr. Bernd Günter, West Germany.

Opposite Page: Ch. Shersan's Bernhugel Hot Gossip, one of the top producing bitches, with co-owner Carolyn Kinley.

Right: Am. Can. Ch. Deerpark Heartlight showing the conformation that made him a top contender. Breeder/owner: Denise Dean. *Carly photo*

Am. Can. Ch. Bigpaws Yoda winning BOB at the 1985 National Specialty. Owners: Martin Quinn and Susan Whiting. *Harkins photo*

This purebred Berner displays the extremely rare red coat color that can occur in the breed. The red color is a disqualification under the standard.

This puppy has the blue eye color that sometimes occurs in Berners and is a disqualification for showing.

The 1985 BMDCA National Specialty Stud Dog Class Winners (left to right): Can. Ch. Bari v. Nydegghoger TT, Can. Am. Ch. Bigpaw's Yoda, and Can. Ch. Bigpaw's Beauregard.

Can. Am. Ch. Alpenblick's Alpine Alpenweide, C.D., winning BOB at the 1989 National Specialty. Owners: Philip and Donna Harness, Canada.
Kohler photo

A Deerpark litter doing time on the woodpile. *Photo by Pat Hatch*

FOUR

The Berner in Other Lands

After a shaky start, the Bernese Mountain Dog prospers again in its native Switzerland. The Berner is also popular in Sweden, Denmark, and Germany, which all have national clubs for the breed that in those countries is known as the Berner Sennenhund.

In Switzerland, the breed association rigidly controls breeding. Only six puppies are allowed to live out of each litter, and only two of the six can be bitches. A representative of the Schweizer Klub für Berner Sennenhunde (SKBS) visits the litter and chooses the puppies to be kept and registered.

In Germany, Berners are part of the Schweizer Sennenhund Verein für Deutschland, which includes all four Swiss mountain breeds — the Greater Swiss, the Berner, the Entlebücher, and the Appenzeller.

The Berner in Great Britain

The Berner was introduced in Great Britain in 1936, when two Samoyed breeders of long-standing reputation, Mrs. Patterson and Mrs. Perry, imported the three-year-old Swiss bitch Senta v. Sumiswald from

Ch. Erno v. Barenbuel, owned by Bev Search, Swiss import and top producer of American champions.

the kennels of Herr Iseli with the aid of the same Mrs. Egg-Leach who had helped Glen Shadow locate and purchase his two Berners. In 1937, Mrs. Perry imported five more dogs from Switzerland, one of which was in whelp and gave birth in quarantine. Mrs. Perry bred three more litters, and Major Stacey, who bought a dog and a bitch from her, produced one litter. These five litters were the extent of Berner activity in the British Isles before World War II. During the war, the Perrys, like most people, were unable to feed so many large dogs. Three were given to the army as mascots, and the others were dispersed to pet homes. The breed died out in England, and the Berner was not reintroduced in that country until 1969.

The new pioneer of Berners after they were reintroduced into Britain in 1969 was Mrs. Irene Creigh, a Mastiff breeder. She had imported a three-month-old male Berner and a one-year-old bitch after seeing a Berner in the background of a picture of a Mastiff. The new imports were bred during the nine-month quarantine necessitated by a rabies scare. Mrs. Coats, an English Setter breeder, bought Dora v. Brentenhoff while the bitch was in quarantine; thus, the first litter of Bernese in Great Britain since World War II carried Mrs. Coats's Nappa Kennel prefix. Dora produced two more litters for Mrs. Coats before she was given to the Guide Dogs for the Blind Association. One of Dora's daughters was the first Berner to work as a guide for the blind in Britain.

Oro de Coin Barre, the male imported by Mrs. Creigh, did much to popularize the breed in Britain by his handsome appearance. The breed was advanced further by Mrs. Lena Robbins when she purchased an Oro x Dora puppy. She developed the breed under her Tarncred Kennel name and bred some of the well-known present-day champions.

The next important dog on the scene was Mrs. Gray's Groll v. d. Leukenbeck. He came to England from Germany in 1971 with his owners, who were returning to Britain from military service. He was not used extensively as a stud, but he did leave two winning sons, Miecklesteine Black Benjamin and Tarncred Drummer.

Mrs. Heather Curtis, already well known for her Takawalk Old English Sheepdogs, contributed to the breed in England when she imported a male, Fox v. Grunenmatte. Although he had to be exhibited in the British version of the Miscellaneous classes, Fox won many admirers with his fabulous outgoing personality. Fox did not live to complete his championship, but he made his mark on the breed through his progeny.

The Berner in Canada

The Berner got its start in Canada in a remarkably similar way to how it was introduced in the United States. Ron Smith of Ontario, while visiting a Newfoundland kennel in 1973 with the intent of buying a Newfoundland, saw a Berner that Mrs. Cummings, the kennel owner, was showing. Smith was so impressed with the appearance and tempera-

Left: Am/Can Ch. Dallybecks Echo Jackson, a top contender for ninety-one honors. Owner: Bobbie Hefner. Breeder: Marjorie Reho.

Below: Left: Can. Ch. Bigpaws Beauregard, son; right: Can. Ch. Bari v. Nydegghoger, father. Owner: Ron Smith. Breeder: Arthur Stockli.

ment of the dog Hugo von Mattenhoff that within a year and a half he was the proud owner of "Blitzen," a Berner bitch bred by Grace Borgh. Once again, the striking appearance and gracious personality of the Berner had won a heart.

Smith spent a frustrating year and a half working to have the Bernese recognized by the Canadian Kennel Club (CKC). Two previous attempts had failed due to lack of dogs and lack of interest. The CKC requires a minimum of twenty-five dogs nationally represented in all provinces in order for a club to apply for recognition in the CKC.

Application was made to the CKC after enough dogs and interested people were found and after the papers from the countries of origin were submitted, along with registration applications for eleven dogs and five litters. Although the CKC adopted a "wait-and-see" attitude about the rare breed, Berner owners in Canada remained resolute and continued to work for the breed until it was recognized in May 1977. The Bernese Mountain

Agility test offered at the 1991 National Specialty.

Left: A boy and his puppy enjoy the 1991 National Specialty.

Below, left: 1991 Specialty Veterans Class Winner models European-style medallion award.

High in trial, 1991 National Specialty. Ch. Zeder Hugle's Raleigh v. Rolo CDX TD/Can CD, owned by Ruth Prenosil.

An early gathering of Canadian Berners and their owners in Ottawa, Ontario, 1979.

Dog Club of Canada (BMDCC) was formed in 1979 with fifty members. Marilyn Lister was elected the first president.

The breed has grown slowly but steadily in Canada. By 1990, a total of 746 Berners had been registered, and the Bernese Mountain Dog Club listed 150 members. There are, as yet, no regional clubs. The BMDCC holds a national specialty in a different province each year. With seven time zones spanning five thousand miles from east to west, coordination of a specialty show can present some unique problems.

Today, the club's major concern is education of both the breeder and the buying public. Like most Bernese clubs, the BMDCC is very concerned with cancer problems in the breed and is in the process of collecting data both independently and in conjunction with the U.S. club. Because specialties usually take place in conjunction with a cluster of two or more all-breed point shows, it is possible to finish a Canadian championship in just one weekend, depending, of course, on the size of the entry.

The 1991 top winners in conformation, as recorded by the BMDCC, were:

1. Ch. San Marco's No Question, owned by Dave and Stephanie Patterson.
2. Ch. Maximum Avalanche v Mt. Tops, owned by Madeline Knowles.
3. Ch. Belinda vom Spitalhof, owned by Dean and Tracy Ricard.

The top Berners in obedience in 1991 were:

1. Sandusky's Cetenis Paribus, CDX, owned by L. Komatsu-Galotti.
2. Sennenhof Housi-Koebi, CDX, owned by Paul Schuppli.
3. Pandabears Admeier Rutli, CDX, owned by Nancy Meir.

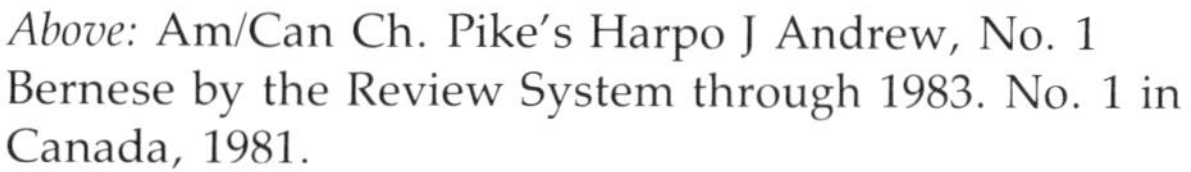

Above: Am/Can Ch. Pike's Harpo J Andrew, No. 1 Bernese by the Review System through 1983. No. 1 in Canada, 1981.
Above, right: Can. Ch. Bigpaws Beauregard, owned by Ron Smith.
Below: Ch. Xodi v. Grüenmatt.

Showing in Canada differs somewhat from AKC events. For example, any dog named Best of Breed or Best Puppy *must* appear in the group ring. Failure to do so may result in loss of the acquired points and/or CKC censure, whereas the AKC does not make group attendance mandatory for breed winners.

The top producers for Canadian-bred or owned dogs and bitches through April 1992 are listed in Tables 4-1 and 4-2.

Table 4-1
Top-Producing Dogs in Canada

Dog's Name	CH	OB	HC	Total
Ami v d Swiss Top Farms	5	6	39	50
Jaycy's Wyatt vom Hund See	0	1	38	39
Bari v Nydegghoger	7	8	16	31
Bigpaws Beauregard	4	3	18	25
Fino v Chaindon	5	2	12	19
Xodi v Grunenmatt	2	4	12	18
Harlaquin's Thor the Bear	3	1	10	14
Ben Vombreiterweg	5	4	4	13
Jaycy's Uri vom Hund See	0	0	13	13
Alpenblick's Alpine Alpenweide	2	1	9	12

Can/Am Ch. Alpenblick's Alpine Alpenweide has won BOB at American Specialty and Canadian Specialty. Owned by Philip and Donna Harness.

First Canadian and North American Tracking Dog Excellent Ch Yuna v. Grünenmatt CD TD TDX OFA. Breeder: Ernst Schlüchter. Owner: Eve Menegoz.

Table 4-2

Top-Producing Bitches in Canada

Dog's Name	CH	OB	HC	Total
Valleyvu's Heidi v Gartenhugl	7	5	12	24
Kala Vombreiterweg	5	2	5	12
Alpenweide's Alpha Heidi	5	2	3	10
Bigpaws Tara	4	1	4	9
Basel's April Image	3	0	6	9
Vombreiterweg's Lady Elsa	2	3	3	8
The Chaletsuizo's Ragamuffin	3	2	2	7
Chelsea v Bernerliebe	2	2	3	7
San Marco's Juliana	3	1	3	7

CH = Champions produced
OB = Companion Dogs produced
HC = Certified hips produced

Valleyvu's Heidi v. Gartenhugl. Owner: Ron Smith. Breeder: Grace Borgh.

Left to right: Am/Can Ch. Bigpaws Yoda and Can. Ch. Annette v.d. Swisstop Farm. Owners: Martin Quinn and Susan Whiting.

Below: OTCh. Chalet Suizo's Fleur, UD, Am CDX (Buffy), first Bernese to obtain Canadian and American Companion Dog Excellent. Am/Can Ch. Alpenweide's Alpha Heidi, Can/Am CDX (Heidi), first Bernese to be a dual champion and obtain Canadian and American CDX. These two were the first and only obedience brace, so far, to win the obedience class at two American Specialties. Both were owned by Coral and David Denis.

Table 4-3
Bernese Entries in Canada, 1990

Province or Territory	No. of Shows	Shows with BMD Entry	No. of Dogs Entered	Average Entry
British Columbia	102	42-41%	136	3.2
Alberta	68	15-22%	50	3.3
Saskatchewan	44	19-43%	44	2.3
Manitoba	37	2-5%	2.0	
Ontario	160	114-71%	397	3.5
Quebec	29	8-28%	19	2.4
New Brunswick	31	7-23%	7	1.0
Nova Scotia	26	12-46%	21	1.8
Prince Edward Island	5	0-0%	-	-
Newfoundland	10	10-100%	10	1.0
Yukon	5	0-0%	-	-
TOTAL:	517	229-44%	688	3.0

Bernese Mountain Dogs in Germany

As in many countries outside Switzerland, the Berner got a late start in Germany compared to other breeds. In 1911, Nanny and Frank Behrens met Dr. Albert Heim at a dog show in Munich. He was there to judge Newfoundlands, but when asked his opinion about which breed to purchase as a guard dog, he recommended a Berner. In the spring of 1911, the Behrens imported the Swiss male Senn v. Schlossgut from Franz Schertenleib, and in 1917, they bought a bitch, Regina v. Oberaargau, from Dr. Scheidegger. Immediately after World War I (January 8, 1919), they had their first litter — one male, one female. The Behrens's kennel name was "v. Sieberhaus."

The Behrens's activities on behalf of the Bernese Mountain Dog led to the founding of the German club for Swiss Sennenhunde on August 3, 1923. The Schweizer Sennenhund Verein für Deutschland (SSV), or Swiss Sennenhund Club of Germany, represents all four of the Swiss Mountain Dogs — the Berner, the Greater Swiss Mountain Dog, the Appenzeller, and the Entlebücher — and maintains the stud books for those breeds.

By 1933, seventeen Berner kennels were active with a total of 182 dogs registered. Today, the club has more than 2,000 members and registers approximately 200 litters every year, totaling nearly 1,000 puppies yearly in all four breeds. The Berner is the most popular of the Sennenhunde represented by the SSV, with slightly more than a thousand individual dogs and almost two hundred litters registered.

BREEDING BERNERS IN GERMANY

Breeding in Germany is very different than in America. In America, in general, quality in dogs is determined primarily by shows, whereas in Germany and throughout Europe, quality is established through a series of tests and evaluations before a dog ever enters the show ring. Dogs and bitches must pass an evaluation (Korung) of correctness of conformation and soundness of temperament before they can be bred.

In order to pass the Korung, a dog must be at least eighteen months of age, be X-rayed clear of hip dysplasia, and earn a grade of Sehr Gut (SG), or "very good," in two dog-show classes (one from the Jungendklasse puppy class and one from the Offene Klasse [open] class).

Korungen (breeding evaluations) are held about four times a year in different places in Germany. Potential breeding stock are judged by a panel of three specialist judges trained and appointed by the Schweizer Sennenhund-Verein (SSV) für Deutschland or the Swiss Sennenhund Club for Germany. The results of all breeding evaluations are published in the stud book along with photographs of each dog that has passed the evaluation. Included is a report on each dog with recommendations as to which strong and weak points should be observed when choosing the dog as a potential sire or dam. Only by passing the Korung can a German Berner be bred. Similar rules apply throughout Europe.

When a litter is whelped in Germany, a club (SSV) officer called the Zuchtwart (breed warden) comes to inspect and grade the litter and the kennel facilities. Since 1973, there have been no restrictions on how many puppies are allowed to live, although voluntary culling is practiced in the case of puppies that are severely faulty or badly mismarked. Puppies with noticeable faults get a stamp on their pedigrees marking them as disqualified for breeding, but they are still eligible for registration.

On the first visit, a few days after the birth of the litter, the Zuchtwart removes dewclaws and records the quality of the puppies. The kennel is checked for cleanliness and adequacy as a breeding facility. When the puppies are about seven weeks old, the Zuchtwart returns to again check the health and quality of the litter. He verifies that the puppies have received their vaccinations and tattoos them in their left ears.

All matings and subsequent litters are reported in the SSV's section of the monthly all-breed magazine, *Unser Rassehund* (Germany's version of the AKC *Gazette*), published by the Verein für Deutsche Hundewesen (VDH), or German Breeders' Association, the German equivalent of the American Kennel Club. Information given includes name of sire and dam of the litter, names and addresses of breeders, number and sex of puppies, hip dysplasia ratings, and titles of sire and dam, if any. In this way, much information about Berners in Germany is readily available to the public at large and represents an ongoing attempt to maintain quality in the breed.

International champion Donar v. Buchsischloessli and owner S. Sollberger take a win at a Swiss show.

Bernese Mountain Dogs in Switzerland

Exhibiting dogs in Europe is quite different than in America. The following story, taken from the April 1988 issue of the *Alpenhorn*, follows Professor Bernd Günter of Germany and his Berner, Max, through showing procedures at a Swiss show. Dr. Günter lets Max tell us about European showing.

> One day a friend suggested that B. G. take me to a dog show sometime. So, when I was about 15 months old, we went to our first show, in Bern, Switzerland. As practically all European shows require, we had to be there

Left to right: Entlebuch Rumpel, Berners "Ursli," Tina, and Xodi. Owner: Eve Menegoz.

at 8 a.m. and were not allowed to leave until 4 p.m.

About 70 or 80 BMDs were at the show. I was in a group called *Jugendklasse* (Juniors, JK, 9 to 18 months). Some were in the *Jüngstenklasse* (puppies, Jük, 6 to 9 months); most, however, were in the *Offene Klasse* (Open Class, OK, from 15 months). As always, one person judged the girls and another the boys, and boys and girls were judged at the same time in separate rings. The judges were — as all judges are in Germany and Switzerland — specialists. As always, they did not judge any breed other than us.

It was great to see so many pretty girls and handsome boys that day. I think that I was the only German there. I wore my comfortable round leather collar and leather leash, just like everyone else. B. G., like all of the other human folks, wore casual clothes, too. In Europe, we never dress up for shows. One or two of my cousins looked as though they had been shampooed the day before (which got them funny remarks and quite a bit of teasing from the others), but everyone else wore the natural Berner sheen.

When it was my turn, B. G. and I walked to the center of the ring. I stood there as still

Fraenzi v. Findlingsbrunnen and Astor v. Buchsischloessli with Sollberger granddaughter, Jacqueline.

Toni v. Burgistein hauls precious cargo at a well-attended agricultural exposition in Bern.

as I could, tail at ease, head up. B. G. even stepped away from me a bit, so that everyone could see me better. The judge first asked my age, and then for about 10 minutes looked me over carefully from the tip of my nose to the end of my tail. He had his hands all over me and even checked the tattoo number in my ear to verify my identity. Then I had to sit down, and B. G. showed him my teeth, for both bite and completeness. After that, we had to run around the ring several times to show how well we could move.

Finally, the judge dictated his critique (about a half-page long) to the ring secretary, who typed it right away. All that time B. G. and I were standing in the middle of the ring. On the report, which later we got to take home, I received an SG (sehr gut, or very good), the highest grade in the Juniors class. The other grades are G (gut, or good) and Gen (Genügend, or acceptable). These two grades actually disqualify a dog for breeding. Anyone can subscribe to all of the reports on all of the dogs in all of the shows, so the judges are pretty much subject to public control, and their judgements are really pretty objective.

After the judge had assessed everyone, those of us who had received an SG had to run round and round the ring in line while the judge watched us. He pulled out one after the other until only four of us were left. After some more running, the judge placed us, first through fourth. Then he justified his decision to the spectators, telling them what he particularly liked about each of us. I was mighty proud to be among the four best dogs in my first show in Bern.

Often at shows I saw one or two dogs that were exceptionally big and handsome, and had a classy air about them. They always drew the biggest audiences and got the most applause. When I asked B. G. why I couldn't be with them, he explained that they were very special dogs called champions, shown in a special class called Siegerklasse (Champion class, SK). They were either national (e.g., Swiss, German) or international champions, or both.

In Switzerland, only 4 shows are held each year; in Germany, about 20. As a result, entries of 15, 20, sometimes as many as 40 males in the Open class are not unusual. The Open class dogs range in age usually from 18 months to 6 or 7 years, making it fairly difficult for a young male to win.

The highest grade in the Open class is a V (vorzüglich, or excellent). From all of the V dogs, the judge places four. Entries at smaller shows may not be sufficient to give four dogs a V. Then the order may be V1, V2, V3, SG4. So the exhibitor really aims first at the V, then placement in the first four, and then, sweet thought, winning the class.

The dog who wins the Open class (OK) must (if he receives a V1) compete against the winner of the Champion class (SK). Very often only one champion is present. If more are entered, they must compete with one another for Best of Champion class (SKV1). Only if the OKV1 dog is chosen over the SKV1 dog, which is fairly unusual, may he be awarded, at the discretion of the judge, a CAC for national champion, or at internation shows a CACIB for international champion. If no champion is present, the judge again may award the CAC and/or CACIB to the OKV1 dog. The judge also may award a Reserve CAC/CACIB to the runnerup dog. Dogs and bitches are judged separately. Thus, it is always the Best of (either) Sex who receives the award.

OTCh Tanja v. Grünenmatt Am. CD (Ursli). Owner: Eve Menegoz; breeder: Ernst Schlüchter.

In order to become a national champion, a dog needs four CACs from three different specialist judges (in Switzerland, three CACs). To become an international champion, a dog must win four CACIBs at international shows (i.e., not regional shows or club specialties) under three different judges, in three different countries, one of which must be the home country of the dog's owner or the breed's country of origin. In either case (CAC or CACIB), at least one year must elapse between the first and the fourth award to qualify for the title.

The national clubs award the title of National Champion without much delay after the requirements are fulfilled. However, after the fourth CACIB is awarded up to a whole year may pass before the Fédération Cynologique Internationale (FCI) officially confers the title International Champion. Considering that a dog can earn a CAC or CACIB only from the Champion or Open class, or in exceptionally rare cases the Working class (obedience - title dogs), one can understand why dogs normally are at least 2 years old (usually much older) before they receive their first certificate. Obviously, then it is next to impossible for dogs to become champions before they are 3 to 4 years old. I, for example, received the title German Champion at 3½ years old and the title International Champion at 4½ years.

I think that currently, as at any time, only four or five German, two or three Swiss, and a half-dozen international champion BMDs are alive.

Ch. Ashley V Bernerliebe CDX, National Specialty Winner 1980, 1982, 1983. Breeders/owners: Joel and Christina Ohlsen.

FIVE

The Best of the Best

Bernese Mountain Dog owners can be proud of the many accomplishments of their breed given the short period of time in which the breed has had AKC recognition and the relatively small numbers of dogs registered.

New records continue to be set. For example, in 1992, Liskarn America Bound Jerry DD, Am. Can. CD, was the first Berner to earn a perfect 200 in obedience competition at the May 3 Kennebecasis Obedience Club Trial in New Brunswick. Ch. Cita V Sagispicher, owned by Kim Behrens, set records in conformation by going Best in Sweepstakes and Winner's Bitch from the six- to nine-month class at the 1991 BMDCA National Specialty. Her second show was the 1992 National Specialty, where she was Best of Winners and Best of Opposite Sex from the Open class. Two weeks later, she finished with a Best in Show at the Ladies' Dog Club in Massachusetts, May 30, 1992.

At the time this book was written, eight Berners have achieved the coveted All Breed Best in Show Award.

Some idea of the growth of the breed and the involvement of BMDCA members can be obtained by looking at statistics provided by the club. In 1981 only 44 Berners earned championships, and only 16 qualified for a Companion Dog (CD) degree. By 1991, 139 Berners were awarded championships, 50 earned CD degrees, 10 earned CDX degrees, 5 Utility degrees, 5 Tracking Dog degrees, 1 Tracking Dog Excellent degree, and 7 dogs earned the Novice Draft Dog title. In 1981 there were 104 litters and 450 individual Berners registered with the AKC. By 1991 those numbers had increased to 326 litters, 1,404 individual dogs. The 1992 registrations were 1,502 individuals — a healthy increase in popularity.

The BMDCA provided the following statistics for Bernese Mountain Dogs from 1937 through 1991:

	Total	**Males**	**Females**
Champions	1,339	639	700
Companion Dogs	529	233	296
Companion Dog Excellents	77	27	50
Utility Dog Degrees	14	5	9
Tracking Dog Titles	46	12	34
Tracking Dog Excellents	3	2	1
Novice Draft Dogs	7	3	4

The Bernese Mountain Dog Club of America tabulates the top winners and producers owned by BMDCA members each year. Top winning conformation dogs are listed in Table 5-1. Top producers of champion offspring are listed in Tables 5-2 and

Ch. Shersan Chang O'Pace v. Halidom CD, BOB, 1986 National Specialty Winner. Sire of twenty-six champions to date and the BMDCA top winning dog in 1984, 1985, and 1986. Owner: Carolyn Kinley. *Callea Photo.*

5-3. Breeders and fanciers will want to learn about the great producers and their offspring. Pedigrees of some of these dogs and bitches are also provided. The influence of a single stud dog can be phenomenal, but when you are planning to breed, look for a bitch with a strong background of top producers. A foundation bitch from a long line of top producing bitches can improve the odds for producing consistent quality and/or performance.

The Bernese Mountain Dog is just coming into its own in performance classes. The first BMDCA Novice Draft Dog competition was held in 1991. Seven dogs qualified for the title NDD. In 1992, Liskarm America Bound Jerry and Olympians Helen of Troy CD went on to qualify for the advanced, or Draft Dog (DD) title.

The lists and tables that follow contain title holders through March 1993.

BEST IN SHOW BERNESE MOUNTAIN DOGS
(published through March 1993)

Dog	Owner/Breeder
Ch Alphorn's Copyright of Echo (D)	Dr DG & Gretchen Johnson/owner
Ch Pike's Harpo J Andrew (D)	James Smalley/Mrs Joe Pike
Ch Shersan Chang O'Pace V Halidom CD (D)	Robert & Carolyn Kinley/Millicent Parliman
Ch Olly Von Tonisbach (D)	Umberto Guido/Fritz & Hilda Schaffer
Ch Rich's Halidom Charlemagne (D)	Richard Ponko/Millicent & George Parliman
Ch Bornedale Puffin V Ledgewood (B)	Kim Behrens/Susan & Michael MacWilliams
Ch Arthos October V Berndash (D)	Sharon Smith/Adele Miller & Richard Volpe
Ch De-Li's Standing Ovation (D)	Lilian Ostermiller/owner
Ch De-Li's Count Down (D)	Lilian Ostermiller/owner
Ch Octobers A Seekin (D)	Judith Cons & Sharon Smith/Sharon Smith
Ch Cita V Sagispicher (B)	Kim Behrens/Marianne Iff
Ch Shersan Jordache In Command (D)	Joanna Sherwin & Carolyn Kinley/ Carolyn Kinley & Patricia Dreisbach

TRACKING DOG EXCELLENT BERNESE MOUNTAIN DOGS
(published through March 1993)

Name (Sex)	Owner/Breeder
Viva's Graemlicher Bischof TDX (D)	Carolyn Gramlich/Carol Arntz
Sandusky's Timely Tabitha UDTX (B)	Michael & Cherie Bjond/Sandra Ongemach
Durbach Bravo Ziggy Stardust TDX (D)	Brenda Sanders/Jerry Uhl

UTILITY DOG BERNESE MOUNTAIN DOGS
(published through March 1993)

Name (Sex)	Owner/Breeder
Ch Dina De L'Armary UD (B)	Mary Alice Horstick/Jean Badertscher
Ch Felicidad's Calypso Of Aspen UD (B)	Kenneth Collier & Elizabeth Farnum/ Elizabeth & Eugene Farnum
Bernfield's Astrea V Car-Mar UD (B)	April & Ervin Rifenburg/Diana & George Tribukait
Elka's Brie Of Kemahtrail UDT (B)	Christopher & Katherine Milar/Janice Sommers
Ch Shersan Brite N Shining Star UD (B)	Jerry Hughes/Robert & Carolyn Kinley
Ch Dallybeck's Destry UD (D)	Bill Hammer/George Coulter & Marjorie Reho
Ch Kemahtrail's Brekke UD (B)	Katherine Milar & Janice Lebeuf/Janice Lebeuf
Rif's Turbo Charger UDT (D)	April Rifenburg/Lynda & Keith Zucca
Ch Arundel's Star Caper UD (B)	Paula Hopkins/Susan & Alan Brightman
Ch Ocooch Mt's Surefire Snowmont UD (D)	Gary & Mary Garbe/Darcy Cummings & Susan Tramp
Ch Ouija V Buttonwillow UD (D)	Elaine Newman/Diane & Ted Russ
Felicidad's Granville Grand UD (D)	Susan Ablon/Cheryl Summers & Phyllis Collier
Seacrest-Bev's Raven V Random UDT (B)	Patricia Losco/Gail & Kevin Whitesell
Sandusky's Mutadis Mutandis UD (B)	Kathleen Galotti & Lloyd Komatsu/ Sandra Ongemach
Sandusky's Timely Tabitha UDTX (B)	Michael & Cherie Bond/Sandra Ongemach
Sandusky's Brighteye Abigail UDT (B)	Deborah Hotze/Sandra Ongemach

NOVICE DRAFT DOG TITLE HOLDERS

Name (Sex, Date Title Published)	Owner/Breeder
Bluesky Matt Dillon V Summit CDX (D, 9/91)	Heun & Roth/Roth
Liskarn America Bound Jerry (D, 9/91)	Dombroski, Jaskiewicz & Mulvey/Bridges
Lupine's Little Tugboat CD (D, 9/91)	Cottle/Muick & Giangarra
Ch Nordstaaten's Emma CDX (B, 9/91)	Ballmer/Barney
Olympians Helen Of Troy CD (B, 9/91)	Allen/Brouck
Ch Sandusky's Promises Promises CD (B, 9/91)	Zipsie & Ongemach/Ongemach
Sudan Neuchatel V Halidom CD (B, 9/91)	Sanvido/Parliman
Bigpaws Banfield (D, 5/92)	Dick/Quinn
Elsa Undertow Of Mt Lore CD (B, 9/92)	Cottle/Bridge
Ch Olympians Oracle Of Delphi CD TD (B, 9/92)	Jaskiewicz & Brouck/Brouck
Ch Pinnacle's Andes V Juster CD (B, 5/92)	Jonas/Jonas
Ch Rosewood Benjamin Von Kayper CDX (D, 5/92)	Morrow & Stewart/Morrow
Schwarzeritter V Mooseberry CD (D, 9/92)	Huber/Elders
Sennenhof Ilaria CD (B, 9/92)	Barney/Menegoz
Ch Shersan's Must Be Magic CD (B, 9/92)	Sanvido & Kinley/Kinley & Dreisbach
Ch Sojourner Shambala CDX (B, 5/92)	Jonas & Armatys/Campbell
V Aiko Von Bernerliebe CDX (D, 5/92)	Benson/Byerly & Ohlsen

DRAFT DOG TITLE HOLDERS

Name (Sex, Date Title Published)	Owner/Breeder
Liskarn America Bound Jerry NDD (D, 9/92)	Dombroski, Jaskiewicz & Mulvey/Bridges
Olympians Helen Of Troy CD NDD (B, 9/92)	Allen/Brouck

Table 5-1
BMDCA TOP WINNING CONFORMATION DOGS AND BITCHES

Year	Dog (points earned)	Owner/Breeder
1976	Dog: Ch Alphorn's Copyright of Echo (1938) Bitch: Ch Zyta V Nesselacker (1133)	Dr DG & Gretchen Johnson/owner Mary Dawson/A Krauchi
1977	Dog: Ch Alphorn's Copyright of Echo (6420) Bitch: Ch Clara's Blass (211)	Dr DG & Gretchen Johnson/owner Marcus & Janice Ahrens
1978	Dog: Ch Alphorn's Copyright of Echo (404) Bitch: Ch Zyta V Nesselacker (56)	Dr DG & Gretchen Johnson/owner Mary Dawson/A Krauchi
1979	Dog: Ch Ashley V Bernerliebe (1953) Bitch: Ch Lady Rowena of White Cross (216)	Christina & Joel Ohlsen/owner Elizabeth Fuller/Dr V Buckley
1980	Dog: Ch Pike's Harpo J Andrew (2392) Bitch: Ch Vari Land Cruiser Miss CD (18)	James Smalley/Mrs Joe Pike Robert & Vicki Groh/ Valerie Weers & Richard Bankhead
1981	Dog: Ch Pike's Harpo J Andrew (3362) Bitch: Ch Broken Oaks Bergita CD TD (59)	James Smalley/Mrs Joe Pike Andrew & Marjorie Reho/Gale Werth
1982	Dog: Ch Pike's Harpo J Andrew (9561) Bitch: Ch Broken Oaks Bergita CDX TD (825)	James Smalley/ Mrs Joe Pike Andrew & Marjorie Reho/Gale Werth
1983	Dog: Ch Pike's Harpo J Andrew (6228) Bitch: Ch Madchen Von Barengraben (671)	James Smalley/ Mrs Joe Pike Harriet & Leon Gehorsam/Edward & Pamela Lloyd
1984	Dog: Ch Shersan Chang O'Pace V Halidom CD (14,167) Bitch: Ch Tauna's Lady Silvertip (627)	Robert & Carolyn Kinley/Millicent Parliman Beverly Search/James Smalley
1985	Dog: Ch Shersan Chang O'Pace V Halidom CD (24,170) Bitch: Ch Bigpaw's Brigitta Alpenweide CD (246)	Robert & Carolyn Kinley/Millicent Parliman Philip & Donna Harness/Susan Quinn
1986	Dog: Ch Shersan Chang O'Pace V Halidom CD Bitch: Ch Jungfrau's Afternoon Delight	Robert & Carolyn Kinley/Millicent Parliman Gretchen Johnson/David Harper
1987	Dog: Ch Deerpark Heartlight (2399) Bitch: Ch Bornedale Puffin V Ledgewood (7229)	Denise Dean/Lisa Curtis & Denise Dean Kim Behrens/Susan & Michael MacWilliams
1988	Dog: Ch Deerpark Heartlight (3437) Bitch: Ch Bornedale Puffin V Ledgewood (9732)	Denise Dean/Lisa Curtis & Denise Dean Kim Behrens/Susan & Michael MacWilliams
1989	Dog: Ch Arthos October V Berndash (6432) Bitch: Ch De-Li's Chase The Clouds (246)	Sharon Smith/Adele Miller & Richard Volpe Lillian Ostermiller/owner
1990	Dog: Ch De-Li's Standing Ovation (8748) Bitch: Ch Deerpark Double Play CD (599)	Lillian Ostermiller/owner Joanne Prellberg & Dan Clay/Denise Dean
1991	Dog: Ch De-Li's Standing Ovation Bitch: Ch Trilogy's Chang O Tempo	Lillian Ostermiller/owner Ian &Cynthia Valentine/Susan Tramp
1992	Dog: Ch. De-Li's Standing Ovation Bitch: Ch Cita V Sagispicher	Lillian Ostermiller/owner Kim Behrens/Marianne Iff

(Note: Winning dogs must be owned by BMDCA members)

Ch. Alphorns Copyright of Echo, 1977 National Specialty Winner. First Bernese in the United States to win an all-breed Best in Show (BIS). BMDCA top winning dog in 1976, 1977, and 1978, and sire of eleven champions. Owner/breeder/handler: Gretchen Johnson. Sired by Ch. Tryarr Alphorn Knight Echo. *Kloeber Photo.*

Ch. Zyta V Nesselacker, 1976 Specialty Winner and top winning bitch that same year. Owner: Mary Dawson.

Table 5-2
SIRES OF TEN OR MORE CHAMPIONS AS OF MARCH 1993

#Ch	Name of Sire (Stud Book Entry)	Owner/Breeder
44	Ch Halidom Davos V Yodlerhof CD (5/77)	Buchanan/Brooks
40	Ch Deerpark Heartlight (5/85)	Dean/Curtis & Dean
37	Ch De-Li's Foreign Touch (1/88)	Ostermiller/Ostermiller
32	Ch Shersan's Black Tie Required (8/86)	Kinley/Kinley
28	Ch Ashley V Bernerliebe (11/80)	Ohlsen/Ohlsen
26	Ch Shersan Chang O'Pace V Halidom CD (10/84)	Kinley/Buchanan
24	Ch Kuster's Jocko Of J Bar (4/76)	Kuster & Johnson/Alpstein Kennel
23	Ch Jaycy's Wyatt Vom Hund See (12/84)	Burney/Rutter
20	Ch Arthos October V Berndash (9/87)	S Smith/Miller & Volpe
19	Ch Alex Von Weissenburg (11/85)	Donohew/Schofer (Switz)
	Ch Ami VD Swiss Top Farm (5/82)	Townsend/Schaer (Can)
	Ch Broken Oaks Dieter V Arjana (5/83)	Werth/Werth
	Ch Majanco Languardo (2/79)	Pike/Lendon-Ludwig (UK)
18	Ch Pike's Chewbacca (9/80)	Kara/Pike
17	Ch De-Li's Standing Ovation (7/89)	Ostermiller/Ostermiller
15	Bev's Black Jack V BB (4/84)	Ostermiller/Burney & Westerlund
14	Ch Argon V Wil-Lancer (7/72)	Reisinger/O'Hagan
	Ch Dallybecks Echo Jackson (10/89)	Hefner/Reho
	Ch De-Li's Special Attraction (2/86)	Ostermiller/Ostermiller
	Ch Olly Von Tonisbach (5/84)	Guido/Schaffer (Switz)
	Ch Wyemede's Luron Bruce (5/79)	Buss/Crawford
12	Ch Alpenblick's Alpine Alpenweide (9/88)	Harness/Denis
	Ch Arak's Bittersweet Beau CD (9/85)	Peterson/Kara
	Ch Bev's Baron V Greybern (5/88)	Burney/Gray
	Ch Sablemate Basko Vom (3/73)	Townsend/Howison
	Ch Sablemate Diplomat (8/75)	Howison/Howison
11	Ch Alphorn's Copyright Of Echo (3/77)	Johnson/Johnson
	Ch Briel's Amorous Amos (7/81)	Edwards & Pickard/Pickard
	Ch Deerpark's Furious Fusion (4/84)	Dean/Dean & Bork
	Ch Donar V Mutschen (10/88)	Hauser/Schrode (Switz)
10	Ch Sanctuary Woods Black Lancer (7/68)	Knight/Knight
	Ch Shepherd's Patch Carl B (9/80)	Mulvey/Horstick

Kilian v Enggistein

Ch. Hektor v Nesselacker

Arthos v Waldacker

Grey v Waldacker

Nora v Bernetta

Ch. Flora v Nesselacker

Gunda v Nesselacker

Ch. Grand Yodler of Teton Valley CDX

Wachter v Konradshaus

Arno vd Grasburg

CACIB Alex v. Angstorf

Rita vd Grasburg

Priska vd Grasburg

Bella's Clara

Bobi v Bauernheim

Bella's Albertine

Bella v Moosboden

CH. HALIDOM DAVOS V YODLERHOF CD

Ch. Alex v Bauernheim

Bari vd Taubenfluh

Eve vd Klosteralp

Sultan v Dursrutti

Kandi v Dursrutti

Ch. Ginger v Senseboden

Astor du Devens

Ch. York v Flühwald

Erna v Nyffelhof

Galan v Mattenhof

Cita v Balmhof

Diana v Moosseedorf

Ch. Alex v Bauernheim

Kaya v Moosseedorf

Cilla v Ranfluh

Ch. Halidom Davos V Yodlerhof, CD, all-time top-producing sire, shown here winning the 1979 National Specialty. Owner: Penny Parliman. Breeder: Jim Brooks.

CH. DEERPARK HEARTLIGHT	Ch. Ashley v Bernerliebe CD	Ch. Galan v Senseboden	Sultan v Dursrutti	Bari vd Taubenfluh
				Ch. Alex v Bauernheim
				Eve vd Klosteralp
				Kandi v Dursrutti
			Diana v Moosseedorf	Galan v Mattenhof
				Ch. York v Fluhwald
				Cita v Balmhof
				Kaya v Moosseedorf
				Ch. Alex v Bauernheim
				Cilla v Ranfluh
		Ch. Dult Daphne v Yodlerhof CD	Ch. Grand Yodler of Teton Valley CDX	Ch. Hektor v Nesselacker
				Kilian v Enggistein
				Ch. Flora v Nesselacker
				Bella's Clara
				Arno vd Grasburg
				Bella's Albertine
			Ch. Ginger v Senseboden	Sultan v Dursrutti
				Bari vd Taubenfluh
				Kandi v Dursrutti
				Diana v Moosseedorf
				Galan v Mattenhof
				Kaya v Moosseedorf
	Deerpark Daisy	Ch. Gunther v Vogel CD	Ch. Halidom Davos v Yodlerhof CD	Ch. Grand Yodler of Teton Valley CDX
				Ch. Hektor v Nesselacker
				Bella's Clara
				Ch. Ginger v Senseboden
				Sultan v Dursrutti
				Diana v Moosseedorf
			Tetons Rocky Mountain Tundra	Ch. Jamars Black Nugget v Wymede
				Ch. Maximilian v Nesselacker
				Wyemedes Sablemate Siren
				Daisy Schneeglockshen
				Ch. Argon v Wil-Lancer
				Buffalo Bon Fromage
		Deerpark Bellesprit d'Azca	Bari de la Truche	Edor du Boiron
				Porthos La Vaux
				Edda v Aarbach
				Flora v Spitzenberg
				Sultan v Dursrutti
				Alma v Grunenmatt
			Ch. Deerpark Iner v Buttonwillow	Ch. Afterberner v Buttonwillow
				Panda Bear v Buttonwillow
				Zodiac's Fancy v Sablemate
				Yodlers Windsong v Bernerhof
				Ch. Grand Yodler of Teton Valley CDX
				Ch. Gerta v Buttonwillow

Am/Can Ch. Deerpark Heartlight, top winning dog in 1987 and 1988 and sire of forty champions to date.
Owner: Denise Dean.
Breeders: Lisa Curtis and Denise Dean.

CH. SHERSANS BLACK TIE REQUIRED

Parents	Grandparents	Great-grandparents	Great-great-grandparents	
Am & Can Ch. Shersan Chang O Pace v Halidom CD	Ch. Halidom Davos v Yodlerhof CD	Ch. Grand Yodler of Teton Valley CDX	Ch. Hektor v Nesselacker	Killian v Enggistein
				Flora v Nesselacker
			Bella's Clara	Arno vd Grasburg
				Bella's Albertine
		Ch. Ginger v Senseboden	Sultan v Dursrutti	Bari vd Taubenfluh
				Kandi v Dursrutti
			Diana v Moosseedorf	Galen v Mattenhof
				Kaya v Moosseedorf
	Ch. Halidom Kali v Muensterplatz CD	Ch. Halidom Kelas Senn	Donar v Zielackerhof	Chlaus v Forst
				Arlette v Zielackerhof
			Ch. Halidom Kela CD	Dumpy v Tiefenhof
				Zusi v Grunhag
		Vreni v Muensterplatz	Ch. Klaus v Kiesenthal	Galen v Mattenhof
				Tilla v Quellbach
			Bella's Clara	Arno vd Grasburg
				Bella's Albertine
Ch. Halidom Keri	Bari les Sommetres	Hako de Chaindon	Porthos la Vauz	CACIB Astor v Chaindon
				Anita v Blasenwald
			Bella v Chaindon	Carlo vd Grandfeybrucke
				Diana v Ruegsbach
		Cybelle les Sommetres	Arko de la Capite	Ares du Bonheyr
				Bety de Trelex
			Kathi Schneggenberg	Alex v Chaindon
				Gabi Schneggenberg
	Ch. Halidom Kara v Davos CD	Ch. Halidom Davos v Yodlerhof CD	Ch. Grand Yodler of Teton Valley CDX	Ch. Hektor v Nesselacker
				Bella's Clara
			Ch. Ginger v Senseboden	Sultan v Dursrutti
				Diana v Moosseedorf
		Ch. Halidom Kali v Muensterplatz CD	Ch. Halidom Kelas Senn CD	Donar v Zielackerhof
				Ch. Halidom Kela CD
			Vreni v Muensterplatz	Ch. Klaus v Kiesenthal
				Bella's Clara

Am/Can Ch. Shersan's Black Tie Required, sire of twenty-two champions to date. Bred and owned by Robert and Carolyn Kinley.

Galen von Mattenhof

Ch. Klaus v Kiesenthal

Tilla v Quellbach

Ch. Clara's Christopher

Arno vd Grasburg

Bella's Clara

Bella's Albertine

CH. KUSTERS JOCKO OF J'BAR

Ultra v Oberfeld

Ch. Sanctuary Woods Black Knight

Gretel v Langmoos

Alpsteins Knight Bell

Bobi v Bauernheim

Ch. Tabea of Altadena

Judy

Ch. Kuster's Jocko of J-Bar, a top producing sire of twenty-four champions, bred by Alpstein Kennel. Owners: Gretchen Johnson and Barbara Kuster. *Olson Photo.*

Ch. Jean Henri La Vaux CD, TD

Bev's Ceasar's Crown v BB

Am & Can Ch. Beukris Brandy Vombreiterweg

Am & Can Ch. Jaycy's Hans v Ben Can CD

Ch. Kuster's Jocko of J'Bar

Am & Can & Bda. Ch. Alphorn's Happy Talk

Ch. Alphorn's Caldonia

Can Ch. Jaycy's Oliver vom Hund See

Ch. Tryarr Alphorn Knight Echo

BIS & Ch. Alphorn's Copyright of Echo

Ch. Tryarr Alphorn Brio

Can Ch. Nordstaaten's Tess v Jaycy Can CD

Ch. Mon Plaisir's Sure Rival

Am & Can Ch. Sunnyhill's Helga v Ulrica CDX & TD

Ch. Sunnyhill's Anna v Jimco

JAYCY'S WYATT VOM HUND SEE

Ch. Edo v Moosseedorf

Ch. Pike's Adonis v Edo

Ch. Bella's Albertine Faymie

Am & Bda. Ch. Darius of Rutherford

Bruno v Bauernheim

Christine vd Speichergasse

Bella v Barenhof

Am & Can Ch. Bev's Jabbering Jodi v BB Can CD

Ch. Clara's Christopher

Ch. Kuster's Jocko of J'Bar

Ch. Alpstein's Knight Bell

Am & Can & Bda Ch. Alphorn's Happy Talk

Ch. Tryarr Alphorn Knight Echo

Ch. Alphorn's Caldonia

Ch. Tryarr Alphorn Brio

Am/Can Ch. Jaycy's Wyatt Vom Hund See finished both championships undefeated in the classes. He is a top producer in both the United States and Canada. Owner: Beverly Burney. Breeder: Larry Rutter.

Ch. Alex v Bauerheim

Bari vd Taubenfluh

Eve vd Klosteralp

Sultan v Dursrutti

Kandi v Dursrutti

Ch. Galan v Senseboden

Astor du Devens

Ch. York v Fluhwald

Erna v Nyffelhof

Galan v Mattenhof

Cita v Balmhof

Diana v Moosseedorf

Ch. Alex v Bauernheim

Kaya v Moosseedorf

Cilla v Ranfluh

CH. ASHLEY V BERNERLIEBE CD

Kilian v Enggistein

Ch. Hektor v Nesselacker

Grey v Waldacker

Ch. Flora v Nesselacker

Gunda v Nesselacker

Ch. Grand Yodler of Teton Valley CDX

Wachter v Konradshaus

Arno vd Grasburg

Rita vd Grasburg

Bella's Clara

Bobi v Bauernheim

Bella's Albertine

Bella v Moosboden

Ch. Dult Daphne v Yodlerhof

Ch. Alex v Bauerheim

Bari vd Taubenfluh

Eve vd Klosteralp

Sultan v Dursrutti

Kandi v Dursrutti

Ch. Ginger v Senseboden

Ch. York v Fluhwald

Galan v Mattenhof

Cita v Balmhof

Diana v Moosseedorf

Ch. Alex v Bauerheim

Kaya v Moosseedorf

Cilla v Ranfluh

Ch. Ashely V Bernerliebe, CDX, three-time National Specialty Winner in 1980, 1982, and 1983, is the sire of 28 champions. Bred and owned by Joel and Christina Ohlsen.

Table 5-3
DAMS OF FIVE OR MORE CHAMPIONS THROUGH MARCH 1993

#Ch	Name of Dam (Stud Book Entry)	Owner/Breeder
17	Ch Trilogy's Title Role (7/86)	Tramp/Tramp
16	Ch Texas Tiffany Vombreiterweg CD (7/79)	Tramp/Townsend
	Ch Shersan Bernhugel Hot Gossip (9/88)	Kinley & Dreisbach/Dreisbach
14	Ch Bev's Jabbering Jodi V BB (8/84)	Burney/Burney
13	Ch Deerpark's Ferkin V Buttonwillow (4/84)	Dean/Russ
12	Ch Sunnyhill's Anna V Jimco (10/75)	Kullman/Cotter
11	Ch Halidom Keri (12/82)	Parliman/Buchanan
10	Ch Alphorn's Happy Talk (7/78)	Burney/Johnson
	Ch Camelot's Hello Dolly (3/81)	Russell/Russell
	Ch Grunberg Iridescent Fire (10/84)	Miller & Volpe/Mulvey
	Pike's Elsa V Siegfried (2/80)	Pike/Pike
	Ch Tonia V Barenried (2/86)	Ostermiller/Jsch (Switz)
	Ch Wyemede's Heidi Vombreiterweg (5/74)	Townsend/Crawford
9	Shamrock's Molly Maguire (5/77)	Kelley/Kelley
	Ch Vombreiterwegs Swiss Lace (10/89)	Hefner/Townsend
8	Ch Alphorn's Caldonia (7/76)	Johnson/Johnson
	Ch Anneliese Vom Bauernhof CD (9/85)	Uhl/Shambeau
	Bella's Clara (9/70)	Howison & Decker/Thompson
	Ch Dallybecks Cresta V Bergita CD (3/87)	Reho/Reho
	Gretel V Langmoos (7/66)	Knight/Balsiger (Switz)
	Ch Gruezi Patty Melt V Reuben CD (4/88)	Getzel/Getzel
7	Bonnie Beaver (11/76)	Salamun/Borgh
	Ch Broken Oaks I-Ching CD (1/87)	Dean/Werth
	Ch Broken Oaks Innisbrook Elata CD (4/87)	McGovern & Milligan/Werth
	Ch Halidom Kali V Muensterplatz (11/77)	Weston & Mueller/Mueller
	Ch Heidi's Gidget Vombreiterweg (6/77)	Bond/Townsend
	Ch Oberland's Heather V Halidom (3/82)	Goodman & Ohlsen/Roth
6	Ch Broken Oaks Butik (3/82)	Werth/Werth
	Ch Halidom Matilda V Davos CD (12/82)	Parliman/Buchanan
	Ch Leisel Vombreiterweg (8/79)	Townsend/Townsend

(continued on page 66)

	Ch Mon Plaisir's Shady Lady CDX (3/77)	Werth/Gagnon
	Ch Nor-Ham's Christine V Wyemede (3/87)	Hamilton/Crawford & Hamilton
	Olympians Goddess Of Love (8/80)	Kolenick & Brouck/Brouck
	Ch Scotsmar's Melody Of Hope CD (5/84)	Sherman & Steinheimer/Werth & Sherman
	Ch Shersan Brite 'N Shining Star UD (6/86)	Hughes/Kinley
	Ch Shersan's Advanced Warning (8/86)	Kinley/Kinley
	Ch Sno-Den's Belle Star CD (11/86)	Ongemach/Perez
	Ch Sunnyhill's Karina V Huldre (6/80)	Kullman/Svendson
	Ch Trilogy's Chang O'Tempo (3/90)	Valentine/Tramp
5	Alpenrose Mountain Mist (3/83)	Fishman & Hostetter/Kobelt
	Ch Alphorn's Harmony (5/79)	Johnson/Johnson
	Ch Alphorn's Honey (7/80)	Burney & Westerlund/Johnson
	Ch Autumn's Michela (4/86)	Lantz/Lantz
	Ch Bernshire Tara Of Arun-Sky (2/86)	Brightman & Groesbeck/Donovan
	Ch Bonnie Haida V Crash (4/79)	Eilers/Salamun
	Ch Broken Oaks Alpy V Copyright (10/79)	Johnson/Werth
	Ch Dagne V Hexliheim CDX (5/79)	Horstick/Dawson
	Ch D Bonhof Sonya Vombreiterweg (5/79)	Townsend/Bond
	Ch Deerpark Cir-Cee (3/83)	Dean & Bork/Dean
	De-Li's Gretchen's Charm (7/89)	Cox & Ostermiller/Ostermiller
	De-Li's Sound Of Joy (8/88)	Ostermiller/Ostermiller
	Ch Franzi V Nesselacker (4/77)	Abrams/Krauchi (Switz)
	Ch Gerta V Buttonwillow (10/74)	Russ & Rector/Russ
	Ch Maren's Winifred V Felderhaus (11/81)	Felder/Ahrens
	Ch Merrimac Mijay's Black label CDX (9/86)	Walker/Mahaffey
	Nikki Vombreiterweg (8/86)	Townsend/Townsend
	Pike's Jewel V Barenried (4/89)	Leist/Pike & Lancaster
	Ch Sablemate Impossible Dream (12/70)	Howison/Welles
	Ch Sanctuary Woods Gloriann (1/71)	Temmel/Knight
	Ch Santera Chastity V Bev's (10/84)	Novocin/Burney
	Ch Shersan Baroness O Bernhugel (10/86)	Dreisbach/Kinley
	Ch Shersan Heartlight Chips Ahoy (11/89)	Kinley/Vogel
	Ch Snow Pals Color My Calliope (4/89)	Stauffer/Abrell
	Ch Tekla's Mandy V Cardiff (1/80)	Pickard/Brown
	Ch Trilogy's Torch Of Snowmont (12/86)	Cummings/Tramp
	Ch Tryarr Alphorn Brio (10/74)	Johnson/Rodgers
	Vreni V Muensterplatz (4/72)	Mueller/Paugh
	Ch Wendy VD Grasburg (12/66)	Howison/Affolter (Switz)
	Ch Windy Knobs Legacy De Grasso (11/88)	Grasso/Hughes
	Wyemede's Sablemate Siren (5/74)	Crawford/Crawford & Howison

Galen vn Mattenhof
Ch. Klaus v Kiesenthal
Tilla v Quellbach
Ch. Clara's Christopher
Arno vd Grasburg
Bella's Clara
Bella's Albertine
Ch. Kuster's Jocko of J'Bar
Ultra v Oberfeld
Ch. Sanctuary Wood's Black Knight
Gretel v Langmoos
Alpsteins Knight Bell
Bobbi v Bauernheim
Ch. Tabea of Altadena
Judy

CH. TEXAS TIFFANY VOMBREITERWEG CDX, TT

Casar v Oberbottigen OFA4
Ch. Sablemate Machs Na
Ch. Wendy vd Grasburg
Am & Can Ch. Sablemate Basko Vom
Ch. Fairplay's Hannibal
Ch. Sablemate Impossible Dream
Bella's Angelique
Am & Can Ch. Ms. Fireball Vombreiterweg
Ch. Sanctuary Woods Black Lancer
Ch. Argon v Wil-Lancer
Ch. Wilhelmina v Neugebauer CDX
Ch. Wyemede Heidi Vombreiterweg
Ch. Marco v Kiesenthal
Ch. Caesar's Legacy For Wyemede
Ch. Wyemede's Marta Von Sablemate

Chlaus v Forst
Zitta v Oberbottigen
Wachter v Konradshaus
Rita vd Grasburg
Egon v Schwandelarain
Heidi vom Altentorn
Bobi v Bauernheim
Bella v Moosboden
Ultra v Oberfeld
Gretel v Langmoos
Ch. Fairplay's Hannibal
Dorli vd Rehweid
Galan v Mattenhof
Tilla v Quellbach
Casar v Oberbottigen
Ch. Sablemate Wendy vd Grasburg

Ch. Texas Tiffany Vombreiterweg CDX, TT, top producer in conformation and obedience. Dam of sixteen champions.
Owner: Susan Tramp.
Breeder: Mary Townsend.

Ch. Galan v Mattenhof
Ch. Edo v Moosseedorf
Kaya v Moosseedorf
Ch.Pike's Adonis v Edo
Arno vd Grasburg
Ch. Bella's Albertine Faymie
Bella's Albertine
Am & Bda Ch. Darius of Rutherford
CACIB Zorro v Mühlstein
Bruno v Bauernbeim
Madi v Münnenberg
Christine vd Speichergasse
Dasso v Schürberg
Bella v Barenhof
Senta v Stygli

AM & CAN CH. BEV'S JABBERING JODI V BB CAN CD

Ch. Klaus v Kiesenthal
Ch. Clara's Christopher
Bella's Clara
Ch. Kuster's Jocko of J'Bar
Ch. Sanctuary Wood's Black Knight
Ch. Alpstein's Knight Bell
Ch. Tabea of Altadena
Am & Can & Bda Ch. Alphorn's Happy Talk
Ch. Sanctuary Wood's Black Knight
Ch. Tryarr Alphorn Knight Echo
Ch. Tryarr Conspiratress
Ch. Alphorn's Caldonia
Ch. Clara's Christopher
Ch. Tryarr Alphorn Brio
Alpstein Knight Dream

Am/Can Ch. Bev's Jabbering Jodi V BB, Can. CD, a top producing dam of ten champions and six obedience titlists.

CH. DEERPARK FERKIN V BUTTONWILLOW	Ch. Klause v Buchsischlossi	York v Bernetta (Swiss)	Wacher v Goldbachtal
			Cresta v Bernetta
		Diana v Buchsischlossi	CACIB Astor v Chaindon
			CACIB Franzi v Findlingsbrunnen
	Ch. Deerpark Brta v Buttonwillow	Bari de la Truche	Edor de Boiron
			Flora v Spitzenberg
		Ch. Deerpark Iner v Buttonwillow OFA	Ch. Afterberner v Buttonwillow OFA
			Ch. Yodlers Windsong v Bernerhof

Great-grandparents
Golf Hof-Wiesental
Tilli v Goldbachtal
Harald vd Denz
Bessi v Nesselacker
Carlo vd Grandfeybrucke
Diana v Ruegsbach
CACIB Wacho v Dursrutti
Desia v Findlingsbrunnen CAC
Portos la Vaux
Edda v Aarbach
Sultan v Dursrutti
Alma v Grunenmatt
Pandabear v Buttonwillow
Zodiac's Fancy v Sablemate
Ch. Grand Yodler of Teton Valley CDX
Ch. Gerta v Buttonwillow OFA

Ch. Deerpark Ferkin V Buttonwillow, a top producing dam of thirteen champions. Owner: Denise Dean. Breeder: Diane Russ.

				Baron de la Baumaz
			Am, Can, Mex Ch. Wunderstrands Arlac v Chavanne CD	
				Can Ch. Gittane de Chavannes
		Ch. Bernhugels Odin von Thor		
				Ch. Halidom Davos v Yodlerhof CD
			Bauerhof's Rika v Davos	
				Shamrock's Molly Maguire
	Ch. Bernhugels Augustus v Thor			
				Ch. Mon Plaisirs Sure Rival
			Ch. Sunnyhills Brig CD	
				Ch. Sunnyhills Anna v Jimco
		Am Bda. Ch. Freyja von Wunderstrand		
				Ch. Halidom Davos v Yodlerhof CD
			Wunderstrands Vera v Fritz	
				Shamrock's Molly Maguire
CH. SHERSAN BERNHUGELS HOT GOSSIP				
				Ch. Grand Yodler of Teton Valley CDX
			Ch. Halidom Davos v Yodlerhof CD	
				Ch. Ginger v Senseboden
		Am & Can Ch. Shersan Chang O Pace v Halidom CD		
				Ch. Halidom Kelas Senn
			Ch. Halidom Kali v Muensterplatz CD	
				Vreni von Muensterplatz
	Ch. Shersan Baroness O Bernhugel			
				Hako de Chaindon
			Bari les Sommetres	
				Cybelle les Sommetres
		Ch. Halidom Keri CD		
				Ch. Halidom Davos v Yodlerhof CD
			Ch. Halidom Kara v Davos CD	
				Ch. Halidom Kali v Muensterplatz CD

Ch. Shersan Bernhugel Hot Gossip, dam of sixteen champions to date. Owners: Carolyn Kinley and Patricia Dreisbach. Breeders: Patricia and Timothy Dreisbach. *Rund Photo.*

CACIB Astor v Chaindon

Porthos la Vauz

Anito v Blasenwald

Hako de Chaindon

Carlo vd Grandfeybrucke

Bella v Chaindon

Diana v Ruegsbach

Bari les Sommetres

Ares du Bonheyr

Arko de la Capite

Bety de Trelex

Cybelle les Sommetres

CACIB Alex v Chaindon

Kathi Schneggenberg

Gabi Schneggenberg

CH. HALIDOM KERI

Ch. Hektor v Nesselacker

Ch. Grand Yodler of Teton Valley CDX

Bella's Clara

Ch. Halidom Davos v Yodlerhof CD

Sultan v Dursrutti

Ch. Ginger v Senseboden

Diana v Moosseedorf

Ch. Halidom Kara v Davos CD

Donar v Zielackerhof

Ch. Halidom Kelas Senn CD

Ch. Halidom Kela CD

Ch. Halidom Kali v Muensterplatz CD

Ch. Klaus v Kiesenthal

Vreni v Muensterplatz

Bella's Clara

Ch. Halidom Keri CD, dam of eleven champions. Owners: Robert and Carolyn Kinley. Breeder: Millicent Buchanan.

Galan v Mattenhof
Ch. Klaus v Kiesenthal
Tilla v Quellbach
Ch. Clara's Christopher
Arno vd Grasburg
Bella's Clara
Bella's Albertine
Ch. Kuster's Jocko of J'Bar
Ultra v Oberfeld
Ch. Sanctuary Wood's Black Knight
Gretel v Langmoos
Alpstein's Knight Bell
Bobi v Bauernheim
Ch. Tabea of Altadena
Judy

AM-CAN BER (BDA) CH. ALPHORN'S HAPPY TALK

Ultra v Oberfeld
Ch. Sanctuary Wood's Black Knight
Gretel v Langmoos
Ch. Tryarr Alphorn Knight Echo
Ch. Hektor v Nesselacker
Ch. Tryarr Conspiratress
Bella's Clara
Ch. Alphorn's Caldonia
Ch. Klaus v Kiesenthal
Ch. Clara's Christopher
Bella's Clara
Ch. Tyarr Alphorn Brio
Ch. Sanctuary Wood's Black Knight
Alpstein Knight Dream
Bonne Amie

Am/Can Ber. Ch. Alphorn's Happy Talk, dam of ten champions, the first Berner to earn a triple championship and first Berner to place in Group in Bermuda.
Owner: Beverly J. Burney.
Breeder: Gretchen Johnson.

Rubis de Childerbrand

Elfi les Platanes

Anette v Oberburzberghof

Ch. Jocky de Vilmoulin

Arkodela Capite

Laika la Vaux

Belle les Delices

CH. CAMELOT'S HELLO DOLLY

Blac de Corbeyier (Import)

Ch Starcrest Attlee v Blac

Ch. Sanctuary Wood's Gloriann

Ch. Starcrest's Carri-On v Attlee

Bella's Axel

Ch. Sanctuary Woods Gloriann

Gretel v Langmoos

Ch. Camelot's Hello Dolly, a top producing bitch owned and bred by Gwen Russell.

Table 5-4
TOP PRODUCING SIRES OF OBEDIENCE TITLE HOLDERS THROUGH MARCH 1993

#Ch	Name of Sire (Stud Book Entry)	Owner/Breeder
19	Ch Halidom Davos V Yodlerhof CD (5/77)	Buchanan/Brooks
15	Ch Jaycy's Wyatt Vom Hund See (12/84)	Burney/Rutter
14	Ch Ashley V Bernerliebe (11/80)	Ohlsen/Ohlsen
11	Ch Pike's Chewbacca (9/80)	Kara/Pike
	Ch Wyemede Luron Bruce (5/79)	Buss/Crawford
10	Ch Ami VD Swisstop Farms (5/82)	Townsend/Schaer (Can)
	Ch De-Li's Foreign Touch (1/88)	Ostermiller/Ostermiller
9	Ch Argon V Wil-Lancer (7/72)	Reisinger/O'Hagan
	Ch Bauernhof's Bear Paws (9/80)	Shambeau/Kelley
	Nova Polaris (9/82)	Shambeau/Pike
7	Can Ch Bari Von Nydegghoger (8/82)	Smith/Stockli (Switz)
	Ch Deerpark Heartlight (5/85)	Dean/Curtis & Dean
	Ch Klaus V Buchsischlossli (8/82)	Russ/Sollberger
	Ch Kuster's Jocko Of J Bar (4/76)	Kuster & Johnson/Alpstein Kennel
	Ch Olly Von Tonisbach (5/84)	Guido/Schaffer (Switz)
	Ch Shersan's Black Tie Required (8/86)	Kinley/Kinley
6	Ch Alphorn's Copyright V Echo (3/77)	Johnson & Johnson
	Ch Bev's Baron V Greybern (5/88)	Burney/Gray
	Ch Jean Henri La Vaux CD TD (2/76)	Horstick/Meister (Switz)
	Mt Chalet's Epic V Lancer (10/72)	Pyle/Pyle
	Rambo VD Schwarzwasserfluh (10/87)	Reufenacht/Zbinden (Switz)
	Ch Shepherd's Patch Czar Wyemede CD (2/82)	Crawford/Horstick
	Ch Wunderstrand's Arlac V Chavanne CD (2/81)	Barney/Fawer (Can)

Table 5-5
TOP-PRODUCING DAMS OF OBEDIENCE TITLE HOLDERS THROUGH MARCH 1993

#Ch	Name of Dam (Stud Book Entry)	Owner/Breeder
6	Ch Bev's Jabbering Jodi BB (8/84)	Burney/Burney
	Ch Gretchen Von Woerner CD (9/80)	Woerner & Ongemach/Kelley
	Ch Merrimac Mijay's Black Label CDX (9/86)	Walker/Mahaffey
	Ch Trilogy's Torch Of Snowmont (12/86)	Cummings/Tramp
5	Ch Broken Oaks Bergita CDX TD (10/81)	Reho/Werth
	Ch Dagne V Hexliheim CDX (5/79)	Horstick/Dawson
	Ch Mon Plaisir's Shady Lady CDX (3/77)	Werth/Gagnon
	Sandusky's Brighteye Abigail UDT (1/89)	Hotze/Ongemach
	Ch Sandusky's My Name Is Helga CDX (9/86)	Ongemach/Ongemach & Shambeau
4	Bauernhof's Rika Von Davos (6/81)	Barney/Kelley
	Ch Broken Oaks Arjana CD (4/80)	Werth/Werth
	Ch Broken Oaks Butik CD (3/82)	Werth/Werth
	Ch Dallybecks Cresta V Bergita CD (3/87)	Reho/Reho
	Ch Dina De L'Armary UDT (7/77)	Horstick/Badertacher (Switz)
	Ch Gruezi Patty Melt V Reuben CD (4/88)	Getzel/Getzel
	Mt View's Mademoiselle Marie CD (10/87)	Peters/Edwards
	Ch Oberland Elian V Bernerliebe (10/84)	Roth/Goodman & Ohlsen
	Sanctuary Woods Color Scheme (7/69)	Pyle/Knight
	Ch Shepherd's Patch Dionne CD (11/83)	Evert & Eschweiler/Horstick
	Ch Stassi's Elka Sommer Schoen CD (10/79)	Sommers/Pennington
	Ch Sunnyhill's Anna V Jimco (10/75)	Kullman/Cotter
	Ch Tanja V Nesselacker CD TD (5/75)	Gruber/Krauchi (Switz)
	Ch Texas Tiffany Vombreiterweg CDX (7/79)	Tramp/Townsend
	Ch Tonia V Barenried (2/86)	Ostermiller/Jsch (Switz)

CH. WYEMEDE HEIDI VOMBREITERWEG OFA

Parents	Grandparents	Great-grandparents	Great-great-grandparents	Great-great-great-grandparents
Ch. Argon v Wil-Lancer	Ch. Sanctuary Wood's Black Lancer	Ultra v Oberfeld	Dani v Ried	Dursli vd Holzmuhle Diana v Bernerland
			Dorette v Schawndelirain	Dursli vd Holzmuhle Greta v Munnenberg
		Gretel v Langmoos	Dani v Senseboden	CACIB Zorro v Mühlstein Berna v Burgstein
			Flocki v Laupenacker	Toni v Oberbottigen Janette v Schlossli
	Ch. Wilhelmina v Neugebauer CDX	Fairplay's Hannibal	Egon v Schwandelirain	CACIB Ch. Beny v Dursrutti Greta v Munnenberg
			Heidi vom Altentorn	Punsch vd Nau Anuschke v Boltenberg
		Dorli vd Rehweid	Goliath v Dursrutti	CACIB Alex v Angstorf Anita v Dursrutti
			Anita v Burgholzli	Echo v d Gotthelfsegg Anita v Oberfeld
Caesar's Legacy For Wyemede	Ch. Marco v Kiesenthal	Galan v Mättenhof	CACIB York v Flühwald	Astor du Devens Erna v Nyffelhof
			Cita v Balmhof	CACIB Beny v Dursrutti Bella vd Petersinsel
		Tilla v Quellbach	Alex v Bauernheim	Max vd Schonau Madi v Munnenberg
			Asta v Falkenberg	Arnold v Belfaux Coquine de Devens
	Wyemede's Marta von Sablemate	Casar v Oberbottigen	Chlaus v Forst	Adam v Dahlihubel Centa v Schneggenberg
			Zitta v Oberbottigen	CACIB Zorro v Mühlstein Ursula v Oberbottigen
		Ch. Wendy vd Grasburg	Wachter v Konradshaus	Barri v Burgistein Asta v Ranflüh
			Rita vd Grasburg	CACIB Alex v Angstorf Priska vd Grasburg

Ch. Wyemede Heidi Vombreiterweg with two of her grandchildren. Dam of ten champions.

			Ch. York v Flühwald
		Galan v Mättenhof	
			Cita v Balmhof
	Edo v Moosseedorf (Swiss Import)		
			Ch. Alex v Bauernheim
		Kaya v Moosseedorf	
			Cilla v Ranflüh
	Pike's Siegfried v Edo		
			CACIB Zorro v Mühlstein
		Bruno v Bauernheim	
			Madi v Münnenberg
	Christine vd Speichergasse (Swiss Import)		
			Dasso v Schürberg
		Bella v Barenhof	
			Senta v Stygli
CH. PIKE'S ELSA V SIEGFRIED			
			Barri v Burgistein
		Wachter v Konradhaus	
			Rita v Ranflüh
	Arno vd Grasburg (Swiss Import)		
			Int Ch. Alex v Angstorf
		Rita vd Grasburg	
			Priska vd Grasburg
	Bella's Albertine Faymie		
			CACIB Zorro v Mühlstein
		Bobi v Bauernheim (Swiss)	
			Madi v Mühnnenberg
	Bella's Albertine		
			Casar v Niederwanben
		Bella v Moosboden (Swiss)	
			Beline v Schnebbenberg

Pike's Elsa V Siegfried, littermate to BIS Ch. Pike's Harpo J Andrew, dam of ten champions. Owner/breeder: Pike.

Ch. Tschuggen's Bosco v. Mt. Lore (right) and Ch. Tschingel von Saanenstrand (left) represent good Berner type. Owned by Linda and Bob Seaver.

SIX

Understanding the Standard

Swiss farmers found uses for type, disposition, and certain characteristics of the Berner Sennenhund, and in time a set of guidelines was developed to help maintain these qualities. This blueprint, known as the breed Standard, provides a verbal picture of the ideal Bernese Mountain Dog. Deviation from the Standard can change the look, or "type," of a breed until it is not recognizable. It is therefore important that every breeder strive to produce only dogs that match the guidelines set forth in the Standard.

Although the original Standard of the Bernese Mountain Dog has changed over the years, the best measure of a Berner's quality is how well he fits the current Standard. The wording of the Standard allows for each breeder to have a slightly different interpretation while still breeding within the range of characteristics permitted by the Standard.

Whether you plan to breed Bernese Mountain Dogs or buy one that someone else has bred, the Standard will serve as the ultimate guide to selecting a dog with the appearance, size, and movement that are correct for this breed. If you are looking for absolute perfection, however, don't expect to find it in any one individual. Every dog has flaws; none are perfect. Use the Standard as a guideline to select the best Berner you can find. Perhaps you will find near perfection in one or two areas and good to excellent qualities in most other characteristics. Balance is important. Never select a dog for breeding or showing that is perfect in one area but defective in another. Instead, look for the best overall specimen.

AKC Standard for the Bernese Mountain Dog

GENERAL APPEARANCE

The Bernese Mountain Dog is a striking, tri-colored, large dog. He is sturdy and balanced. He is intelligent, strong and agile enough to do the draft and droving work for which he was used in the mountainous regions of his origin. Dogs appear masculine, while bitches are distinctly feminine.

SIZE, PROPORTION, SUBSTANCE

Measured at the withers, dogs are 25 to 27.5 inches; bitches are 23 to 26 inches. Though appearing square, Bernese Mountain Dogs are slightly longer in body than they are tall. Sturdy bone is of great importance. The body is full.

HEAD

Expression is intelligent, animated and gentle. The eyes are dark brown and slightly oval in shape with closefitting eyelids. Inverted or everted eyelids are serious faults. Blue eye color is a disqualification. The ears are medium sized, set high, triangular in shape, gently rounded at the tip, and hang close to the head when in repose. When the Bernese Mountain Dog is alert, the ears are brought forward and raised at the base; the top of the ear is level with the top of the skull. The skull is flat on top and broad, with a slight furrow and a well-defined, but not exaggerated stop. The muzzle is strong and straight. The nose is always black. The lips are clean and as the Bernese Mountain is a drymouthed breed, the flews are only slightly developed. The teeth meet in a scissors bite. An overshot or undershot bite is a serious fault. Dentition is complete.

NECK, TOPLINE, BODY

The neck is strong, muscular and of medium length. The topline is level from the withers to the croup. The chest is deep and capacious with well-sprung, but not barrel-shaped, ribs and brisket reaching at least to the elbows. The back is broad and firm. The loin is strong. The croup is round and smoothly rounded to the tail insertion. The tail is bushy. It should be carried low when in repose. An upward swirl is permissible when the dog is alert, but the tail may never curl or be carried over the back. The bones in the tail should feel straight and should reach to the hock joint or below. A kink in the tail is a fault.

FOREQUARTERS

The shoulders are moderately laid back, flat-lying, well-muscled and never loose. The legs are straight and strong and the elbows are well under the shoulder when the dog is standing. The pasterns slope very slightly but are never weak. Dewclaws may be removed. The feet are round and compact with well-arched toes.

HINDQUARTERS

The thighs are broad, strong and muscular. The stifles are moderately bent and taper smoothly into the hocks. The hocks are well let down and straight as viewed from the rear. Dewclaws should be removed. Feet are compact and turn neither in nor out.

COAT

The coat is thick, moderately long and slightly wavy or straight. It has a bright natural sheen. Extremely curly or extremely dull-looking coats are undesirable. The Bernese Mountain Dog is shown in natural coat and undue trimming is to be discouraged.

COLOR AND MARKINGS

The Bernese Mountain Dog is tri-colored. The ground color is jet black. The markings are rich rust and clear white. Symmetry of markings is desired. Rust appears over each eye, on the cheeks reaching to at least the corner of the mouth, on each side of the chest, on all four legs, and under

Figure 6-1
POINTS OF CONFORMATION

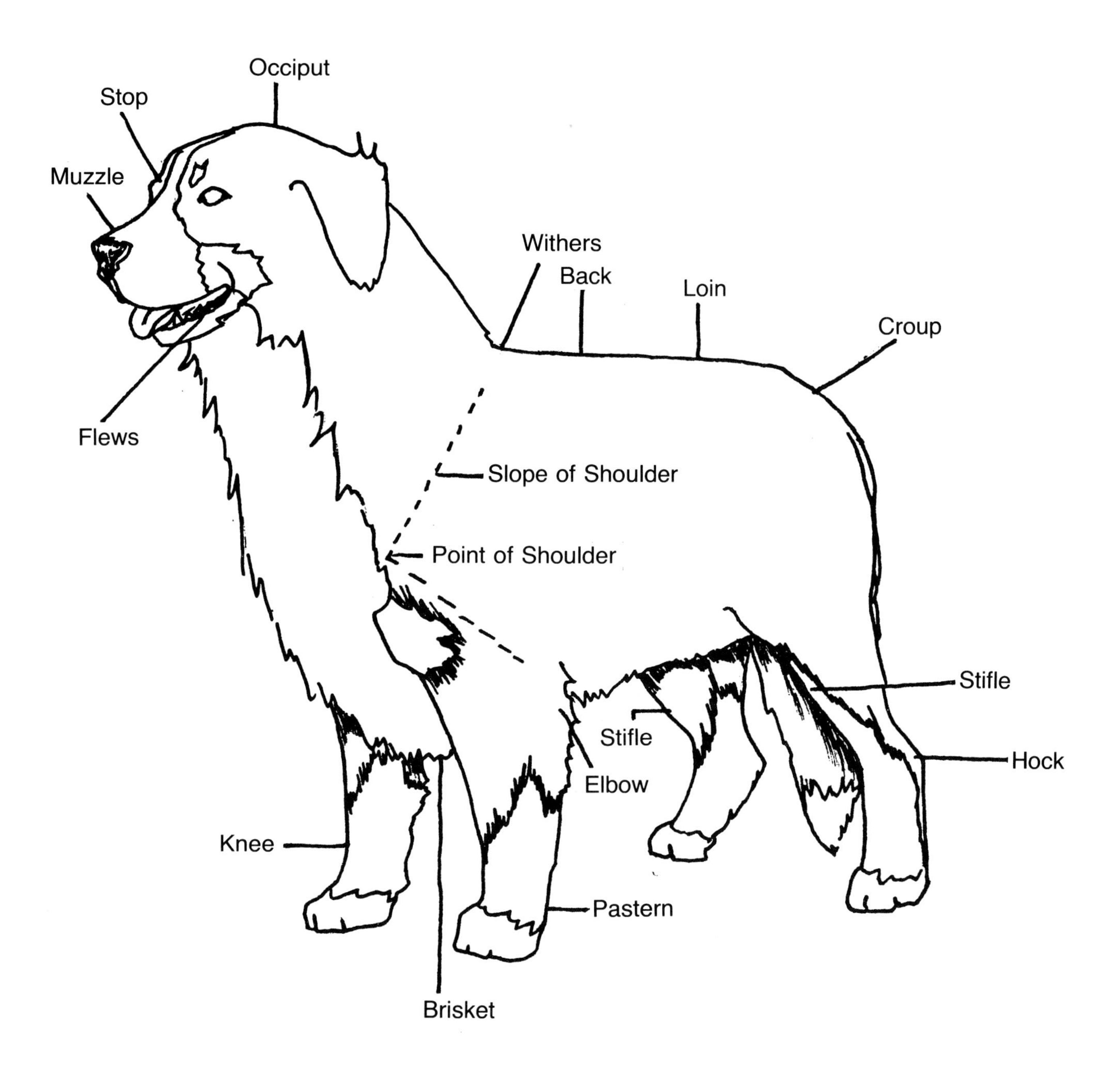

the tail. There is a white blaze and muzzle band. A white marking on the chest typically forms an inverted cross. The tip of the tail is white. White on the feet is desired but must not extend higher than the pasterns. Markings other than described are to be faulted in direct relationship to the extent of the deviation. White legs or a white collar are serious faults. Any ground color other than black is a disqualification.

GAIT

The natural working gait of the Bernese Mountain Dog is a slow trot. However in keeping with his use in draft and droving work, he is capable of speed and agility. There is good reach in front. Powerful drive from the rear is transmitted through a level back. There is no wasted action. Front and rear legs on each side follow through in the same plane. At increased speed, legs tend to converge toward the center line.

TEMPERAMENT

The temperament is self-confident, alert and good natured, never sharp or shy. The Bernese Mountain Dog should stand steady though may remain aloof to the attentions of strangers.

DISQUALIFICATIONS

Blue eye color.

Any ground color other than black.

Approved 1-10-90

Effective March 28, 1990

The Berner is a sturdy, strong-boned dog with an appearance of strength. Dogs appear masculine while bitches are distinctly feminine. Ch. Heartlight Baby Grand shows the strength and sturdiness called for by the standard for a male.

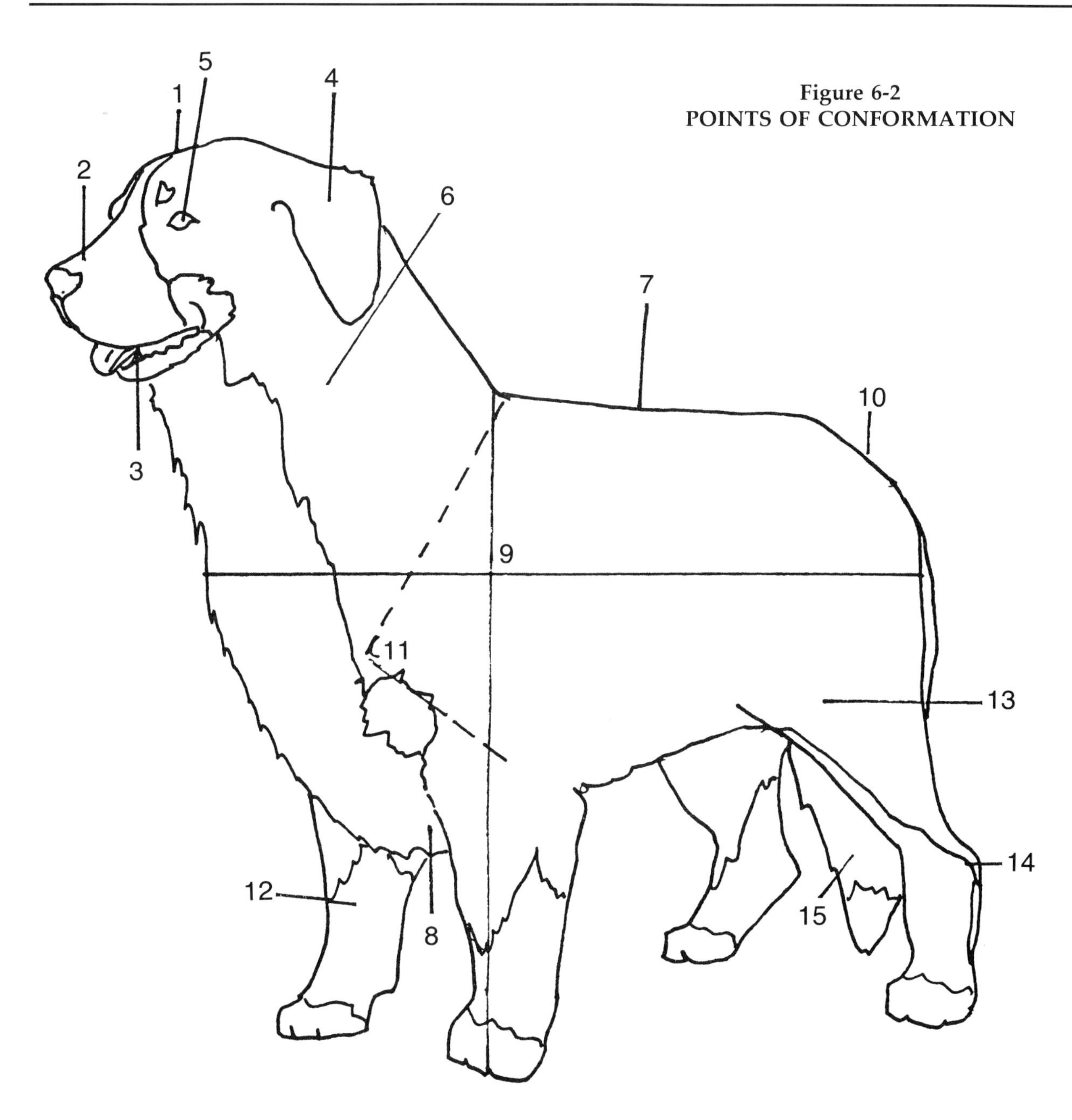

Figure 6-2
POINTS OF CONFORMATION

1: Skull, flat on top, slightly longer than muzzle and broad, with slight indentation running from stop to crown.
2: Muzzle, strong and straight, appearing blunt.
3: Lips, clean and flews only slightly developed.
4: Ears, medium size, set high, triangular with round tips.
5: Eye, dark brown, slightly oval in shape. Blue color is a disqualification.
6: Neck, strong, muscular, and of medium length.
7: Back, broad and firm, level from withers to croup.
8: Chest, deep, capacious with well-sprung ribs.
9: Length to height, slightly longer in body than is tall.
10: Croup, round and smooth to tail insert.
11: Shoulder lay back, moderate.
12: Front legs, straight and strong, elbows well under.
13: Thighs, strong and muscular.
14: Hock, well let down and straight as viewed from rear.
15: Tail, bushy, carried low when in repose, upward swirl when dog is alert.

Ch. Shersan's Chang' O' Pace v. Halidom shows symmetry and balance in proportion.

Body length slightly greater than height. Ch. Alphorn's Trio v. Jocko owned by Sal Vendrillo, bred by Gretchen Johnson, Alphorn Kennels.

Ch. Anneliese vom Bauernhof shows a beautiful female head. Owned by Jerry Uhl. *Photo by Janet Wissmann.*

Sally and Joe Walsh's Olympian's Atlas of Saljo has a well-balanced masculine head.

Minimum white markings on face. Ch. Vari Cherokee Du Barskey CD, owned by Linda Williams.

Maximum white markings on face and head. Ch. Yodler's Konig v. Bernerhof owned by Susan Hostetter. Shown here at ten years of age.

Above: Diane Russ's Ch. Klaus v. Buchsischloessli as a youngster, showing the inverted cross chest marking — the "Swiss cross."

Left: Diane Russ with Shenandoah v. Buttonwillow, a young bitch who shows a level topline and correct neck.

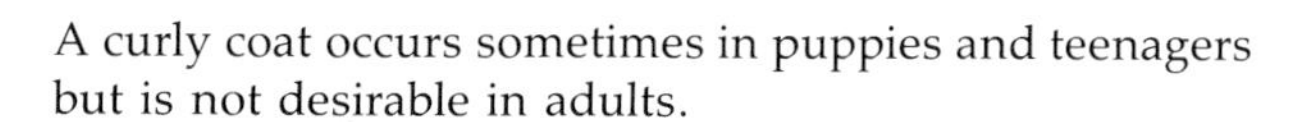
A curly coat occurs sometimes in puppies and teenagers but is not desirable in adults.

Ch. Deerpark Advocate of Talknet owned by Denise Dean shows a correct, balanced side gait at the trot with a "loosely spread M" clearly visible. *Photo by Patrick Hatch.*

Interpreting the Standard

It takes time and experience to begin to form a mental picture of the ideal Berner from the written words of the breed Standard. Watch the breed in the ring at dog shows, ask questions of more experienced fanciers, and visit as many kennels or breeders as possible. Try to evaluate each dog against the breed Standard as you understand it. Remember to make allowances for the tendency of all owners to see the good in their own dogs and to overlook the flaws.

GENERAL APPEARANCE

The two words that set the tone for the Bernese Mountain Dog are "sturdy" and "balanced." The Berner should be a strong animal with bone and muscle sufficient to do draft and herding work over rough terrain. "Balance" refers to the appearance that each part of the dog is in proportion to all other parts. A dog is "balanced" when he presents a pleasing, symmetrical picture.

These characteristics, in conjunction with the striking black, tan, and white coloring, make a Berner identifiable at first glance. In addition, males

Figure 6-3
COLORING

1: Ground color, jet black. Any ground color other than black is a disqualification.
2: Rust, over each eye, on cheeks reaching to corner of mouth, on each side of chest, on all four legs, and under tail.
3. White, blaze and muzzle band, on chest forming an inverted cross, on feet, not extending higher than pastern.

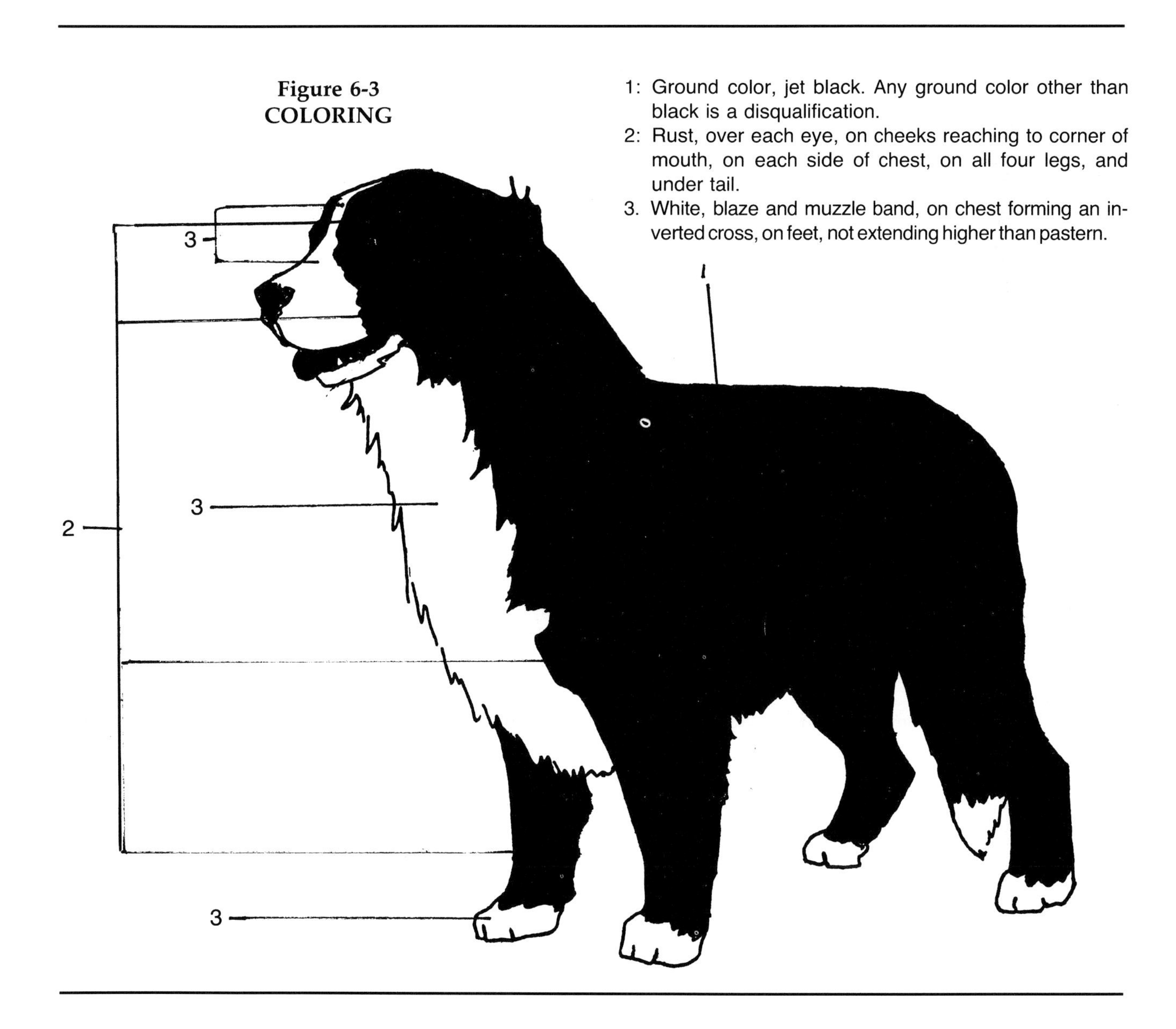

should be easily recognizable, with a proud, confident look and more body mass. Bitches should have a softer appearance.

SIZE, PROPORTION, AND SUBSTANCE

Measured at the withers (topmost point of the shoulders), dogs should be twenty-five to twenty-seven and one-half inches; bitches, twenty-three to twenty-six inches. Although Bernese Mountain Dogs appear square, they are slightly longer in body than they are tall. An ideal actual measurement of the Berner would show a 9:10 ratio; that is, for nine units of height, he should have ten units of length. A truly square Berner would be predisposed to faulty movement, such as overreaching or crabbing. Sturdy bone is of great importance.

The Berner's body is rounded and stocky. He is a visibly large dog, and he should have the substance to match his size without appearing coarse or awkward. Basic type, soundness, and balance, however, are more important than height. Dogs that fall within the height requirements and maintain breed type and sound movement are to be preferred over those that are simply large. Berners above or below the limits stated in the Standard should be faulted in direct proportion to the extent to which they deviate.

The Berner bitch typically has a soft expression. *Art by Janet Wissmann.*

HEAD

The characteristics of the correct Berner head continue to separate the breed from any other tricolored or other Swiss mountain breed. While the dark brown eye color is the hallmark of the Bernese Mountain Dog, expression is extremely important, and a vicious or frightened expression should never be evident in a Berner. The eyes of a Berner should show a lively, loving expression indicative of his gentle nature, although when he stands his ground before a threatening strangers or animal, there should be no doubt in anyone's mind that he will steadfastly protect his people and his territory. The slightly oval shape of the Berner's eye adds interest to his expression, but a rounded eye, while not desirable, is not as faulty as either a sunken or a protruding eye. Eyelids turned inward so that the lower eyelashes irritate and ulcerate the surface of the eye (entropion) or eyelids that turn outward, leaving a pouch for infection to occur in exposed tissues (ectropion) are not only serious faults but pose a danger to a Berner's health and eyesight.

The size, set, and carriage of the ears are critical in determining expression and can make the difference between an outstanding appearance and a mediocre one. Ears set on too low give a "houndy" look, as do heavy ears. A Berner's ears should be mobile, lifting easily to show his attitude and alert expression. Earset, ear carriage, and shape can make a difference in the look of quality and can help to define breed "type."

The head (skull) should be in proportion to the rest of the dog's body. It should be neither too small nor too large in comparison to the rest of the dog. The backskull in adults should be flat and slightly longer from front to back than the muzzle. The furrow mentioned in the Standard is an indentation running from the stop to the crown of the backskull in the adult, and it gives the Berner a soft expression.

The muzzle is strong and straight, appearing blunt, and the mouth is dry (no drooling), with fully pigmented lips held close to the gums. The Bernese Mountain Dog Standard calls for the dog to have complete dentition, meaning that he should have forty-two teeth, including twelve incisors, four canines, sixteen premolars, and ten molars. Only the molars are uneven in number; there are two upper molars and three lower ones on each side of the jaw.

The correct bite is when the top incisors snugly overlap the bottom ones. The outer sides of the lower incisors touch the inner sides of the upper incisors. Incorrect bites are undershot, in which the top incisors touch behind the lower ones, and overshot, where the top incisors greatly overlap the bottom ones, leaving a space between the upper and lower teeth. The level bite, in which the incisors meet exactly, edge to edge, is also incorrect. This is less serious than overshot or undershot bites.

NECK, TOPLINE, AND BODY

The neck should be in balance with the rest of the dog and set on the body so that there is a smooth flow from neck into back. The set and length of the neck are affected by other structural features, particularly shoulder layback. A neck that is too short and that appears to be set right on the shoulders may indicate an upright shoulder blade that will give an incorrect, choppy stride.

The back should be broad, with a firm, level topline from withers to croup, and the chest should reach at least to the elbows at the brisket. A broad, deep chest is needed for adequate heart and lung space, which gives a dog endurance to do his work, but the chest should not be so round and broad that it gives the appearance of a barrel. A barrel-shaped chest will cause the elbows to turn outward

Figure 6-4
DENTITION

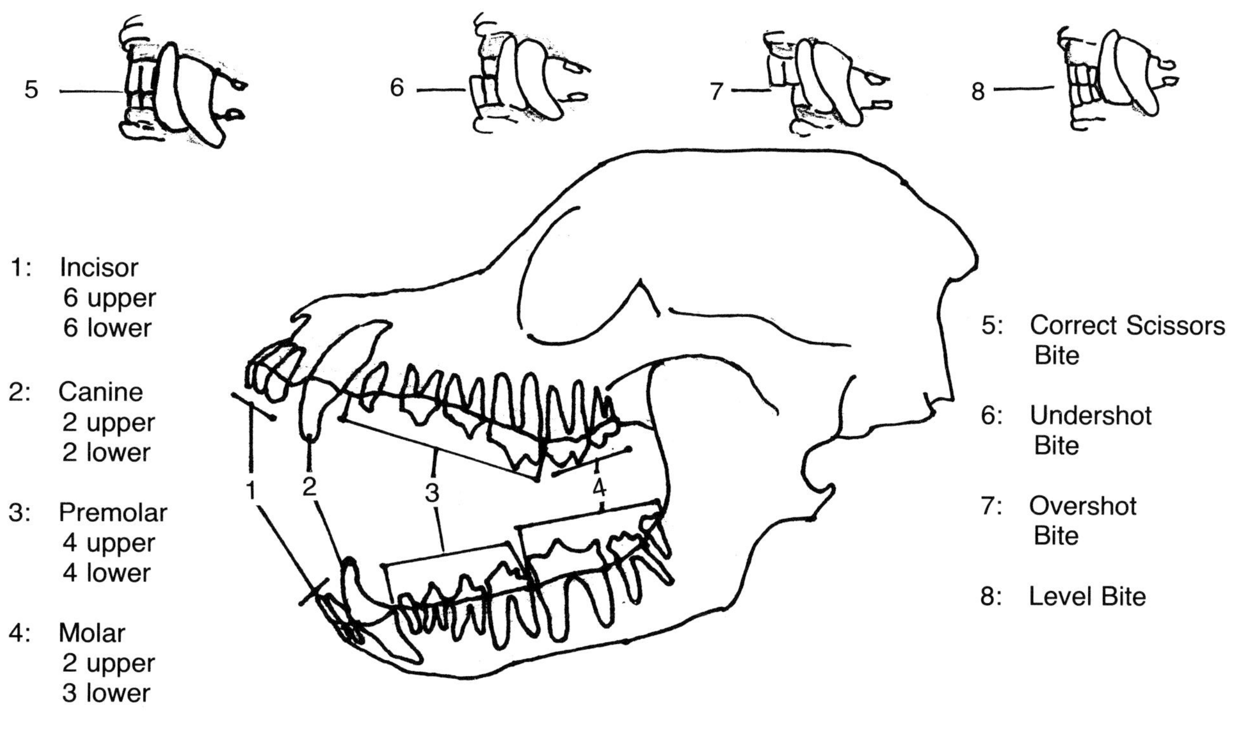

5 6 7 8
1 2 3 4

1: Incisor
6 upper
6 lower

2: Canine
2 upper
2 lower

3: Premolar
4 upper
4 lower

4: Molar
2 upper
3 lower

5: Correct Scissors Bite

6: Undershot Bite

7: Overshot Bite

8: Level Bite

and interfere with correct movement of the forelegs.

The loin, that short section between the last rib and the croup, plays an important part in the Berner's ability to perform the function for which he was originally bred. A broad, strong loin of proportionally short length is necessary in a draft dog. Berners with a weak or long loin will lack strength and will tire easily. Similarly, the slope and width of the croup influence the dog's ability to work. The Berner's broad, slightly rounded croup gives him the room for musculature needed to move loads as well as the necessary pelvic angulation to enable him to trot without tiring when he is acting as a drover.

The Berner's tail should be long and should look like a soft, plush bottle brush with no appearance of feathering. He expresses himself gently with a waving tail, rarely wagging it wildly. If a kink is present, it can most often be found by running your hands along the bone of the tail. Young dogs often carry their tails with an upward swirl at the end, which should not be confused with a kink. A puppy may carry his tail high, especially in play; however, as he matures, the tail usually returns to its correct position, sweeping low or hanging straight downward.

FOREQUARTERS

The Berner's front assembly denotes his dual heritage of draft and droving. The moderately laid-back shoulder is muscled enough to move heavy loads, but free-moving and flat enough to permit the free, easy stride needed by a herding dog. The forelegs are straight and strong, with elbows set well under the shoulders. The pasterns slope slightly, but not so much as to cause weakness. Correct shoulder placement and slope of pastern act as shock absorbers and allow a dog to work longer with less fatigue.

Figure 6-5
THE FOREQUARTERS

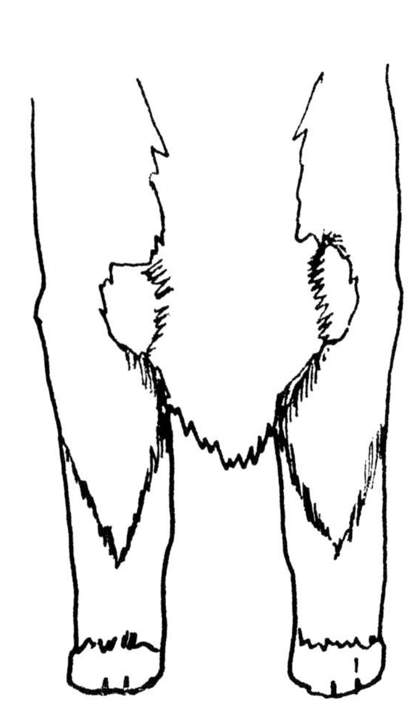
Correct Front

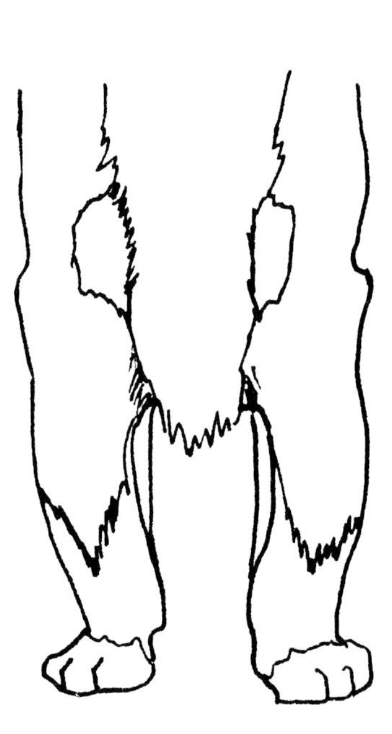
Fiddle Front

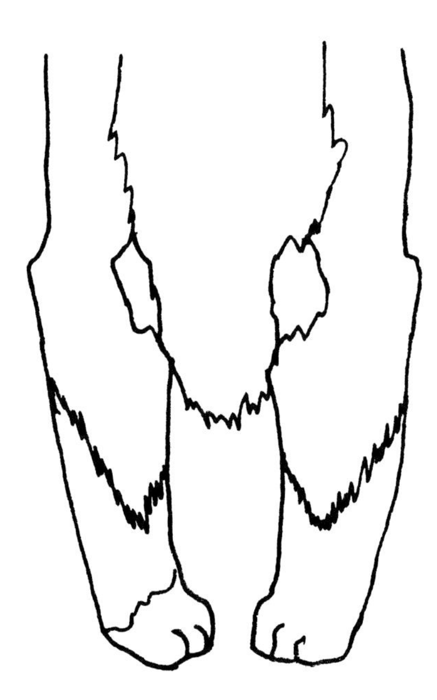
Out at Elbows / Toed In

The feet should be round and compact with well-arched toes and thick, resilient pads or "leather" on the bottoms of the feet that also cushion each stride. Dewclaws may be left in place on front legs, but removing them will give a tidier appearance and prevent the tearing of a dewclaw on rough ground, which causes much pain for the dog and necessitates medical attention.

Faults in the front assembly include toeing in or out, fiddle front, out at elbows, and straight shoulders. Faults in the shape of the foot are hare foot or splay foot, instead of the preferred round, compact shape.

Figure 6-6
THE FOOT

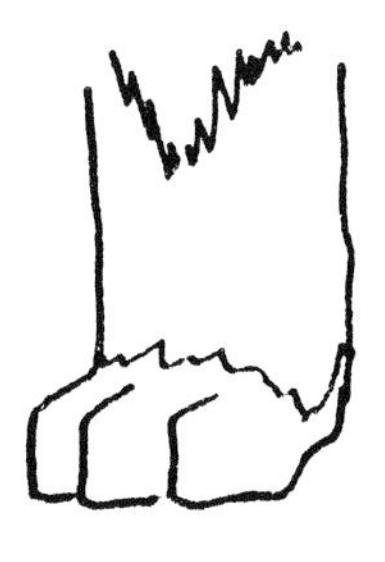

Correct Foot

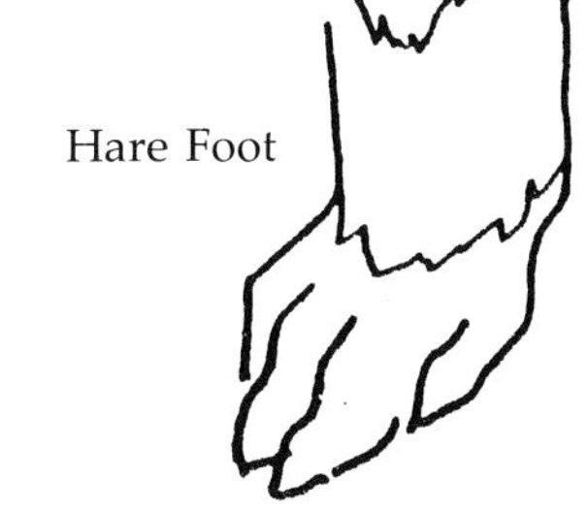

Hare Foot

HINDQUARTERS

The hindquarters of the Bernese Mountain Dog are his power train. All of the characteristics should allow for draft work. Wide, strong thighs and moderate stifle angulation provide strength and the straight transmission of thrust needed to pull loads.

A hock is well let down when it is short compared to the length of the leg from hock joint to hip joint. A short hock is conducive to the smooth transmission of power. For that reason also, the hocks should be straight when viewed from behind. Hocks that turn inward (cow hocks) or outward (bow hocks) are incorrect because they waste effort and energy and misdirect the transmission of power.

Dewclaws should be removed from the rear legs. Although some puppies are born without rear dewclaws, Berners may also have double or triple rear dewclaws. Not only are these unsightly, but they may be painfully torn, rendering the dog lame.

Figure 6-7
THE HINDQUARTERS

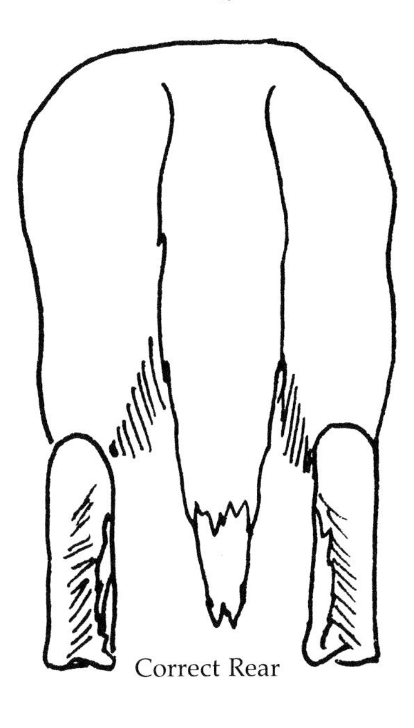

Correct Rear

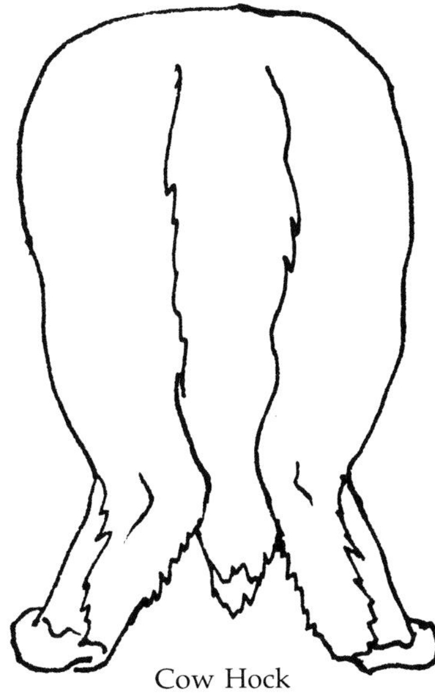

Cow Hock

COAT

The Berner's coat is intended to protect him in all kinds of weather, from hot summer sun to winter snows. The silky, slightly wavy or straight coat with its thick undercoat protects against extremes of weather. A curly or soft coat or a coat with insufficient undercoat is undesirable because it allows ice and snow to penetrate to the dog's skin and absorbs dirt and water. A proper coat will shed dirt and not form mats easily, making grooming a much easier task than you would first suppose. In warm weather, the Berner will shed his undercoat, leaving only the shiny outer coat, which will sometimes be quite short.

COLOR AND MARKINGS

The Bernese Mountain Dog is a black dog with rich russet and clean, white decoration. The width

Overseer v. Buttonwillow at five months.

Overseer v. Buttonwillow at one and a half years of age showing the shrinkage of white markings on the face.

of the blaze and the amount of russet on the head may vary within the restrictions of the Standard, but both russet and white markings should be symmetrical. Freckling in the white on the muzzle is not a serious fault, although clear white is preferred. White on the chest typically forms the inverted cross, often referred to as a "Swiss cross," but an irregular pattern is acceptable. Russet on the feet and legs must separate white and black markings. White above the pastern, running up inside a leg, is undesirable, as is black bleeding down the legs onto the feet. Any bleeding or blending of colors is undesirable, including a reddish or brownish cast to the black coat or a gray shading of the breeches. The only exception to this is during shedding.

GAIT

The Berner's trot should appear easy and powerful, and he should display good reach and powerful drive from the rear transmitted through a level back with no wasted action. Support is on opposing limbs — with the right front/left rear and left front/right rear legs on the ground at the same time. As the dog comes toward you at a trot, the front legs should present a straight line from shoulder to pad, with both legs converging toward the center line

Am./Can./Bda. Ch. Alphorn's Happy Talk, owned by Bev Burney, was the first American Berner to win a triple conformation title.

Figure 6-8
SIDE GAIT

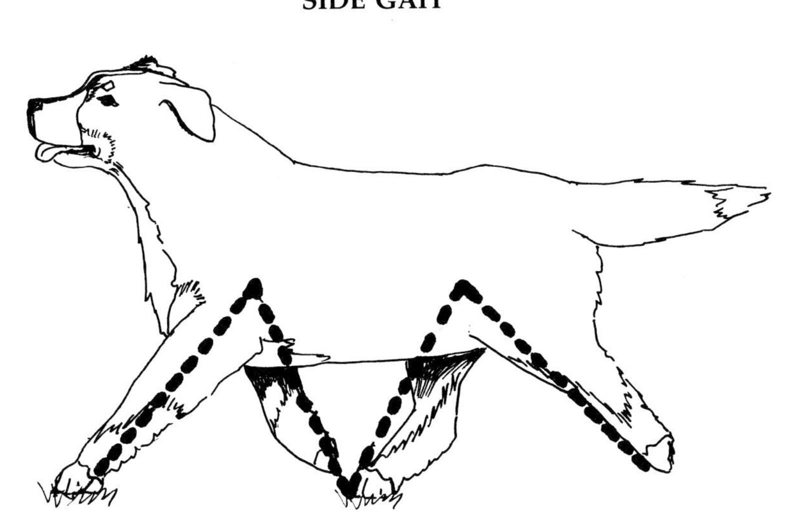

Correct, balanced side gait can be thought of as a loosely spread "M." There should be equal distance between the outer "legs" of the "M," and the feet should not overlap in the center of the "M."

in a "V." From the rear, the hocks (metatarsi) also converge toward the center line of the body, forming a straight line from point of hip to pad.

Correct, balanced side gait can be thought of as a loosely spread "M" with equal distance between the "legs" of the "M" with the inside "legs" not overlapping. When viewed from the side, the hocks should present an open angle demonstrating adequate extension of the rear leg at the hock joint. This should be visible at the maximum point of extension just as the dog finished one stride and begins to step underneath himself for the next stride (see Figure 5-18).

The "M" configuration is also visible in the pacing gait, although pacing is faulty movement. In pacing, both legs on one side of the dog's body move forward at the same time while the opposite side legs move back. A dog may pace due to extreme fatigue, but pacing in the show ring is usually a result of poor structure. A pacing dog exhibits a crisscross, rolling motion unlike the smooth flow of correct movement.

Overreaching, another faulty gait usually generated because of poor fronts, too-short bodies, or overangulated rears, is when the inside legs overlap. In another movement fault known as crabbing, the dog goes beyond overreaching to display a sidewise movement much like that of a crab; thus, the name. Both rear feet travel outside the plane of the front feet. This is sometimes a structural fault but at times can be improved by adept handling. Movement may also be faulty by virtue of a too-wide front, which causes a side-to-side rolling motion, or by cow hocks, which rob the dog of the power to cleanly transmit the driving force of his rear legs.

TEMPERAMENT

The correct disposition for the Bernese Mountain Dog is alert and somewhat suspicious of strangers around home but agreeable to being handled by strangers away from home. The good-natured Berner is wary and accepts strangers slowly, admitting them into his circle when his master has told him that it is acceptable to do so. Away from home, the Berner should be congenial, self-confident, and never shy or timid.

Faults in temperament include shying from or being aggressive toward judges or people who approach in a friendly, nonthreatening manner. Growling, snapping, or lunging at any nonthreatening dog or person, especially a child, is out of character and absolutely unacceptable.

The Canadian Standard: A Brief Introduction

The Canadian Standard for the Berner differs in subtle ways. Although the wording may be a little tighter in some areas, it still describes an ideal Bernese Mountain Dog and accounts for the freedom we have to show back and forth across the Canadian and American borders. A good Berner will be able to win in either country.

Canadian Kennel Club Breed Standard Effective January 1, 1988

ORIGIN AND PURPOSE

The Bernese Mountain Dog takes its name from the canton of Bern in Switzerland, its native land. It is one of the four Swiss tri-colour breeds known by the collective name Sennenhunde, the only one of the four with a long coat. The Bernese Mountain Dog and his ancestors lived for many generations as farm dogs, with occasional use as draft dogs. From this background developed a hardy, natural, good-natured working breed that today is known principally as a faithful family companion.

GENERAL APPEARANCE

Large, sturdy, well-balanced working dog of substantial bone. Square in appearance from withers to ground and withers to tail set. Heavy-coated with distinctive characteristic markings. In comparison with the opposite sex, dogs appear masculine, bitches feminine, without loss of type.

TEMPERAMENT

The Bernese temperament is one of the breed's strongest assets. Consistent, dependable, with a strong desire to please. Self-confident, alert, good natured. Attached and loyal to human family; may be suspicious of strangers, but never sharp or shy. A dog must stand for examination when required to do so by its handler.

SIZE

Dogs 24.4-27.6 in. (62-70 cm) [best size 26-26.8 in. (66-68 cm)]; Bitches 22.8-26 in. (58-66 cm) [best size 23.6-24.8 in. (60-63 cm)]. Height measured at the withers. The stocky, well-balanced appearance must be maintained.

COAT AND COLOUR

The adult coat is thick, moderately long, possibly with a slight wave but never curly. It has a bright natural sheen. In texture it is soft rather than harsh, but is weather resistant, easily kept and resists matting. There is a soft, seasonal undercoat. Compulsory markings: Jet black ground colour. Rich russet markings (dark reddish brown is most favoured) appear on the cheeks, in a spot over each eye, in a patch above each foreleg, and on all four legs between the black of the upper leg and the white of the feet. Clean white markings as follows: On chest extending uninterrupted to under chin, also a slight to middle-sized blaze extending into a muzzle band which is not so wide as to obliterate the russet on the cheek (and which preferably does not extend past the corners of the mouth). Preferable markings: White feet with white reaching at the highest the pasterns and a white tip of tail. Mark-

Bartlett's Berners -- Things not mentioned in the Breed Standard

The nose nudge or Bernese Mtn Bump...

the Big Swiss attack...

Houseguest hospitality...

Critter sitter...

ings should be symmetrical. Too little white is preferable to too much.

SKULL

Flat and broad with a slight furrow; defined but not exaggerated stop.

Muzzle: Strong and straight; roughly square proportions, tapering only very slightly. Muzzle is slightly shorter than length of skull. Lips are fairly clean and tight; black in colour.

Teeth: Jaw is strong with good teeth meeting in a scissors bite. Dentition should be complete.

Nostrils: Well open and black in colour.

Eyes: Dark brown in colour, almond shaped, and well set apart; tight eyelids. Expression is intelligent, animated and gentle.

Ears: Middle-sized, triangular in shape with rounded tip. Set above eye level high on side of head; hanging close to the head in repose, brought forward at the base when alert.

NECK

Strong, muscular of medium length, well set on. Dewlaps are very slightly developed.

FOREQUARTERS

Shoulders are well-muscled, flat lying and well laid back. Forelegs are straight with substantial bone; parallel stance. Elbows are well under shoulders. Pasterns are slightly sloping, but not weak. Feet are proportionate in size, round and compact. Dewclaws are preferably removed.

Two Berners socialize while their people watch the 1991 BMD Specialty.

BODY

Approximately square from withers to ground and withers to tail set. The body is sturdy. The chest is broad, with good depth of brisket reaching at least to the elbows; ribs are well sprung. The back is firm and level. Loins are strong and muscular. The croup is broad, well-muscled.

HINDQUARTERS

The hindquarters are powerful, with broad, well-muscled thighs and substantial bone. Stifles are well-angulated. Hocks are well let down, turning neither in nor out. Pasterns are wide and straight, standing parallel. Feet are proportionate in size, round and compact. Dewclaws must be removed in the first few days of life.

TAIL

Bushy, hanging straight, with bone reaching to the hock joint or slightly below. Carried low in repose, higher when the dog is in motion or alert. An upward arc is permissible, but the tail should never curl over itself or be carried over the back.

GAIT

The natural travelling gait of the breed is a slow trot, but it is capable of speed and agility. Good reach in front. Strong drive from the rear; flexing well at the stifles. The level backline is maintained; there is no wasted action. Front and rear feet of each side travel in lines parallel to direction of motion, converging toward a centre line at increased speeds.

FAULTS

A fault is any deviation from the standard, to be weighed in accordance with the degree of deviation. In addition and in particular: Major Faults — ectropion or entropion; undershot or overshot mouth; tail rolled over back. Minor Faults (subject to degree of fault) — deficiency of type, particularly lack of substance; overly long or thin body; light or round eyes; level bite; incomplete dentition; too narrow or too snipey muzzle; too massive or too light head; too light russet markings or impure colour; grey colouring in black coat; nonsymmetrical markings, especially facial; white neck patch; white anal patch; curly coat in adult dog; splayed feet; kink in tail.

DISQUALIFICATIONS

Cryptorchid or monorchid males; split nose; absent markings as described in Compulsory Markings; white neck ring; blue eye colour; ground colour other than black.

Ch. Deerpark Iner v. Buttonwillow, owner Denise Dean, breeder Diane Russ. This lovely young bitch grew up to be a top producer. *Photo by Patrick Hatch.*

Some things get better and some things get worse, but puppies are always cute. Sylvia Howison has a lapful of cute babies who aren't in the least worried about such things.

SEVEN

Choosing A Puppy

Before You Decide on a Berner

Before you look at puppies, be sure that a Bernese Mountain Dog will suit your family's life-style and preferences. Dogs have been bred for centuries for specific tasks that have shaped their personalities. When you find the personality that best satisfies your needs and wants, you will have a dog that you will enjoy. An excellent book in the personalities and dispositions of all breeds is *The Perfect Puppy* by Dr. Benjamin L. and Lynette Hart. If you're convinced that a Berner is the breed that suits you, you are ready to choose a puppy.

Selecting a Berner puppy is a very important decision. You are deciding to bring a new member into your family, and you will need to consider how the rest of your family, including other pets, will react to the new arrival. Keep in mind that a puppy is a baby. Like all babies, they need special attention. They need long rest periods, proper food, and constant access to plenty of fresh, clean water. While it is wonderful for the puppy to socialize with the family and visitors, after a short while he should be allowed to go to his quiet place to rest. This lets your puppy learn about the world of people, plus he learns that there's a time for play and a time for quiet.

Contacting a Breeder

Before you begin looking at Berner puppies, contact several breeders, and before you talk price, find out what guarantees they offer on the puppies and adults that they have for sale. A responsible breeder will offer a limited guarantee on general health and will have records of vaccinations and health care received by the puppies. The guarantee should include some provision for replacing the puppy if he should have a genetic defect, such as hip dysplasia, although the guarantee may be different for show-quality dogs and breeding stock than for pet prospects.

A Berner labeled "pet quality" is not necessarily an inferior specimen of the breed. "Pet quality" usually means that the dog is a good representative of the breed but may lack the symmetry of markings, substance of bone, or movement characteristics that would make him really competitive in the conformation ring. A reliable breeder should willingly explain why a puppy has been graded as a pet. If you do not intend to show in the conformation (breed) ring or breed your Berner, this may be just the individual for you.

Berners can shine in the obedience ring, where the thrill of competition is just as intense and the winning just as satisfying. If this is the case, dispo-

SALES AGREEMENT

This agreement accompanies the Contract of Sale of one Bernese Mountain Dog to ______________ ______________________________. It is the intent of this agreement to clarify the rights and guarantees of the Breeder and Purchaser, both of whom must agree to the conditions set forth herein.

1. HEALTH: The Breeder guarantees the health of this dog for a period of 48 hours. The Purchaser agrees to take dog for a veterinary checkup within this time. The Purchaser agrees that he will maintain all necessary shots as recommended by the veterinarian, and will maintain the animal according to the highest possible health care standards. See back of Agreement for up-to-date shot record. This portion of the Sales Agreement *excludes* death from accident or improper handling of dog.
2. HIP DYSPLASIA: A) The Purchaser guarantees to X-ray the dog for hip dysplasia at the age of 2 years, or sooner if symptoms appear. B) Purchaser also guarantees to submit the above X-rays to OFA in Missouri for possible certification. C) Breeder guarantees that if the dog becomes crippled from hip dysplasia, she will replace the dog with a like-quality puppy, in which case the dysplastic dog must be returned. If the Purchaser wishes to keep the dog, Breeder will sell the Purchaser another dog of the same quality for one-half the purchase price. D) Purchaser agrees to neuter dog with severe dysplasia, *but prior to any such action* guarantees to discuss the matter with the breeder. E) *Purchaser guarantees to feed the dog in strict accordance to Breeder's instructions* and the above section will be considered void if this is not done.
3. PET QUALITY PUPPIES: Anyone purchasing a pet-quality puppy which has characteristics deemed detrimental to the breed at large if bred, guarantees to neuter this dog at the age of 6 months.
4. BREEDING RIGHTS: Breeders hold the right to use all males produced by this kennel at stud for one-half a reasonable stud fee.
5. CHANGE OF OWNERSHIP: Purchaser agrees that if at any time he wishes to sell the dog, the Breeder will have first right to purchase the dog back at a reasonable price.
6. KENNEL NAME: Purchaser agrees to use the kennel name, Buttonwillow, and the prefix letter of this litter.

CONTRACT OF SALE

The Breeders hereby sell one Male/Female Bernese Mountain Dog from the ________ Litter, whelped on ____ to:

Name: ______________________________

Address: ______________________________

City, State, Zip: ______________________________

Phone: ______________________________

The sale price is $ ________, to be paid in full on the date of the signing of this contract, unless other arrangements, to be specified below, have been made.

Buyer(s) signature below indicates that he/she has read and agreed to all the conditions of the Sales Agreement and Contract of Sale.

______________________	______________________
Date	Buyer
______________________	______________________
Breeder	Buyer

SPECIAL CONDITIONS

____

____

SHOT RECORD

Distemper/measles ____________	six weeks	Rabies ____________	four months
DA2PL/parvo ____________	nine weeks	Parvo ____________	eighteen weeks
DA2PL/parvo/corona ____________	twelve weeks	DA2PL/parvo ____________	eighteen weeks

FEEDING INSTRUCTIONS

Feed a good puppy food with no more than 26% protein, and keep the puppy thin. NO SUPPLEMENTS!

sition and personality are particularly important. Choose your Berner puppy carefully for the temperament that will suit you best. The breeder should still offer a guarantee of general good health and soundness and special provisions against hip dysplasia. Some breeders, however, only guarantee replacement of the dog or a refund of money in the event of crippling from dysplasia.

A guarantee of replacement or refund of money in the case of hip dysplasia is very important. Hip dysplasia is a crippling disease of the hips that affects many large breeds, and Berners, as a large breed, are susceptible. (For more information on hip dysplasia, see Chapter 13.)

Remember, too, that you are buying a registered, purebred dog. Make sure that the breeder has sent the litter registration to the American Kennel Club, and obtain a written agreement that the individual registration form ("blue slip") for your Berner will be given to you when you pick up your puppy, or sent at a later date if it has not yet been processed by the AKC. When no document is available, the AKC requires a breeder to provide the following information: breed, sex, color and markings, date of birth, litter number (when available), names and registration numbers of the sire and dam, name of the breeder, and the date sold or delivered. For a dog that is already registered, written documentation must include the registered name, the registry number, and the date sold or delivered.

Left: Decisions, decisions. Which one will I choose? *Art by Janet Wissmann.*

Below: At first glance, littermates are nearly indistinguishable, but differences are soon apparent. The Buttonwillow "O" litter.

Making Your Selection

There is nothing cuter than a litter of Berner babies. At first glance, they look like carbon copies of each other. On closer inspection, you will find a variety of distinguishing features. There will be differences in the amount and placement of white markings on the face and feet. Some puppies will be larger and some smaller; some will be quiet and some will be boisterous.

Be sure that you know whether you want a dog to show or a pet. Read the Bernese Mountain Dog Standard and have an idea of the Berner that you want. If you don't know what you want, even an experienced breeder will have difficulty helping you choose the best puppy for you. If you are not sure whether you want a pet or a show prospect, choose the show prospect; however, you should be aware that show puppies are priced higher than companion dogs.

Perhaps you will see one puppy whose appearance attracts you more than the others. When choosing a puppy on appearance, keep in mind what the Standard says about how the Berner should look. White markings should be symmetrical, although the amount of white is a personal choice. White on the feet should not extend above the pasterns. On young puppies, large white areas will appear to shrink as the puppy grows, and the russet will expand. If you prefer more white on an adult, choose the puppy with substantial white markings. You can estimate where the markings will extend on the face by feathering back the hair at the margin of the blaze. A solid white line will show how far the white will extend when the puppy is grown. Also, a white mark often appears at the back of the neck; this spot is not usually large and disappears in a few months. Small amounts of some larger markings may remain into adulthood, but this is not regarded as a serious flaw. More important are the amount and placement of russet markings; if you plan to show your dog, choose a puppy whose russet cheek patches come at least to the corners of the mouth.

If you choose a puppy by size, look first at the parents to get an idea of how large the puppy may grow. The Standard allows some variation in size; therefore, size may not be critical in choosing a

The bleeding of black into the russet on this four-month-old's forelegs is not desirable but will almost totally disappear, and she will also grow to fit her ears.

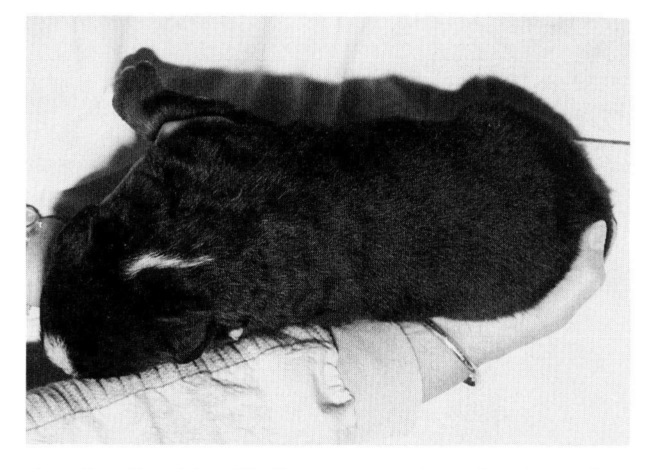

A stripe like this will disappear, perhaps leaving only a few hairs to mark its presence.

Ch. Beauty v. Buttonwillow showing symmetry of markings on face, chest and feet with the help of a young friend.

A black mark like this will remain, but if it is low enough, it will not be visible. If visible, it may be counted as a minor fault.

typical Berner. Signs of potential for large size include larger feet and a longer tail when compared to littermates. The size of the legs in Berner puppies is not a real indication of the puppies' potential adult size because Berners tend to have large legs anyway.

Whether you are interested in pet or show quality, temperament is of paramount importance. Try to notice how outgoing or reserved the individual puppies are. Some will come to you right away and demand your attention; others will be reserved and will come only after they are accustomed to your presence. If a puppy appears to be shy, keep in mind that it takes special handling to bring a shy individual to full potential; therefore, this puppy may not be a good choice for a novice owner.

Male or Female?

Another important consideration in choosing a Berner puppy is sex. Do you want a male or female? If you choose a female, she will come in season twice a year. During those times, she must be kept separated from *all* males to prevent unwanted pregnancy.

Differences in personality between sexes in Berners are slight. Both sexes are usually outgoing and amiable and train easily. Instances of stubbornness occur on an individual basis regardless of sex. If you intend to breed, you'll want a bitch, of course. If you plan to breed eventually, but just want to show and train your Berner for a while, a male is a better choice; he doesn't have to miss obedience or conformation handling classes two months out of the year because he is in heat. If you plan on spaying or neutering your dog, the sex that you choose makes little difference. Males are larger than females; therefore, if space is at a premium at your house, you may prefer a female.

Choosing a Show Puppy

When choosing a show prospect, look for clear, bright colors of black, rust, and white on a symmetrically marked, stocky puppy with straight front legs and a broad, deep chest. The head should be broad with a short muzzle and a fairly deep stop. It should be wide at the cheeks and have good width between the ears. The eyes should be tight-lidded and dark in color. Look for short hocks and a well-bent stifle. The tail should be set low and carried moderately low; puppies will carry their tails up and gay when playing, but the tail should not be carried curled over the back and should hang straight when the puppy is calm.

Sylvia Howison, long-time breeder and judge of Bernese Mountain Dogs, suggests that breeders use

Above: Ch. Hallelujah v. Buttonwillow shows the symmetry of markings and substance of a future champion. Owned and shown by Debbie Goldbey.

Below, left: Am/Can Ch. Gruezi Dear Abby CD and Ch. Gruezi Earl of Sandwich, two show-quality puppies.

Below, right: Joe Fridy, a potential show puppy, displaying clear colors, symmetrical markings, broad head, well-defined stop, and stocky build. Owned by A.B. Davis and Jerry Uhl, bred by Jerry Uhl.

the following guidelines in picking a show puppy. First, keep notes on each and every litter bred, including information on the parents, the grandparents, and earlier generations if they have been seen. Photos and videos are useful, but the camera (and each person who looks at a dog) often sees something different. Record all of the traits — good and bad — that you remember about the puppies' ancestors.

Next, when the puppies are six to eight weeks old, wet each puppy thoroughly — all that fuzzy puppy coat can hide the structures underneath it. With the puppy sopping wet, notice the structures of the head, the spring of the ribs, and the rear angulation.

On the head, are the lengths of the muzzle and skull about equal? Is there plenty of room between the ears? Is there a bit of dome to the skull? If so, the head is probably going to be structured correctly. Check the teeth and the eyes. The teeth should meet in a loose scissors bite. The lower jaw grows more slowly than the upper jaw, and a small amount of room is needed for the lower jaw to catch up without becoming level or undershot. Eye color is difficult to evaluate in a pup less than eight weeks of age; however, a light blue iris, a disqualification for show dogs, is evident when the puppy is five weeks of age or older. Check to see that the lower eyelids are tight, with no drooping or red haw showing. The eyes should be set well into the skull, not protruding, and should be set well apart.

Continuing to the body, there should be an apparent neck. Not only will a lack of neck give the appearance of a bunched-up adult, but a lack of neck is often a first indication of faulty shoulder structure that will result in choppy, incorrect movement. The ribs should have a definite spring but should taper in underneath the chest and not be round like a barrel. The back of even the young puppy should be fairly level and not roached up (if the pup is wet and cold, let him walk around a little before deciding whether the back is roached). A rule of thumb says that no more than two fingerwidths of loin (space between the last rib and the hipbone) should be present on the eight- to ten-week-old puppy. More or less space could indicate an adult with a too long or too short body.

All kids love a cuddly puppy. Kate Rogers and three-month-old Deerpark Kameo.

Shoulders should lay back a bit and not poke up like tent poles. Rear legs should be sturdy and not overangulated. Rear legs that look like jackrabbit legs are overangulated and will be weak. Feet should be round and tight and should never be splayed.

The next evaluation can be done with the puppy dry and rested. In a hallway or similar area, have someone hold a puppy while you go to the other end. Call the puppy to you calmly; you would like the puppy to trot, not run. Observe his movement as he comes toward you. He should move straight at you with no rolling in at the pasterns. Elbows should not turn out as the front feet come down.

Wyemede's Valais von Alpenrose at four and a half months of age shows typical teenage conformation.

Irresistible Berner puppies.

This lanky teenager turned out to be Ch. Shersan Chang' O'Pace v. Halidom CD. (See what he turned out to look like on the next page.)

Ch. Shersan Chang' O' Pace v. Halidom, a top winning Berner. "Pacer" is shown here winning Best in Show.

Now, have your helper call the puppy so that you can watch his rear movement as he goes away from you at a trot. Hind legs should move cleanly and straight ahead. Hocks should point neither in toward the center nor outward, and the action should be the same on both sides.

To evaluate movement from the side, watch two or three puppies in a large area. Agile, free movement is important, even in the very young puppy. The show puppy must move smoothly, with balanced (equal) drive from the rear legs and extension of the front legs. Jerky action may be an indication of orthopedic or structural problems.

Observe puppies as they get up from a resting position, too. A puppy that *always* sits up in front from a prone position and then pulls himself to a stand by using his front may be dysplastic. A puppy should be able to bound up off of the ground on all fours. An unsound puppy will want at least two feet and more likely three on the ground at all times.

Along with structure and movement, evaluate the temperament and disposition of show prospects. Puppies should be confident and outgoing, although any puppy can have an off day. A puppy that constantly "freezes" when introduced to new surroundings may turn out to be timid. It may be possible to improve this puppy's attitude by removing him from the litter and giving him special attention from six to ten weeks of age. Pick him up often and touch him all over; however, this puppy will need a special, understanding home where he can get the needed attention. It is important to note that a timid individual — no matter how sound and correct his movement and structure — will often be at a disadvantage in the show ring, where charisma and a bolder attitude catch the judge's eye.

Sylvia Howison also lists traits that may either improve or worsen as the puppy matures. These characteristics apply to the eight- to ten-week-old puppy.

TRAITS THAT MAY IMPROVE

Insufficient angulation
Curly coat
White neck spot (usually disappears if smaller than a quarter)
Gray fringes on puppy coat
Smooth, short coat
Light eyes (may darken somewhat)
Slightly overshot bite
Slightly roached back
Slightly long loin
Slightly light bone

TRAITS THAT PROBABLY WILL NOT IMPROVE

Variation in rust markings
Large areas of excessive white
Fine, weak muzzle
Overangulated rear
Very long loin (more than four fingers' width)

Snuggle up close, kids, it's cold out here. Deerpark "B" litter. Breeder: Denise Dean.

At six months of age, these four typical teenagers show the lanky stage that Berner puppies often go through.

Very fine, slender bones
Size at six weeks of age less than half that of the largest puppy

TRAITS THAT PROBABLY WILL WORSEN
Undershot bite
Very short neck
Straight shoulders
Splayed feet
Too little white on face
Wry mouth

Not every eight- to ten-week-old show-prospect Berner will mature into a top show dog, but if you choose these characteristics and a sound temperament, you will have a head start toward a quality Berner. Furthermore, a pedigree of dogs that have produced quality offspring is more likely to produce a competitive show Berner than one that does not.

If you are choosing a Berner puppy to show, keep in mind that he will go through growth stages. The stocky, chubby puppy may become tall and lean; his body may appear more like that of a setter than like that of a proper draft dog. A puppy's body grows at different rates; the topline may sag and his front end might appear to belong to a different dog than does his rear. Movement may appear loose and gangling, and the adolescent Berner may look insubstantial. But take heart — at about eighteen months of age, he will begin to "come back together." By the time he is two to three years old, he will have reached his full potential, and hopefully he will have recaptured the good looks and potential that he showed as a puppy.

Art by Janet Wissmann.

Temperament

With the exception of the guidelines on temperament, these suggestions have been aimed especially at the person who intends to show his or her Berner. For the Berner owner who wants only a pet and companion, less perfection is acceptable, and temperament may be the most important factor.

A good guide to a puppy's temperament is his score on a puppy aptitude test (PAT). Developed by Jack and Wendy Volhard in the late 1970s, this series of nine developmental measurements can determine whether a puppy is dominant or submissive, outgoing or introverted, and can give you a clue regarding his potential for obedience training. Each puppy is tested separately and is scored on a six-point scale where a score in the middle of the range is optimum. The ideal time to do the aptitude test is at seven weeks of age. If the breeder from whom you are buying has not already tested the puppy that you are considering, ask if you may perform the test yourself.

Writing in the February 1988 issue of the *Alpenhorn,* breeder/trainer Melissa Bartlett stated, "Puppies are tested at seven to ten weeks old by an unfamiliar person in an unfamiliar place. If the puppies are tested earlier, the tests may not be accurate, and if they are tested later, the environment influences the scores." The PAT has been proven to be a useful tool for matching the right dog to the right person. An experienced tester can help you find the Berner puppy that will fit your life-style and household. (See pages 112-113 for the test criteria.)

Older Berners

This chapter has been about choosing a puppy, but sometimes an older dog is a good choice. While it is a wonderful adventure to watch a puppy grow, an older Berner that already knows his manners can bring much pleasure to a home needing a quieter, more settled dog. And, surprisingly, the mature Berner adjusts readily to a new home, bringing all the love and loyalty that he showed his former family to his new one. Breeders often have older dogs that they want to place at a reasonable price as companions.

Choosing the right Berner may appear to be a great deal of work, but it will be worth the effort. The right dog will be a joy to the household and a pleasure throughout the years.

Take the picture, quick! Ten Bernerhof puppies won't stay still long. Breeders: Harriet Rector and Diane Russ.

Oh, the things a guy has to put up with on the road to fame and glory! Ch. Taliesin Ruff Stuff, "Dash," poses as a "Pup in a Cup" in this photo by Bob Abrams.

Temperament

With the exception of the guidelines on temperament, these suggestions have been aimed especially at the person who intends to show his or her Berner. For the Berner owner who wants only a pet and companion, less perfection is acceptable, and temperament may be the most important factor.

A good guide to a puppy's temperament is his score on a puppy aptitude test (PAT). Developed by Jack and Wendy Volhard in the late 1970s, this series of nine developmental measurements can determine whether a puppy is dominant or submissive, outgoing or introverted, and can give you a clue regarding his potential for obedience training. Each puppy is tested separately and is scored on a six-point scale where a score in the middle of the range is optimum. The ideal time to do the aptitude test is at seven weeks of age. If the breeder from whom you are buying has not already tested the puppy that you are considering, ask if you may perform the test yourself.

Writing in the February 1988 issue of the *Alpenhorn,* breeder/trainer Melissa Bartlett stated, "Puppies are tested at seven to ten weeks old by an unfamiliar person in an unfamiliar place. If the puppies are tested earlier, the tests may not be accurate, and if they are tested later, the environment influences the scores." The PAT has been proven to be a useful tool for matching the right dog to the right person. An experienced tester can help you find the Berner puppy that will fit your life-style and household. (See pages 112-113 for the test criteria.)

Older Berners

This chapter has been about choosing a puppy, but sometimes an older dog is a good choice. While it is a wonderful adventure to watch a puppy grow, an older Berner that already knows his manners can bring much pleasure to a home needing a quieter, more settled dog. And, surprisingly, the mature Berner adjusts readily to a new home, bringing all the love and loyalty that he showed his former family to his new one. Breeders often have older dogs that they want to place at a reasonable price as companions.

Choosing the right Berner may appear to be a great deal of work, but it will be worth the effort. The right dog will be a joy to the household and a pleasure throughout the years.

Take the picture, quick! Ten Bernerhof puppies won't stay still long. Breeders: Harriet Rector and Diane Russ.

PUPPY APTITUDE TESTING

1: Social Attraction

The tester sits on her heels and calls the puppy to her

2: Following

The tester walks away, verbally encouraging the puppy to follow.

3: Restraint

The puppy is gently rolled onto his back, and one hand gently restrains him for 30 seconds.
Eye contact and relaxedness are noted.

4: Social Dominance

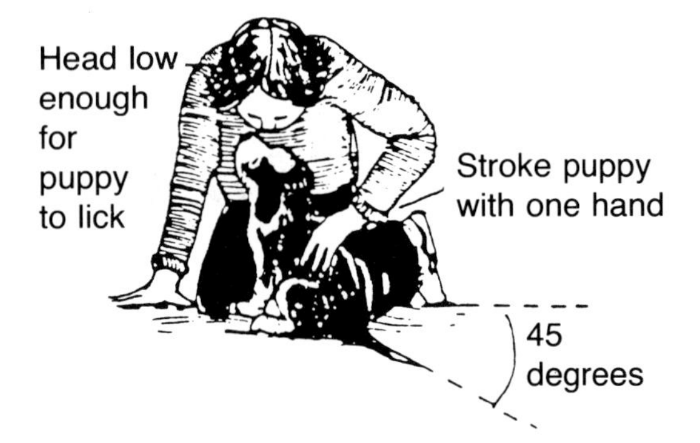

With the puppy sitting at a 45-degree angle in front of the tester, he is stroked gently from head to tail.

5: Elevation Dominance

The tester laces her fingers under the puppy's rib cage and lifts the puppy so that all four feet are off the ground. The puppy is held in this position for 30 seconds.

6: Retrieving

After the puppy starts toward the paper, the tester moves back and encourages the puppy

After getting the puppy's interest, the tester tosses the crumpled paper 2-4 feet away.

7: Touch Sensitivity

The tester cradles the leg in one hand and squeezes the webbing between the toes with the other. Squeezing with increasing pressure, the tester counts to ten.

8: Sound Sensitivity

Puppy faces away from tester

The tester bangs a metal spoon against a metal pan.

9: Chase Instinct

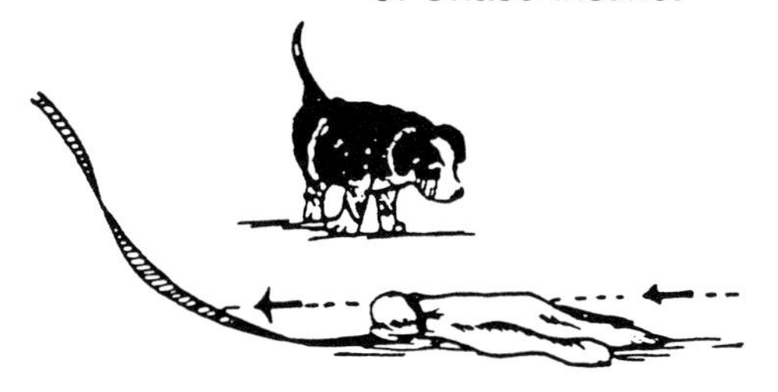

The tester jerks a towel across the floor in front of the puppy.

10: Stability

Tester pops open umbrella, then sets it down. Tester encourages pup to investigate the umbrella by tapping it and saying, "What's this, pup?"

Closed umbrella is held 4 ft away from the pup and perpendicular to the direction the pup faces. Puppies often startle when the umbrella is opened. They are scored on their response after umbrella is set down.

11: Energy Level

Watch pup's activity level on the testing and check with the breeder for confirmation.

Oh, the things a guy has to put up with on the road to fame and glory! Ch. Taliesin Ruff Stuff, "Dash," poses as a "Pup in a Cup" in this photo by Bob Abrams.

EIGHT

Bringing Up Baby

Preliminary Preparations

The groundwork for caring for your Berner puppy begins even before you bring the puppy home. Once you have selected your pup and made the arrangements, find out what type of puppy food the breeder has been feeding and purchase some of the same brand. Prepare a place for your puppy to sleep, eat, and play. Most people like to bring the young puppy into the house and fix a place for him in the kitchen or rec room, where he will have plenty of exposure to family activities for the first few weeks. You can make or purchase a four-foot-square pen for his "playpen." A large box or a crate will provide a secure place for him to sleep at night. Your puppy will be happier and will bond more quickly if his bed is placed near your own bed at night for the first few weeks.

Choosing A Veterinarian

Next, check into veterinarians in your area and select one with whom you have good rapport. Ask for recommendations from other dog owners and, if possible, from other Berner owners. You will be working with this person on a number of occasions and will need to trust him or her in an emergency. It is therefore important to select a veterinary clinic that is within reasonable distance of your home with a qualified staff.

It is important that you be aware of and discuss with the veterinarian when making your selection that Bernese Mountain Dogs often do not react to anesthesia the same way as other dogs of their size. In general, they need *smaller* doses of injected anesthetic agents than other breeds of their size and weight. If possible, inhalation anesthesia should be used on Berners, because it does not sedate the dog as deeply and is quickly reversible. A vet who is aware of this tendency in Berners can safely anesthetize your dog when necessary. If a veterinarian is not aware of this tendency and is not interested and willing to learn, keep looking.

First Day in the New Home

You have purchased your beautiful Berner puppy and brought him to his new home. The first few days with you are crucial to his adjustment. He should be given a place of his own right away and allowed some quiet time to explore, sleep, and adjust to new people, noises, and smells. His senses will be almost overloaded with the new experiences. A towel, sock, or toy from the breeder may help him feel at home. If none were provided, give him a soft toy (with all buttons removed so that he won't swallow them) to cuddle. Leave a radio for him, or place him where you will be working.

Art by Janet Wissmann.

Stroke and cuddle your puppy often.

If you have children, this is the time to teach them how to hold and handle the puppy, and then teach them to leave the puppy alone to take a nap. Don't allow the puppy to become overtired or overstressed the first few days by energetic young children.

Provide free access to water during the day, and feed according to the breeder's instructions, usually three or four times a day for an eight-week-old puppy.

How to Handle Your Puppy

Stroke, cuddle, and talk to your puppy often so that he will bond to you, but take great care when lifting him. Never pick up a Berner puppy by his front legs or underneath his shoulders. Three-fourths of a Berner puppy's weight is supported by tender shoulder cartilage. Picking him up under the "armpits" like you would a human baby could damage that cartilage severely, possibly causing movement problems or even crippling the dog.

The proper way to lift a puppy is to lift the front with a hand between the forelegs, holding the chest, and with the other hand or arm underneath the rump, lift the rear simultaneously, thus distributing the weight evenly. Your puppy will feel more secure, plus this method will prevent injury.

When petting the young puppy, be gentle, especially over the hips and shoulders, which can be injured by hearty thumps. Never punish the young puppy by swatting him on the rump. Heavy blows,

The correct way to pick up a puppy.

even given in love, damage soft cartilage in these areas. If your puppy jumps up on you, do not shove him down roughly, because this may injure him. Instead, push him gently back to the ground with a hand on his chest and immediately bend down to his level to give him attention. You may wish to tell him "Off!" as you push him down, and teach him a command for the "down" action, but praise in the form of your bending or stooping to pet him should follow immediately.

And because the Bernese Mountain Dog is a very rapid-growing dog that will reach his adult weight before his body is fully developed to carry it adequately, it is important that your Berner puppy not run up and down long stairways or jump off of any high place. This does not mean that you shouldn't own a Berner if your house is reached by a long stairway, but until your Berner is five or six months old, he should go up, and especially down, stairs slowly. In fact, his tender shoulder cartilage can best be preserved if he can be carried down very long stairways until he is too heavy or too large to be carried easily.

The watchword with your young Berner is "slowly." Although he will want to bound and jump and run with the exuberance of his youth, he should be restrained from putting forth all his speed and energy on stairs and jumping off of anything higher than himself. On flat terrain, your puppy can run and bound to his heart's content; however, it is not advisable that he be allowed to play roughly with larger, older dogs. And anytime that you see your young Berner limping after exercise, crate him or keep him at rest in a quiet place until all signs of pain or limping from overexercise are gone. If he is still limping after three or four days, he may need veterinary attention.

The First Veterinary Visit

As noted earlier, a breeder's warranty may specify that you must have your puppy examined by your own verterinarian within a specified time, usually forty-eight to seventy-two hours after taking the puppy home. Whether required or not, this is the recommended practice for all new puppies. You need to be absolutely sure that you are starting out with a healthy dog.

Take along any information on puppy shots or worm medication given by the breeder. The veterinarian will note these on your puppy's record and will be better able to advise you when booster shots and rechecks are needed. If no vaccinations have been given, the veterinarian will start you on a schedule that is right for your puppy. When you get home, make up a file folder for your puppy's records and place your sales contract, veterinary records, pedigree, and other papers safely in the file for future reference.

Quiet time. This young Berner takes time out for needed rest.

Naming and Registering Your Puppy

The breeder will most likely have supplied you with a "blue slip," or litter registration form, for your puppy. If you purchased an older dog or a show prospect, the dog's name may have been chosen by the breeder. Otherwise, you must choose a name and complete the litter registration *within six months of the date of birth.* After this date, the litter registration will not be honored by the American Kennel Club.

Because the Berner is a Swiss breed, some people like to name their puppy in the Swiss tradition. German is the primary language in Switzerland. You will often see the letters "v" and "vd" in the names of Bernese Mountain Dogs. These letters are an abbreviation for the German word "von," meaning "from," and "von der," "von den," or "von dem," all meaning "from the." In Switzerland, these are used to denote the region or the kennel where the dogs were born. In America, "vd" is seldom used, but "v" used before a kennel name that occurs as a suffix is very common. It is used to indicate the kennel that bred the dog. For example, *Ashley v Bernerliebe* is a dog from the Bernerliebe kennels.

Kennel names may be used as suffixes or prefixes and may be used interchangeably. A few kennel names are registered with the AKC; however, this is not required. If a name is registered, the breeder must give permission in writing on the registration application in order for you to use the kennel name as part of the dog's name. Unregistered names do not require the breeder's written permission. The breeder may require in the sales agreement that you use or do not use the name of the kennel.

When selecting a name, choose one that is unique, that fits the dog, and that does not rhyme with a command or with the name of a member of your household. For example, "Beau" rhymes with "No" and may be confusing to the puppy. Consider the length of the name and the ease of saying it clearly. The AKC requires that the puppy's registered name be no longer than twenty-five letters, including spaces. It is nice to take part of the registered name as the call name for your pup. Of course, you can always choose to call him something totally unrelated to his registered name.

You may glean some ideas for naming your dog by looking at his pedigree. A pedigree is the "family tree" of your puppy's ancestors. On the top half you will find the name of his sire (father), the sire's parents, the grandparents, and perhaps the great-

The amount of white on a Berner is a personal choice. Two Bernerliebe puppies have found satisfied owners.

grandparents. Other information, such as OFA (Orthopedic Foundation) numbers, eye certification numbers, or coat color, are sometimes given. The bottom half of the pedigree traces that same information on your puppy's dam (mother). It is incorrect to use kennel names from your puppy's ancestors other than the breeder's (owner of the dam's) kennel name. However, you may find individual names that can be combined or modified that would indicate relationship with the dogs in the background of your puppy. Or, they may spark an idea for a totally unique name of your own.

After you have chosen a name, complete the rest of the registration form and mail it to the AKC with the requested fee. In four to six weeks, you should receive an individual registration paper for your dog. It will list you as owner and your chosen name as the official registered name for your dog.

Note that there are two kinds of registrations offered by the AKC. In addition to the regular registration form, there is a Limited Registration. If the breeder supplied a Limited Registration paper with your puppy, no puppies can be registered from this dog or bitch. The dog may still compete in obedience or performance competitions but not in the breed classes at AKC shows. While there is no requirement to spay or neuter the dog, the Limited Registration stays with the dog when it is sold. However, the *breeder* of the dog may revoke the Limited Registration if the dog is later deemed to be of show/breeding quality. If you plan to breed or show, remember to check out the type of registration being provided with your puppy *before* you sign the purchase agreement.

A Berner likes to be close to his people, and this fellow takes his duty literally.

Cool water, a cool, dry place to lie, and a friend to share it with make a wonderful life.

Your Puppy's Crate

A crate is important in several ways. It keeps the puppy out from under foot, it teaches him the meaning of quiet time, it provides a safe car restraint when he travels, and it restricts unsafe roaming at shows, motels, or when you can't be with him. In addition, it is a great aid in housetraining. A crate is not a "jail"; it is a necessity for the puppy's discipline and safety. Although a pup may protest going into the crate for the first few times, he will soon accept it as his haven of safety. For this reason, never scold or punish your puppy in or near his crate.

Purchase a crate that is large enough for your puppy to grow into. For a Berner, a crate approximately twenty-four inches wide, thirty-six inches deep (long), and twenty-seven inches high is recommended. A wire crate will permit better air circulation and is preferred over the plastic airline crates. Crates can be purchased at most pet-supply stores, at some discount stores, and through many dog-supply catalogs.

Pad the bottom of the crate with a blanket or carpet remnant. Give the puppy a Nylabone or large rawhide chew toy, and he will be content to sleep in his crate. Just remember not to leave him there too long — a couple of hours at a time is maximum for a puppy. An older dog can be crated safely for about one-half day or during the night.

Feeding the Berner Puppy

Choose a balanced, nutritionally complete dog food with 24 to 26 percent protein for your Berner puppy. Choose a growth formula or a food that is certified nutritionally complete for all life stages by National Research Council standards. The breeder who sold you your pup will probably suggest a good ration that is readily available in your area. No additional supplements should be needed. If your young Berner is hesitant to eat the kibble in dry form, moisten it with a little hot water or broth. *No* added calcium should be given, but if your veterinarian recommends it, a multivitamin supplement can be used. Table scraps, except for perhaps very small portions put over the dry kibble, are to be avoided, because they are not nutritionally balanced.

Breeders' experience has shown that Berners, both puppies and adults, will grow and prosper better on a diet containing a moderate amount of protein than on a high-protein diet. The only time that I have had problems in my dogs was when I fed a highly recommended 30-percent protein food.

Remember that a healthy puppy is not necessarily a fat puppy. Berner puppies should ideally be a little on the thin side to minimize stress on hip and shoulder joints. Some Berner breeders stipulate in their sales agreements that feeding a high-protein diet to puppies will nullify the breeder's guarantee against hip dysplasia (HD) and osteochondrosis dessicans (OCD). Evidence indicates that the feeding of a "hot," high-protein food can push a puppy's growth until he becomes susceptible to nutritional and environmental causes of HD or OCD.

Excessive weight causes stress on shoulders and hips. The fat puppy can easily injure himself in normal movement while the cartilaginous growth plates are being replaced by bone tissue. For that same reason, a Berner puppy should not be allowed to jump from high places like porches or steps, or to go up and down high flights of stairs. A fast-growing, large breed like the Bernese Mountain Dog is most prone to develop OCD or panosteitis during the intense four- to nine-month growth period. During this stage, it is especially important to feed a moderate protein food with a balanced amount of fat. If limping or other signs of lameness occur, reduce the protein level of the puppy's feed and restrict his activity.

After your puppy has reached nine months of age and this rapid growth period has passed, fit your puppy's diet to his life-style. The more active he is, the higher the protein level, perhaps up to 26 percent.

Signs of a well-fed but suitably slim Berner puppy include being able to just feel his ribs and a slight hollow behind the ribs. A puppy with a potbelly that lingers long after mealtime may have a roundworm infestation. His stool sample should be checked for parasites by your veterinarian.

FEEDING SCHEDULE FOR PUPPIES

Now that you know what to feed, you need to establish a consistent feeding schedule. *When* you feed can be almost as important as *what* you feed. A seven-week-old puppy will need three meals a day. When the puppy is five months old, the daily ration may be divided into two meals, one in the morning and one in the evening. These are only guidelines, of course. You shoud suit the feeding schedule to the needs of your particular puppy. Some puppies will do better on three or four feedings a day for a much longer period than the averages listed here.

HOUSETRAINING

To use a crate as a housebreaking aid, you must

In training to be a mountain dog. *Photo by Bobbie Hefner.*

have the crate available as soon as you bring your puppy home. The puppy will need to evacuate his bladder and/or bowels after waking, playing, and eating. Take your puppy to a designated area in the yard. If he goes, praise him with a light, high-voiced, "Good puppy!" If he does not go, take him back to his crate, wait for a short time, and give him an opportunity to go again. Do this as many times as necessary until he relieves himself. When he has done his business, let him out in the house or yard again.

If he should have an accident, do not shout or punish him severely. A firm "No!" and taking him to the right spot outdoors will usually be enough to correct the situation. Punishment should be done only at the time of the infraction, not after the fact. Under no circumstance should a puppy's nose be rubbed in his mistake. Quite a few people have the incorrect notion that this is a way to housebreak. *It is not.*

Remember, too, that a puppy can't hold his movements as long as a grown dog. Offer him the "potty" area several times during the day if he is in the house most of the time. If he is to be in the house at night, he should sleep in his crate and not be allowed to wander around unsupervised. He will let you know if he needs to go out. It is important to understand that a crate is a training device and a bed. Keep your Berner out with you as much as possible so that he will become a member of the family.

Take your dog with you when you can. Seeing new places and new faces helps him become sociable.

Socialization and Discipline

In addition to vaccinations, health care, and physical exercise, your Berner puppy needs socialization. Take him to as many places as he is welcome. A trip to the park or to a friend's house, or a walk around a shopping center will teach your puppy about the world beyond his home and will allow him to develop a friendly attitude toward the outside world. Called socializing, this visiting away from home helps a dog develop into an emotionally balanced member of your family, secure and posed in all situations.

Berner puppies and adults, as a rule, do not require severe or even moderately severe discipline. The breed tends to be sensitive to harsh corrections, but discipline fairly given is rarely forgotten. The most important point to remember about disciplining a dog is to give a correction only at the time of the offense. If punishment or discipline is given long after an infraction, your Berner will not know why he is being punished, and he will become confused and distrustful of you.

In most instances of misbehavior, a stern "No!" or "Ah-ah" suffices to clue a Berner that his behavior is not acceptable. For the hard-headed individual that stands off and defies you, a scruff shake may be in order. Take a good hold on the hair and skin on either side of the neck, look your Berner straight in the eye, and tell him, "No!" in a quiet, firm voice. The tone of your voice and your expression will tell him more surely than the grip on his neck that his behavior has been unacceptable.

The other side of discipline is praise. An encouraging "good dog" will do much to reinforce desired behavior. If your Berner is scolded for tearing up the trash or digging up the roses, no praise should be given after the correction. However, when teaching a command, such as in obedience, if your Berner requires a snap on the leash to reinforce the idea of coming to you, praise him once he has come — even though you had to make him do it. A rule of thumb is to let your dog know when he's right and when he's wrong.

Basic Puppy Training

There is an old adage, "A trained dog is a happy dog." The corollary to that is, "A trained dog makes a happy dog owner." The Berner takes well to training. He has a natural desire to please you and learns easily. As soon as you get your puppy, you can begin training him a little each day — no, not formal, strict training, but basic facts of life that will allow him to develop into a good canine citizen.

Begin by teaching your puppy manners. The first thing that a puppy should know is to come when he is called. This also can be a time of special bonding, Berner to family. Call your puppy's name in a happy voice and bend down to him as he comes. You may have to pat your knees or clap your hands to give him the idea if he is not yet familiar with his name, but put a smile on your face and in your voice, and he will soon get the idea. When he comes, bend or kneel to be on his level and give him a small treat while praising him. Make coming to you a pleasant experience, and your Berner will come to you easily under any circumstance. However, *never* call your Berner to you and punish him! If you must punish a Berner, go to him to do it, and let the punishment fit the crime.

Of equal importance is that you should only punish him at the time of his transgression. If you arrive home after several hours absence to find an object broken or chewed, refrain from punishing your puppy. Instead, try to catch him in the act and make your displeasure known at that time. The Bernese Mountain Dog has a great sense of fairness and will resent unjust punishment. For the Berner, a shake of the neck scruff and a sharp reprimand are more than enough to stop unwanted behavior.

When your puppy is coming to you consistently, you can teach him how to walk with you on lead (leash). This can be done by letting *him* first take *you* for a walk. Fasten a flat buckle collar (nylon or leather) on your puppy and attach a leather or nylon lead (no chain) to it. Let your puppy go out to an area where he likes to explore and follow along with him, holding the lead. Put gentle pressure on the lead from time to time; if your puppy looks back to you at this, praise him, and let him continue exploring.

Two fifteen-minute sessions should be sufficient to accustom a Berner puppy to slight pressure on the lead, and you can begin to break the news to him that he has to walk with you where you go. While putting steady, gentle pressure on the lead, pat your leg and call your puppy to you. If your Berner struggles against the lead, as some will do, keep steady, gentle pressure on the lead and coax him to you, praising him lavishly when he finally makes it to you.

When your puppy has come to you, praise him and change direction again with pressure on the lead, encouraging him to follow you by patting your leg and calling his name. Praise your Berner as he changes direction and comes with you. Repeat this exercise, gradually shortening the lead until he has only enough lead to be at your left side on a loose lead. Continue praising him when he follows the pressure on the lead; encourage him with leg pats and voice until he stays at your side consistently. Praise him especially when he looks at you. When his eyes meet yours, and he gives you his full attention, tell him that he is wonderful — because he is. And the more you tell him, the more he will be.

These daily lessons at home over the next few weeks will prepare you and your puppy for formal obedience training later on. Whether you train for competition or just for socialization and manners, the training process will build bridges between you and your dog that will last a lifetime.

Ch. Ashley v. Bernerliebe finishing his CD a few days before his death. His special effort is an example of the dedication and courage the Berner brings to the human-canine relationship.

NINE

A Lifetime of Loving Care

The Bernese Mountain Dog is not a breed that can be confined to the backyard and forgotten. These dogs prefer human companionship and do not do well as kennel dogs. A Berner that is not given daily personal attention is likely to become a miserable, shy, large, problem dog.

Because of their size, body mass, and thick coat, and the sun-absorbing qualities of their black coat, Berners are susceptible to heatstroke. Young dogs may need to be restrained from exercising too much in hot weather. All Berners need shade and plenty of fresh drinking water. A child's wading pool provides a great way for the Berner to cool off. Although Berners live in the warm climate of our southern states, most will seek the comfort of their owners' air-conditioned homes. Alternately, they dig a cool subterranean den.

In fact, all Berners tend to dig, so it is important to provide an approved digging area for your dog. If you bury a rawhide chew or other favorite item there, your dog will be encouraged to dig in this area and not in your favorite flower garden.

Grooming

A dog with bright eyes and a shiny coat is a joy to behold, and the Berner coat has an especially eye-catching sheen. A double-coated breed, the Bernese Mountain Dog has a soft, wooly undercoat and a harsher outer coat. This weatherproof coat does not mat readily, and mud or dirt slips right out.

All that is needed to keep your Berner neat and clean is an occasional bath and frequent brushing. If your life is busy, one-half hour every week will suffice. This special time that you reserve to be alone with your Berner will benefit both of you.

The Bernese Mountain Dog will shed. The hair is easily removed from clothing or furniture with a velvet lint brush. A daily brushing will help to reduce the amount of loose hair about the house.

Tools for grooming the Berner are simple and few. Unless you are getting your Berner ready to show, a basic set of grooming tools consists of a pin brush, a slicker brush, and nail clippers. A grooming table is handy but is not absolutely necessary. However, you may find it easier to groom your Berner while he is standing on some high surface, where he may not be as apt to wiggle while being groomed.

Weekly grooming should consist of an overall brushing. Pay special attention to the area just behind the ears, where mats will form most readily, if at all.

Check your dog's toenails twice a month to see if they need clipping. Toenails are clipped to the edge of the pink line, or "quick," that shows

Above: Grooming table.

Left: Basic grooming tools include: slicker brush (Universal), pin brush, and nail clipper.

through white nails; on black nails, estimate the same distance and don't clip beyond it.

Ideally, nail clipping is started in the young puppy so that he becomes at ease with the procedure. By using fingernail clippers on the one-week-old Berner, you can prevent his clawing his mother's underside as he nurses. Weekly clipping will accustom him to the handling of his feet.

Regardless of the age of the Berner, use caution during the procedure. A quicked nail is very painful and will bleed; therefore, it is important to avoid cutting into the quick or your dog will become fearful of nail clipping. If you do cut the quick and the nail bleeds, you can use a preparation called Kwik Stop® to stop the bleeding (in a pinch, you can use flour).

Your Berner will also need his teeth cleaned periodically. Among the new products for dogs are toothpaste and a toothbrush that, if used daily, will help prevent tartar buildup. You can purchase a scaler and learn from your veterinarian or from a

Mountain Boy v. Buttonwillow gets groomed, and an ordinary table makes a good platform.

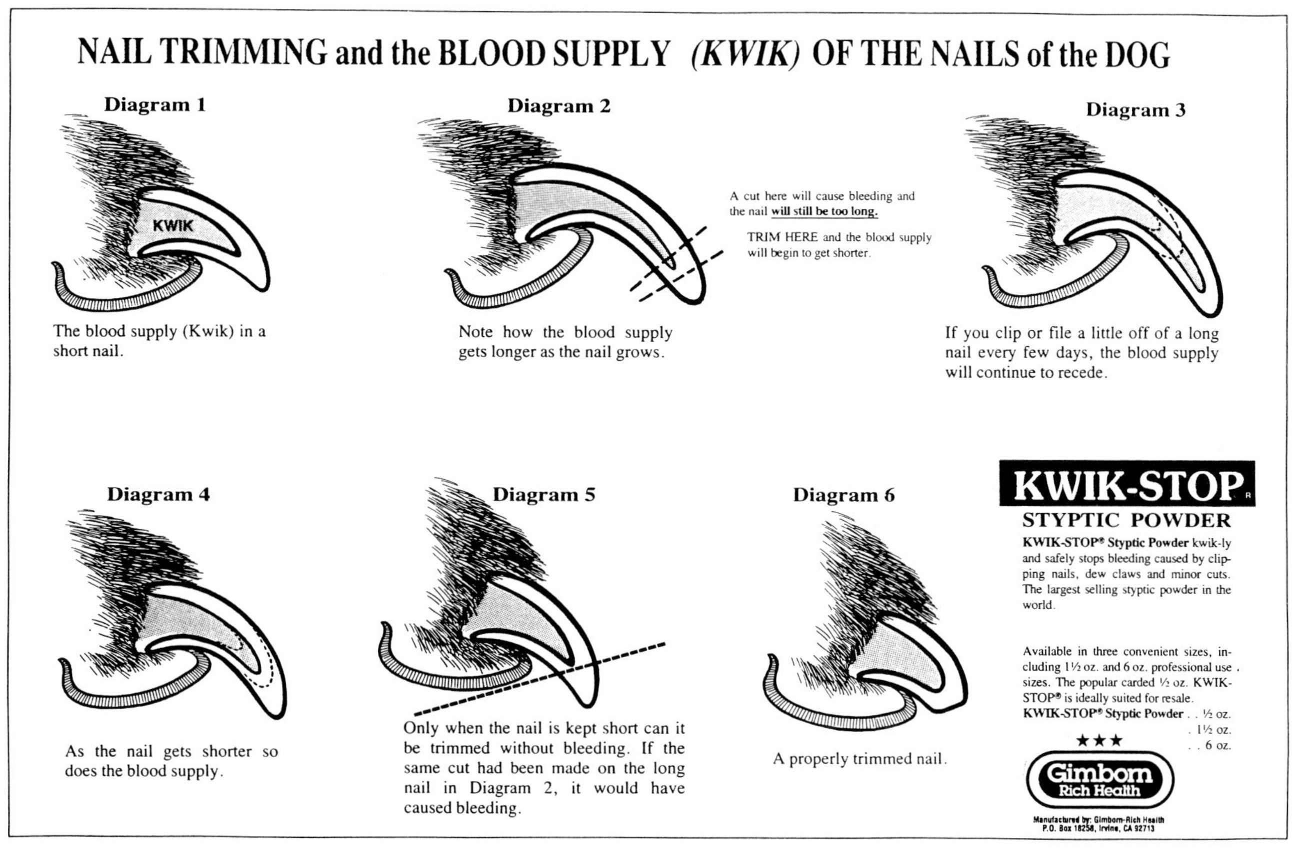

Used with permission.

Well-groomed Berner. *Art by Janet Wissmann.*

Berner breeder how to scrape the tartar off the outsides of the teeth. If you choose not to use either of these methods, your veterinarian will need to clean your dog's teeth periodically, especially as your Berner ages. Bad teeth and infected gums are the leading causes of heart problems and systemic infections in older dogs. Keeping the teeth in good condition is one way to ensure a healthy, relatively long life for your Berner. You should be aware, however, that veterinarians will insist on anesthetizing the dog before doing any dental procedures, and anesthesia carries a special risk for Berners.

Training

One of the most important aspects of your life with your Berner is the time you spend training him. This is a time of fostering a common language between the two of you and learning to communicate with each other. When your Berner puppy is at least three months old and has had time to bond to his new family, he is ready for puppy kindergarten. These classes are simple obedience lessons for the young dog usually offered by a local kennel club or obedience-training club, although they may be given by an individual. Often, they will be advertised in local newspapers, and veterinarians will post notices of upcoming classes on their bulletin boards.

Obedience training teaches you to teach your dog. In puppy kindergarten, most programs teach a sit, a down, and a heel lesson, along with some general information about care and feeding of puppies. The aim of kindergarten classes is to help you

Ch. Kaylin's Bridgette Bardot UD has gone far in obedience. She is shown here with owner Dorothy Lademan, receiving her High Scoring Dog award for a score of 199½.

learn to teach your dog good manners and to teach *you* how to communicate with your dog. They also prepare you and your dog for formal obedience training and provide needed socialization.

Formal obedience training can be started at six months, and classes are available from the same organizations or individuals as for puppy kindergarten. The lessons will be stricter versions of the puppy classes. As well as teaching sit, down, and heel, your dog will learn to stay and stand on command and to stay sitting and lying for an extended length of time while you are separated from him but not out of sight.

An important point to remember about training Berners is that they are willing workers and want to please you. They are also very sensitive. Harsh corrections and training methods will confuse them and hurt their feelings. Never allow anyone else to work with your dog unless you are absolutely certain that they will not use heavy-handed corrections. One nice working Berner was used by a competent but no-nonsense instructor to demonstrate an obedience lesson. When the Berner was hesitant to leave his owner, the instructor gave him a sharp jerk, or correction, to bring him into position, and the dog refused to work at all. What the instructor failed to realize (and perhaps the owner as well) is that Berners are aloof to strangers, and this outgoing, good-natured male wasn't prepared to work for someone whom he didn't know. Even now, this dog is wary of similar-looking men. In fact, it has been difficult for him to finish his obedience and conformation titles, because shows had to be picked that would avoid judges who resembled that instructor.

Remember, too, that Berners, especially puppies, are large dogs that grow very rapidly. At some growth stages, their bodies are too large for their immature muscles to move briskly. For this reason, don't demand quick sits, rapid departs into heeling, and snappy downs from your young dog. Many obedience instructors and their assistants are more familiar with smaller, lighter breeds such as Labrador Retrievers, Golden Retrievers, Shelties, and Border Collies and thus may not understand the Berner's special requirements during this time. Be patient with your instructor and explain your Berner's situation. Be patient with your Berner and

Dual titled Ch. Ouji v. Buttonwillow UD with owner/handler Elaine Bunn.

continue training at a pace that he can accommodate, but don't allow him to take advantage of his special status.

Above all, obedience training should be pleasant for the dog. It is a good socializing experience, and your Berner will learn to greet strangers happily away from home if you ensure that those people are polite and courteous. This is not to say that he will welcome unfamiliar people into his home territory or even people whom he has met previously away from home with open arms. He will be protective of his home and family when he is home and will probably "woof" at newcomers.

Housing

The Berner is an easy dog to care for and needs little special care and handling. Housing for your Berner is a simple matter. If he doesn't live in the house with you, a sturdy dog house sized to fit him will accommodate him. Berners are suited to cold weather; no special housing is necessary in most cases, although you should provide shelter from the winter winds.

The Bernese Mountain Dog is more susceptible to hot weather than to cold. He can live successfully in hot climates if he receives some special attention in very hot weather. Shade and a supply of cool water are essential. It is not necessary that he come inside to air-conditioning, but a fan placed outside to circulate the air in a shady spot will help him keep cool on the hottest days. If a Berner is going to dig, this will be the time. The breed is not noted for digging up the flowerbeds, but some will dig to get to cooler earth in the summer.

Fencing

Bernese Mountain Dogs do not need high fences, because they are not fence jumpers, yet some type of sturdy, four- or five-foot-high fencing is necessary. Many breeders will refuse to sell a puppy to a home that does not have a secure fence.

A kennel area for Berners also does not need to be elaborate. In the absence of a fenced yard, a kennel for a Berner should allow enough area for exercise. It should provide large enough space to allow him his bathroom area and still have room

Berners are at home anywhere their people are. Mountain Boy v. Buttonwillow relaxes aboard the fifty-three-foot boat where he lives with Harold and Bea Den Bleyker.

left over for romping. The kennel should be placed under shade and, if possible, near your house. As mentioned earlier, the Bernese Mountain Dog cannot be kenneled extensively and still maintain an outgoing personality.

In the *temporary* absence of kennel or fence, the Berner could be chained or tied as long as he has shade, shelter, and water. While we have never heard of Berners being tied out, we do not believe it would be harmful for a *short* time. During this time, take precautions to ensure that your dog will not be mistreated or teased. Do not tie or chain your Berner indefinitely. Remember, this is a breed that craves human companionship.

If, however, your gate is accidentally left open and your Berner walks out, there is usually no need to panic. Berners are homebodies that prefer to stay in their home territory. On a farm, Berners will seldom stray far from the house. This is the heritage of the farm dog that the Berner is bred to be.

Art by Janet Wissman.

Basic Nutrition

Food for your dog provides the raw materials for growth and body maintenance and the energy to support life and activity. A dog requires six major nutrients — protein, fats, carbohydrates, vitamins, minerals, and water. The need for each nutrient is different depending on your dog's life stage, whether the stage be growth, maintenance, work, pregnancy, or lactation.

Proteins, the most expensive components of any dog food, are also the most important. From the breakdown of protein, the dog derives several of the essential amino acids that he cannot make in his own body and must have for growth and maintenance. Both plant and animal proteins are used in commercial dog foods. Muscle meat, meat by-products (organ meats, hooves, feathers), bone meal, eggs, cheese, milk, fish, wheat, corn, and soybean meal are typical. A quality commercial dog food will list proteins as its first three ingredients. A good commercial food containing at least 24 percent protein is a good choice for the Bernese Mountain Dog.

The next most essential element in your Berner's diet is fat. Fat provides the energy that your dog needs in order to use the amino-acid-building blocks of the protein in his diet. Though much has been written about fatty-acid deficiency in dogs and its effect on the quality of the coat, there is little cause for concern in a diet adequate in fat content. Twelve to 16 percent fat in a dry dog food is adequate to provide energy in your Berner and keep his coat in condition.

Carbohydrates (sugars and starches) make up a large portion of a commercial diet. Sugars are easily digested by dogs without special processing, but starches such as corn, wheat, oats, or potatoes must be cooked in order to be digested. In this way, the dog can use a wide variety of carbohydrates in his diet. In fact, many dogs survived on cooked potatoes during World War II in England.

Vitamins and minerals, although they are not foods, are the dietary elements that enable proteins, fats, and carbohydrates to be used properly in the dog's body. With a good-quality commercial dog food, there is absolutely no need to supplement any vitamin or mineral, and this is especially true for the Bernese Mountain Dog.

All of the nutrients above provide energy and a basis for growth and maintenance in your Berner; however, none of them will suffice if he doesn't have continuous access to clean, fresh water. Water is not only necessary for transporting nutrients to the body's cells and for eliminating toxic waste products, but it acts as a coolant in warm weather when your Berner pants. The dog's body can lose all of its fat and half of its protein and still live, but if one-tenth of the total water content is lost, he will die.

If you are new to dog feeding, all of this may seem confusing. Be guided by the recommendation of your Berner's breeder until you have enough experience to see what food best promotes your dog's health and well-being. The most important point to remember about feeding your Bernese Mountain Dog is to keep him healthily slim.

Just watching. Pike's Rumple-Hochi v. Rex keeps an eye on seven-week-old Tyler Siceloff.

DIET-RELATED CONDITIONS

The Bernese Mountain Dog has a tendency toward two growth and/or physical conditions that plague all fast-growing, large breeds — osteochondritis dessicans (OCD) and panosteitis. Some breeders believe that these diseases are affected by the Berner puppy's diet. Symptoms of OCD include lameness or stiffness in the affected joint. It may affect many joints in the same individual, although the shoulder is the most commonly affected. The elbow, hock, and knee are less commonly affected.

While the two main causes of OCD are often presented as being genetic and environmental, one veterinarian at the University of Tennessee at Knoxville believes that OCD is a genetic condition only so far as it occurs in breeds heavier than sixty pounds. Research into environmental causes has strongly linked a high-protein diet and overexuberant exercise in the young dog with the development of OCD in Berners. Treatment includes immediately reducing the protein level of the puppy's diet and restricting his activity, especially jumping. Surgery may also be required. Obviously, you should consult your veterinarian. Keep in mind, however, that surgery will disqualify your Berner from being shown.

A little bit of hero worship. Mountain Boy v. Buttonwillow and German Shepherd friend prove that Berners are compatible with other breeds.

The second inflammatory condition that can occur in Berner puppies that are fed excessive protein is panosteitis. Similar to "growing pains" in children, panosteitis is an inflammation of every part of a bone and is characterized by limping on one or both front legs. Restriction of high protein levels and activity, such as in treating OCD, is also helpful in treating panosteitis. (For more information on panosteitis and osteochondritis dessicans, see Chapter 13.)

Feeding Ault Berners

Feeding the adult Bernese Mountain Dog is as simple as offering a nutritious, moderate protein food. A well-balanced, 24-percent protein dry food is adequate for the normally active adult Berner.

It is not even necessary to radically change the diet of the pregnant or lactating bitch. A good-quality, 24- to 26-percent protein diet, perhaps supplemented with a daily multivitamin, usually ensures a healthy pregnancy and strong babies. The only difference in feeding the pregnant/nursing bitch is that as her daily ration increases, it should be given in two or three feedings.

Coat luster and texture are good indicators of how well your Berner is assimilating the nutrients in his food. In the absence of internal parasites, a dull, harsh coat (except during shedding) is often a sign of poor nutrition. If the coat simply lacks luster, it may just be that a food with a higher fat content is needed.

Risk of bloat and gastric torsion can be minimized by feeding your Berner his daily quota of food in two small feedings rather than one large meal. Also, limit water consumption immediately before and after feeding.

Simply put, bloat is the swelling of the stomach with gas, and torsion is the turning of the stomach in the thoracic cavity so that the gas is trapped and the stomach enlarges like a balloon. The condition is life-threatening and is very painful to the dog, and you will note that he is in extreme distress. This is a *medical emergency*. Take the dog to the veterinary clinic *immediately*.

Another factor that puts a Berner at risk for bloat is the habit of gulping his food. Although not all Berners gulp their meals, for those that do, the divided-meals feeding system may be a lifesaver. In addition, a Berner should not be allowed or invited to play boisterously or to exercise strenuously after eating.

Guess who came to dinner! Sollberger Berners Fraenzi and Farah share a meal with Mutz the cat.

The importance of fresh, clean water cannot be overemphasized. Water is an essential nutrient in dogs, just as it is in people. Without it, other nutrients cannot be broken down and transported to the vital organs and tissues to promote and sustain life. Clean, fresh water, available at all times, good-quality food, and your love are all that your Berner needs to live a long, healthy life.

The Older Berner

In the absence of disease, the average life expectancy of a Bernese Mountain Dog is about eight years, and some live to ten or eleven. The Berner does not go through a period of failing health and senses in old age, as most other breeds do. There is usually no cataract development or loss of hearing, and there is no gradual diminishing of heart and kidney function. The Berner slows down and becomes more mellow until one day he is gone from you with no regrets and no long goodbyes. In any case, there are few "old" Berners in the general population.

Large dogs age more rapidly than smaller ones, but one rule applies to all: the better the care and nutrition, the more gradual and less dramatic the aging process. Signs of aging in the Berner include slowing of activity, more willingness to remain in the coolest or warmest spot in the house, and a little less tolerance of boisterous puppies. The elder Berner becomes even closer to his human family; he tolerates separation poorly, particularly boarding and hospitalization. If your older Berner requires simple medical attention, it is better to treat him at home with your vet's guidance and cooperation than subject him to the stress of separation. Any noticeable change in health should be brought to the vet's attention. The older Berner may need a complete health exam once or twice a year, and that may include a urinalysis, a complete blood count (CBC), and possibly an EKG and liver and kidney function tests.

Arthritis in joints may be present in the older Berner, but he can be made more comfortable with

Ch. Majanco Languardo lived to eleven years of age. He is pictured at ten years of age with owner Mrs. Joe Pike.

Ch. Yodeler's Konig v. Bernerhof carries his ten years gracefully, showing the quiet dignity of the older Berner.

moderate exercise, a padded sleeping area that is free of cold drafts, and buffered aspirin as recommended by your vet. His coat mats more easily, and his skin may become dry and scaly due to reduced activity of oil-producing glands. Small, nonmalignant skin tumors are common in the older Berner. Frequent, thorough grooming will keep his coat attractive and will help eliminate the musty odor so often acquired by the old dog. Bathing with mild shampoo when necessary will keep the coat and skin healthy, too, but special care should be taken to prevent chilling while the dog is wet. Towel him and keep him in a warm room that is free of drafts until he is completely dry.

NUTRITION AND THE OLDER BERNER

The older dog is subject to tooth and gum disease that may interfere with eating. A Berner's incisors sometimes wear down rapidly, and his teeth may require cleaning. Any loose and broken teeth should be removed to make it possible for him to eat without pain. Regular plaque removal and brushing during your Berner's life can prevent serious periodontal problems such as loss of teeth and bad breath. An experienced breeder or veterinarian can show you how to clean your dog's teeth.

The older Berner needs to have his daily quota of food divided into two feedings to prevent the possibility of bloat, and he requires fewer calories than when he was young and active. You may feed one of the commercially available "low-calorie" dog foods, but adjusting the amount of his normal diet and keeping track of how much padding is on his ribs and hips by daily inspection will accomplish the same goal.

EUTHANASIA (PUTTING YOUR BERNER TO SLEEP)

Your aging Berner may have no serious health problems throughout his later years; but if the older dog is in constant pain or poor health and he has no quality of life, there is a final kindness that you can offer your old friend. This is the last responsibility that you have for your Bernese Mountain Dog — to let him go if necessary. Nothing can ever take his place, but somewhere there will be another Berner waiting for your heart.

BIS Ch. Arthos October v. Berndach with his namesake rocking "horse" made by Ron Young.

TEN

When Your Berner Is Ill

The healthy Bernese Mountain Dog displays energy appropriate for his age and has alert, shining eyes and a soft, lustrous coat. He pursues his daily routine with undiluted joy, his waving tail and smiling face signaling his happiness in being part of your life.

The sick Berner is lethargic. His coat may appear dull, and he will probably show a loss of appetite. His nose may be dry (a warm nose does not necessarily signal illness in the dog), and he may have a fever. The normal temperature for a Bernese Mountain Dog is approximately 102 degrees F. Just feeling your dog's skin is not a clue to whether his temperature is normal. Your vet doesn't need to know every time your Berner coughs, sneezes, or yelps, but some symptoms need immediate veterinary attention. They are:

Bleeding: Blood in stools or urine or bleeding from any body part.

Convulsions: Violent shaking of the head or legs; dazed appearance.

Lethargy: Lack of usual energy or playfulness or a reduced tolerance for exercise.

Change of eating habits: Refusal of food, eating significantly more or less for a prolonged period without good reason (such as hot or cold weather).

Weight loss: Dramatic change in body weight over a short or long period when food intake remains constant.

Vomiting and/or diarrhea: Multiple occurrences over a short period of time or continual occurrences over a long period of time. Loss of fluid and dehydration are life-threatening in puppies or elderly Berners.

Changes in thirst and urination: Inability to satisfy thirst, increase in volume or frequency of urination, straining or inability to urinate, urinating in the house after a proven period of being housebroken, any change in urinating habits without cause or explanation.

Coughing: Any prolonged coughing, purulent-appearing nasal discharge, or a dry, scaly nose.

Pain: Limping or favoring a leg other than signs of panosteitis, pain upon being touched or lifted.

Injury or abnormality of the eye: Redness of conjunctiva (lining of the eye), excessive discharge or tearing of any kind, squinting, filmy appearance of the eye, difficulty seeing. Put a soft cloth or gauze over the injured eye until your vet can see your dog. This will reduce the amount of injury caused by the dog scratching at the eye or blinking excessively. Severe injury or disease may be referred to a canine ophthalmologist.

Lumps and bumps: Any unexplained lump or thickening is suspicious, but especially one that grows rapidly or bleeds.

Scratching: Continual scratching or gnawing on the body, the legs, or the tail, pawing at the face or ear, or frequent tilting and/or shaking of the head.

These symptoms are not meant to alarm, and it would be rare for a dog to exhibit all of them. However, if they do occur, they are signs that something out of the ordinary is going on with your Berner. Briefly inspect your dog each day, by sight and by touch, all over. Knowing what is normal for him will help you to distinguish between the need for an emergency trip to the vet and a quiet evening at home.

Viral Diseases

The major viral diseases in dogs are distemper, leptospirosis, hepatitis (adenovirus), parainfluenza, parvovirus, and coronavirus. Protection from these diseases is provided by the DA2PL (distemper, adenovirus 2, parainfluenza, leptospirosis) vaccine and the parvo and corona vaccines.

DISTEMPER

Distemper is not prevalent today, because most dogs are vaccinated regularly against it. Occasionally, however, a case does occur in spite of inoculation or due to the owner's forgetting to get the dog's booster shot. The symptoms of distemper can include rapid rise in temperature, loss of appetite, increased thirst, chronic cough, mucus discharge from eyes and nose, diarrhea, and sometimes seizures.

Antibiotics and careful home care are used to treat mild cases of distemper with noninvolvement of the central nervous system. Unfortunately, even when the dog survives, there may be permanent reminders of the disease. The dog's teeth are left discolored and often unsound, and there may be permanent scarring and damage to the lungs as well as seizures and permanent damage to the central nervous system.

LEPTOSPIROSIS AND HEPATITIS

Leptospirosis (a bacterial disease affecting the kidneys and liver) and hepatitis (adenovirus) are of particular interest because they can be transmitted to people. Both diseases affect the liver and produce the jaundice effect familiar to anyone who has seen hepatitis. Symptoms and treatment are similar to those for distemper, with the additional symptom of yellow or jaundiced gums, conjunctivae, and skin. Vaccination can prevent the disease in both man and dog.

KENNEL COUGH (CANINE COUGH)

Technically known as tracheobronchitis, canine cough is an upper-respiratory infection characterized by a persistent dry, hacking cough. It may occur with exercise or in a resting dog and is highly

Table 10-1
Suggested Vaccination Schedules for Puppies and Adults

Vaccination	When to Give
Puppies	
Distemper-Measles	6 weeks
DA2PL/Parvo	9 weeks
DA2PL/Parvo, Corona	12 weeks
DA2PL/Parvo, Rabies	16 weeks
Parvo	18 weeks
After 18 weeks, go to adult schedule	
Adults	
DA2PL	Yearly
Parvo	Yearly
Rabies	According to the law of your state (every 1-3 years)

Check with your veterinarian frequently, because the availability of new vaccines or the results of new research may initiate a change in recommended types and schedules of vaccinations.

contagious. Most dogs with kennel cough do not have a fever, are bright and alert, and have a good appetite. The persistent dry cough may be followed by bouts of deep, harsh coughing and gagging that sometime produce foamy mucus. The best protection against canine cough is by vaccination beginning at six weeks and by following a complete schedule.

This infection gets its name from the fact that many dogs present symptoms after being boarded in a commercial kennel. Puppies and young adults are most susceptible, and the most serious complication is pneumonia. To help prevent development of pneumonia, dogs with kennel cough should be rested and kept in a relatively warm environment away from other dogs to prevent spread of the disease. In mild cases, treatment may not be needed, and the cough will clear up in about two weeks. However, if your dog is feverish and lethargic with loss of appetite and has discharge from the nose or eyes and/or difficulty breathing, suspect pneumonia and take him to your vet.

Canine cough can be caused by one of the following organisms: canine parainfluenza virus (CPI), canine adenovirus type 2 (CAV-2), or bordatella bronchiseptica bacteria. There are thirteen known components of this disease complex that cause kennel cough, but parainfluenza, bordatella, and adenovirus 2 are the only ones for which there are vaccines. Vaccines with DA2PL or DA2LP offer protection against the parainfluenza and adenovirus 2. Topical vaccines such as Intra-Trac II®, Naramune®, or Coughguard-B® give protection against bordatella.

PARVOVIRUS AND CORONAVIRUS

Parvovirus and coronavirus are the viral diseases most dreaded by puppy owners. The affected puppy or young dog first shows signs of lethargy, then is beset with severe vomiting and diarrhea. The hallmark of both diseases is the inability to keep down food and water and a bloody or foul-smelling diarrhea. Most very young puppies do not survive parvo, and many older puppies and adults do not. The potential for survival is higher in cases of coronavirus, although survival is not assured in either disease.

Both diseases may be treated symptomatically with intravenous fluid replacement and rest until the virus works its way through the puppy's system. However, prevention is much preferred to infection and survival, because residual effects may cloud your Berner's potential to live a normal life.

Prevention of parvo and corona is as simple as having your puppy vaccinated. The vaccination schedule for parvovirus typically consists of four shots, with two shots needed for coronavirus. The first parvo vaccination is usually given at nine weeks. Although this seems too long to wait before vaccinating against parvo, most bitches of breeding age have now built a sufficient level of antibody protection through vaccination or actual exposure

Figure 10-1
FIRST AID

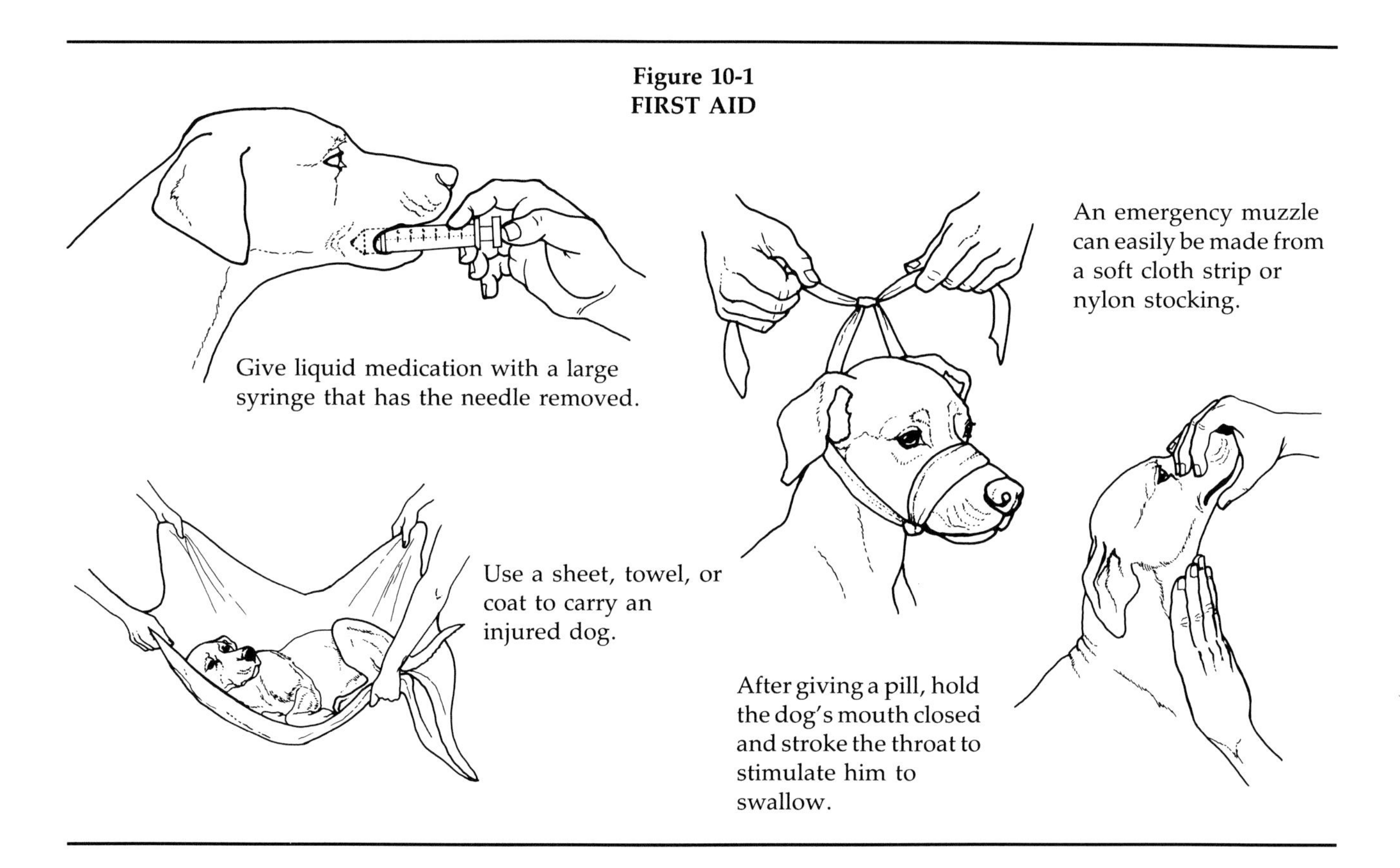

to the disease and can pass on these antibodies to their unborn puppies. Thus, puppies typically are born with adequate protection until maternal antibodies deteriorate at about nine weeks.

Another point to remember is that should your Berner contract parvo (or corona), he has a much improved chance of surviving the disease if he is free of internal parasites.

Rabies

Due to stringent state regulations regarding vaccination of dogs and cats against rabies, most pet owners have never seen a case of rabies. Rabies is a viral disease that is transmitted by the bite or urine of an infected animal. Dogs are usually infected by the bite or urine of a wild animal (skunk, fox, squirrel, bat, or raccoon), and a person can contract the disease if bitten by the infected dog or if saliva or urine from the infected dog enters a cut, scratch, or open wound.

The classic concept of the rabid dog is one that is aggressive and combative; however, that is not always the case. There are two forms of rabies — "furious," in which the dog is aggressive and combative, and "paralytic," in which the dog drools and is uncoordinated. Both forms start with a personality change. The dog may seem overly affectionate or markedly shy, or he may appear restless or become aggressive. He may then develop only one of the types of rabies or a combination of both. The result of both types is death. Because rabies is wholly preventable by vaccination (every three years or once a year, according to state regulation), there is no reason why your Berner should be at risk for this progressive, fatal disease.

Internal Parasites

INTESTINAL TRACT WORMS

Internal parasites, or worms, are not usually life-threatening, but they can drain the vitality out of your Berner. The internal parasites that inhabit the canine intestinal tract include hookworms, roundworms, whipworms, and tapeworms. They do damage by attaching to the intestinal lining and sucking blood. A large number of worms over a sufficient length of time can cause serious blood loss. Internal parasites are potentially life-threatening in young puppies or elderly dogs.

Treatment is generally given by worming the dog with pills, pastes, or liquids once the type and quantity of parasite have been determined by microscopic examination of fecal material. Regular fecal exams, every three to six months, followed by worming medication as prescribed by your veterinarian, are an important part of your dog's health regimen.

Signs and symptoms of tapeworm infestation include loss of energy and coat condition. In severe cases, blood loss may be apparent by loss of color in the gums and eye rims. Normally healthy pink skin will be pale, and your Berner will be quite lethargic. Even in the absence of other symptoms, the presence of what appear to be small grains of rice (tapeworm segments) in the stool are proof of tapeworm infestation.

Tapeworm infestation, while debilitating to the dog, is easily eliminated by worming with Droncit®, Cestex®, or some similar anthelmintic agent available through your veterinarian.

HEARTWORMS

Another type of internal parasite, the heartworm, is life-threatening in dogs of any age. The immature heartworm (microfilaria) is transferred to the dog during the bite of an infected mosquito. The microfilaria migrate for several months through the dog's tissues, eventually reaching the heart and pulmonary arteries. In the dog's heart, they can grow to a length of fourteen inches and can cause significant damage to the heart, the lungs, and other organs.

The affected dog tires easily, has a chronic cough, and experiences weight loss; however, these signs do not appear until the disease is well advanced, by which time severe damage may have occurred. The end result of heartworm infestation is either a dog that lacks the energy to take part in your life or the death of a fine canine friend. Once present primarily in the South, heartworm infestations now occur throughout the United States.

The current treatment for heartworm infestation is a daily injection of an arsenic compound for a week and several weeks of confinement. This treatment is as life-threatening as the disease itself. Furthermore, treatment is not permanent protection. In order to keep a dog free of heartworm infestation, daily or monthly preventatives must be given.

First, however, the dog must be tested to see if he harbors the microfilaria or the mature heartworm. A small blood sample is taken for microscopic examination. Giving the medication without testing is dangerous to your dog's health.

Several types of heartworm preventatives are available. They come in tablets, liquid, or chewable tablets. Most types are given daily, but at least one medication can be given once a month. You may start your puppy on heartworm preventative as early as nine weeks of age. Your veterinarian can prescribe the preventative of choice for your area.

External Parasites

External parasites include fleas and ticks that cause your Berner to chew, scratch, and lose coat and condition. These parasites bite the dog and suck his blood. However, it's not what they take from your Berner but what they leave him with that causes the most trouble. Fleas can deposit tapeworm eggs that hatch and mature into bloodsucking internal parasites. Ticks infected with the spirochete Borrelia burgdorferi pass on Lyme disease, a debilitating condition that affects people as well as dogs. Signs and symptoms of Lyme disease in the dog include fever, loss of appetite, and an arthritis-like condition manifested in swelling, pain, and warmth of affected joints, along with lameness. The usual sign is lameness, and attacks typically last just a few days. Recurrence is common. Antibiotics such as tetracycline, erythromycin, and penicillin have been used to treat existing cases, but the best news is that a vaccine is available to prevent the disease. Prevention also includes tick control through avoidance of tick-infested areas and the use of insecticides.

Ch. Shersan Chang' O' Pace displays the striking movement that made him a center of attraction in the ring.

ELEVEN

Understanding A Dog Show

There are two broad areas of competition in dog showing: conformation and obedience. Conformation competition evaluates the dog's structure and movement according to the breed standard, while obedience competition measures a dog's ability to be trained and to work with you. Many Berners compete well in both conformation and obedience.

Although it's not always evident, the original purpose of conformation dog shows was to have a breed expert evaluate the dogs and bitches brought before him or her and choose the one dog and bitch from the entire group that best represented the Standard for that breed. Theoretically, these dogs should produce offspring that would go on to maintain and improve the breed. This is why neutered and spayed animals are not allowed to be shown in conformation or breed competition, although they may be shown in obedience. Ideally, breed competition should determine which dog and bitch, among all those present, can best fulfill the purpose for which the breed was originally intended as set forth in the breed Standard.

Types of Dog Shows

There are four general types of conformation events — the fun match, the sanctioned A or B match, the licensed all-breed show, and the licensed breed specialty. Both conformation and obedience competition are generally offered at each type of show.

Fun matches, put on by a local kennel club, give everyone an opportunity to get experience without the higher entry fees and pressure of a licensed show. The fun match gives the novice exhibitor a chance to practice the skill of showing a dog in a more relaxed atmosphere. A novice can get pointers from fellow exhibitors and even from the friendly judge. This is a good time, too, to get your puppies out (after they have had all of their vaccinations) and let them socialize, that is, become accustomed to seeing lots of different people and dogs. Most fun match rules allow puppies to be shown at three months of age. Entry at fun matches may be "day of show," and classes are determined by the club giving the match. No championship points or obedience titles are earned at the fun match.

A handsome winning brace, Can. Ch. Bigpaws Beauregard and Can. Ch. Bari v. Nydegghoger with owner Ron Smith.

The sanctioned A or B match is regulated by the AKC in a similar manner as a licensed show except that no championship points or obedience titles may be earned. The B match, like the fun match, is the smaller and less pressured of the two, but its aim is to prove to the American Kennel Club that the presenting club is seriously pursuing the ultimate — the licensed event. At the B match, nonregular classes such as the three- to six-month Puppy class and the Brace class may be offered, and entry may be the day of the match or by pre-entry. In the A match, only regular classes may be offered, and all dogs must be at least six months old to enter. Regular and nonregular classes are described in greater detail later in the chapter. Entries for the A match are accepted only prior to the match. This event is run like a licensed show in every way except that points toward championships and obedience "legs" (qualifying scores) are not earned. No dog that is already a champion or that has a CDX obedience title may compete with untitled dogs for awards at a match.

The AKC licenses both all-breed and specialty shows. A dog must be six months of age or older on the day of the show in order to be eligible. The biggest difference to the exhibitor between matches and shows is that in shows, points toward a championship or qualifying obedience scores may be awarded. Entry is by pre-entry only, and fees are higher. There is a certain amount of pressure to be quick in setting your dog up to show, because judges are allowed only a limited time to evaluate or go over each dog. Because licensed shows are more businesslike than matches, the atmosphere is usually more serious, but this doesn't mean that you won't have fun.

The Bernese National Specialty is held once a year and rotates each year to a different area of the United States. The Bernese Mountain Dog Club of America customarily sets a progression of locations, such as the East, the Midwest, and the West, so that people in each region of the United States have relatively convenient access to the show at some time. Entries are by pre-entry only, and Berners from all over the United States and Canada are represented, as well as a few from other countries. It is a great honor for a Berner to place in his class at the specialty, but it is high praise, indeed, to take points or finish a championship at the Berner National Specialty.

Regional breed clubs may also hold specialty shows.

Denise Dean and "Sparky," Am/Can Ch. Deerpark Heartlight, are an unbeatable team setting a pace that reminds everyone that a Berner should be able to move with speed and confidence.

Stud Dog Class. Stud dog Ch. Ashley v. Bernerliebe CD with two of his offspring, Ch. Derrick v. Bernerliebe and Ch. Deerpark Cryssocola.

Entering Your Berner

Entries for licensed shows are taken only by pre-entry with the show superintendent. A closing date is set approximately two to three weeks before the date of the show. In filling out entry forms, you will have to list certain information about your dog. If you are entering on the day of the show at a match, you will want to have a copy of your dog's registration or litter form with you so that you have easy access to the information. Don't rely on memory.

When you fill out the entry form for showing your Berner, you will have to list the dog show class in which you plan to show, for example, Open Dog or Open Bitch. Because you are showing a Bernese Mountain Dog, you may leave the blank marked "Variety" empty; it is used for breeds that divide classes by color or size, and Berners are shown in one color only with no separation by size. Otherwise, fill in each blank with the information requested, including the age (six to nine months, nine to twelve months, twelve to eighteen months) for Puppy classes. Never enter your Berner in more than *one* of the five regular classes. Check the premium list to find requirements for entering any nonregular classes offered. The goal of each exhibitor is to be eligible for points toward his or her dog's championship. The only exception to this is the Junior Showmanship class.

Dog Show Conformation Classes

REGULAR CLASSES

The regular classes in which you may enter your Bernese Mountain Dog are: Puppy 6-9, Puppy 9-12, Puppy 12-18, Novice, Bred by Exhibitor, American Bred, Open, and Best of Breed competition. Definitions of the classes and which dogs may be entered are:

Puppy 6-9. All puppies from six months to less than nine months of age may be shown in this class. The puppy must be six months old on the day of the show or before. A puppy nine months old on the day of the show must be shown in the next Puppy class.

Puppy 9-12. This class is for all puppies nine months to less than twelve months of age on the day of the show. Once a puppy is past his twelfth month, he must be shown in another class.

Puppy classes may be combined (six months to twelve months competing together) or shown separately. If classes are separated, specify the age division on entry forms, because the show superintendent will not do it for you, *and your dog will not be*

Ch. Fozie Bear v. Buttonwillow takes a five point major at an Arizona show with owner/handler Diane Russ.

OFFICIAL AMERICAN KENNEL CLUB ENTRY FORM

All Breed Dog Show & Obedience Trial 93458301

DECATUR ALABAMA KENNEL CLUB, INC.

Point Mallard Ice Rink 1800 Point Mallard Drive SE Decatur, Alabama

SATURDAY, OCTOBER 23, 1993

ENTRY FEE (including 50 cent AKC recording fee) is **$15.50** for the first entry of each dog except Puppy Class which is **$12.00.** Each additional entry of the same dog is **$12.00.** When a dog is entered in more than one class, the highest priced class is considered the first entry. Junior Showmanship Competition ONLY is **$10.00** or **$5.00** as an additional entry.
BREED ENTRIES CLOSE WEDNESDAY NOON, OCTOBER 6, 1993 at Superintendent's Office.
OBEDIENCE ENTRIES CLOSE WEDNESDAY NOON, OCTOBER 6, 1993 or when the numerical limits have been reached, if reached prior to this date at Superintendent's Office. (See Obedience limits on page 1)
MAIL ENTRIES with Fees Payable to **JACK ONOFRIO**, P.O. Box 25764, Oklahoma City, Oklahoma 73125.

NOTICE: PLEASE PUT BREED & NAME OF SHOW ON CHECKS. I ENCLOSE $ 15 50 for entry fees.

IMPORTANT - Read Carefully Instructions on Reverse Side Before Filling Out. Numbers in the boxes indicate sections of the instructions relevant to the information needed in that box. (PLEASE PRINT)

BREED: BERNESE MT. DOG | VARIETY (1) | SEX: FEMALE

DOG (2) (3) SHOW CLASS: BEST OF BREED | CLASS (3) DIVISION Weight, Color, Etc.

ADDITIONAL CLASSES | OBEDIENCE TRIAL CLASS | JR. SHOWMANSHIP CLASS

NAME OF (See Back) JUNIOR HANDLER | JR. HANDLER AKC #

FULL NAME OF DOG: CH. DEERPARK IDEM V. BUTTONWILLOW

Enter number here

☒ AKC REG. NO. / ☐ AKC LITTER NO.: WG 432563
☐ ILP NO.
☐ FOREIGN REG. NO. & COUNTRY

DATE OF BIRTH: OCT 1 1990

PLACE OF BIRTH: ☒ USA ☐ Canada ☐ Foreign
Do not print the above in catalog

BREEDER: DENISE DEAN

SIRE: CH. DEERPARK HEARTLIGHT

DAM: CH. BROKEN OAKS I-CHING

ACTUAL OWNER(S) (4): DIANE RUSS, DENISE DEAN
(Please Print)

OWNERS ADDRESS: RT 12 BOX 557

CITY: ATHENS STATE: AL ZIP +4: 35611

NAME OF OWNER'S AGENT (IF ANY) AT THE SHOW | CODE #

I CERTIFY that I am the actual owner of the dog, or that I am the duly authorized agent of the actual owner whose name I have entered above. In consideration of the acceptance of this entry, I (we) agree to abide by the rules and regulations of the American Kennel Club in effect at the time of this show or obedience trial, and by any additional rules and regulations appearing in the premium list for this show or obedience trial or both, and further agree to be bound by the "Agreement" printed on the reverse side of this entry form. I (we) certify and represent that the dog entered is not a hazard to persons or other dogs. This entry is submitted for acceptance on the foregoing representation and agreement.

SIGNATURE of owner or his agent duly authorized to make this entry: M. Diane Russ

Telephone (205) 729-1563

entered. Age need not be specified for combined classes, and the premium list will tell you whether Puppy classes are to be combined or separate.

Puppy 12-18. A regular class offered at specialties and some all-breed shows. It does not have to be offered, but it is a good place to show a young dog

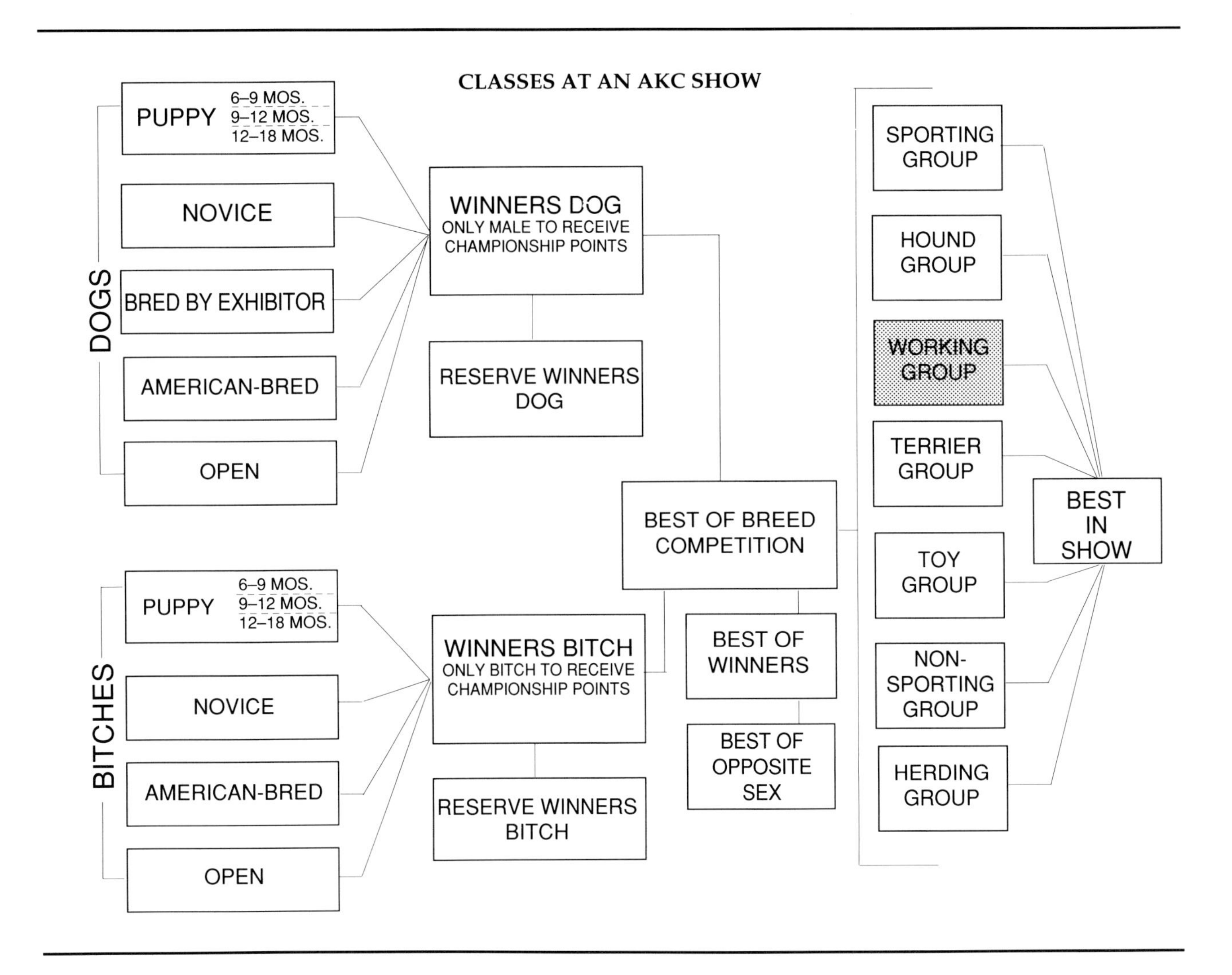

of quality that is not yet ready for competition against mature dogs.

Novice. This is a class for the dog with limited show experience. A dog may show in Novice unless he has won three blue ribbons in that class or one blue in any other class, or unless he has received one or more points toward his championship prior to the closing of entries for the show in which he is being entered. The dog may enter this class at any age greater than six months but must have been born in the United States or Canada.

Bred By Exhibitor. This class is for dogs six months of age or older that are owned wholly or in part by the person who is the breeder or co-breeder of the dog. The "Bred By" dog cannot be a champion and must be shown by the breeder(s) or immediate family of the breeder(s), which the AKC defines as husband, wife, father, mother, son, daughter, brother, or sister. The dog must have been born in the United States. Dogs whelped in Canada may be shown if they are individually registered with the AKC stud book.

Open. The Open class is just what it says — open to all dogs. Any dogs older than six months may be shown here, but this is the only class where foreign or imported dogs can be shown except for Puppy classes.

Best Of Breed. Abbreviated as BOB, this class is for any champion regardless of place of birth as long as he is registered with the AKC.

NONREGULAR CLASSES

Nonregular classes are those that, with the exception of Junior Showmanship, are not typically offered at licensed shows. As a rule, these classes do not count toward a dog's championship. Nonregular classes are generally offered at matches and specialties.

Junior Showmanship. In this class, offered at most shows, the handler aged ten to sixteen is judged on his or her ability to show a dog. The dog is not judged and may compete without penalty in the Winner's class, even if the junior handler does not win his or her class, as long as the dog has won his class that day.

Sweepstakes. For puppies only, this class lets the winner take a percentage of the entry fees for the class. "Sweeps" includes the usual divisions, six to nine months and nine to twelve months, and adds a twelve- to eighteen-months class.

Stud Dog. At least two of each stud's progeny must be exhibited along with the stud. The winner is determined not only by his qualities but by the excellence of the dogs that he has produced, represented by those shown with him. Progeny shown may be either male or female. The competing stud dogs need not be champions to be in the class. Championship points may not be earned from this class.

Brood Bitch. This class duplicates the Stud Dog class. Bitches and their progeny are shown to evaluate the production of each bitch. Offspring

Kenet's Gara Agrippina and Kenet's Germanicus Augustus going Best of Breed and Best of Opposite Sex at Ladies Kennel Association of America show in 1975.

shown with their dams may be either sex, and the competing bitches need not be champions. Championship points may not be earned from this class.

Veterans. This class is for Berners more than six years of age regardless of whether they have a championship. Both sexes are shown together, and the winner goes on to Best of Breed competition. At a specialty, the winner of this class may take points toward his championship if he wins Best in Speciality.

Brace. Brace competition is held in both conformation or obedience. It is offered at many matches and specialties and frequently at licensed shows. In this class, two almost identically marked dogs are shown simultaneously, always coupled together by a special brace leash. If all goes according to training, both dogs move in synchrony, and the effect is thrilling.

Parade of Champions. This class is generally offered only at matches but may be held at specialties. This is not a competitive event. The exhibition of champions of either sex is done for the enjoyment of the crowd. Breeders and exhibitors get an opportunity to show their accomplishments, and novices get to see quality individuals.

Progression of Dog-Show Classes

Classes are divided by sex — dogs (males) and bitches (females). Dogs are always shown first, and the classes take place in the order in which they were listed in the preceeding section. All of the first-place winners of the five classes are shown together in a Winner's Dog class; the best dog is chosen, as well as an alternate, which is referred to as Reserve Winner's Dog. Then, the bitches are shown in the same order.

In the event that the Winner's Dog or Winner's Bitch from that day is found to be ineligible or disqualified for the points, the Reserve is awarded those points. All second-place class winners should

Brood Bitch Winner at the 1988 National Specialty. *Left to right:* Dam Am/Can Ch. Bev's Jabbering Jodi with offspring Mija's Starbuck v. Bev CD and Am/Can Ch. Jaycy's Wyatt Vom Hundsee.

Handler Ronald Pemberton gaits Ch. B. Albertine's George at a 1975 show.

stand by at ringside during the Winner's class; if the first-place dog or bitch in your class is chosen as Winner's Dog or Winner's Bitch, you will be called into the ring to compete for the Reserve Winner's award.

It is only in the Winner's class where points toward an AKC Championship can be earned. The highest number of points that can be earned in any one show is five, and a dog may earn from one to five points depending on the number of dogs of your breed entered in the show. Points earned in groups of three, four, and five are known as majors. A dog must gather fifteen points to become a champion, and two sets of those points must be majors earned under two different judges.

After both Winner's Dog and Winner's Bitch have been chosen, those two compete in the Best of Breed competition along with the champions of record. The champions in the Best of Breed class are known as Specials. Three awards are given. First place is Best of Breed (BOB), and it need not be a Special. Although the proven champions usually do go up as BOB, sometimes a really good class dog will go over them. The second award is called Best of Winners and concerns only the two Winner's class Berners. The Winner's Dog and Winner's Bitch are compared against each other, and the better of the two is chosen Best of Winners. The third and last award given in Best of Breed competition is Best of Opposite Sex. This individual is the best of the opposite sex to the Best of Breed winner.

At an all-breed show, the Best of Breed winner goes on to Group competition. For the Bernese Mountain Dog, this is the Working Group, where the Berner currently competes against the Best of

Breeds from eighteen other working breeds. Ideally, each dog in Group competition is an excellent specimen of its breed, and competition is stiff. Four places are chosen in Group, but only the first-place winner goes on to the grand finale, the Best in Show (BIS) competition.

Best in Show competition always gathers a crowd. It is the last event of the show. The winners from all eight groups compete for the award. it is a thrilling event to watch.

Showing in Canada

If you want to add titles to your Berner's name and you've exhausted the possibilities in the United States, you might consider a trip to Canada. Requirements for acquiring a Canadian championship or obedience degree differ from AKC requirements, as do the shows and trials. David Denis, president of the Bernese Mountain Dog Club of Canada, supplied the following comparisons between AKC and CKC events.

At CKC shows, the show secretary distributes all armbands; at AKC shows, exhibitors receive them at the ring. A dog named Best of Breed or Best Puppy *must* appear in the group ring. Failure to do so may result in loss of points acquired and CKC censure. The AKC does not require attendance in the group ring.

CKC boosters parallel AKC-supported entries. BMDCC specialties usually take place in conjunction with point shows over two to three days. In addition to the specialty show, exhibitors may enter each point show, so it is possible to acquire a Canadian championship in one weekend, depending on the entry. Exhibitors must submit entry forms for *both* the BMDCC specialty and the host club shows.

Obedience Trials

Any purebred dog eligible for AKC registration may enter into obedience competition at AKC shows and matches. Unlike conformation competition, in obedience the dog's appearance and movement are not judged. However, your Berner is on display all the same, and he should be *clean and neatly groomed.*

In obedience competition, the dog and handler are both judged on how well they perform a series of exercises ranging from a heeling pattern to a scent discrimination exercise. In the beginning levels of competition, the exercises are simple but become more difficult and complex as the dog advances. It cannot be stressed strongly enough that the best way to prepare to compete in obedience is to attend organized classes taught by instructors knowledgeable in training methods and in how to show at the various levels of competition.

Deciding which obedience class to enter is simple. By the time you are ready to show your Berner in obedience competition, you will probably already know that obedience competition consists of Novice, Open, and Utility classes. If you have attended obedience-training classes at your local kennel club or obedience-training club, your instructor will probably have explained to you which class you and your Berner are ready for. The following are the regular obedience classes and their requirements.

NOVICE

Novice competition is divided into two sections, Novice A and Novice B. Novice A is for dogs that have never won an obedience title and whose handlers or co-owners have not completed requirements for any obedience title. Novice B is for dogs that have not won a title, that are being shown by someone who has titled another dog, or that are handled by a novice but co-owned by someone who has titled a dog.

The required exercises are the heel on-lead, the heel off-lead, the figure-8 on-lead, the stand for examination, and the off-lead recall with finish. A one-minute sit-stay and a three-minute down-stay are done off-lead with the handler across the ring from the dog. Two hundred points is a perfect score. A dog must earn at least 170 points without failing any exercise to qualify for a "leg" toward a Companion Dog (CD) obedience title. Three qualifying scores earned under three different judges in Novice competition will qualify your Berner to carry the title "CD" after his name.

Clearing the bar jump is Ch. Dina de l' Armary, UTD. Owned by Mary Horstick Eschweiler, she was the first Bernese Mountain Dog to earn a utility title.

Liberty's Belle CDX, owned by Ruth Ballmer, soars over the broad jump.

OPEN

Open competition is also divided into two sections, Open A and Open B. Open A is for dogs that have won a CD title but have not yet won the Companion Dog Excellent (CDX) title. Open B is for dogs that have a CD or a CDX, or even a Utility Dog (UD) title.

The heeling exercises in the Open class are the same as in Novice except that all work is done off-lead. In addition, the dog must retrieve a dumbbell on level ground and over a high jump. He must also leap a broad jump consisting of a series of low hurdles that are spaced out. During the recall, the dog must drop into the down position on command about halfway back to the handler. The sit-stay lasts three minutes and the down-stay five minutes. Both the sit and down are done with the handler out of the ring and out of sight of the dog. They are true tests of a dog's trust and willingness to work with and independently of his handler. A perfect score is 200, and three qualifying scores of 170 or above, with passing scores on all exercises, earned under different judges are required for your Berner to have the title Companion Dog Excellent (CDX) placed after his name.

UTILITY

As in Novice and Open obedience, Utility is divided into two sections, A and B. The Utility A division is for dogs that have not yet won a UD. Dogs with a UD must compete in Utility B. In Utility competition, not only must your Berner work off-lead in every exercise, but many of the directions to the dog are given in the form of hand signals with no verbal commands. This displays cooperation and obedience at their highest levels. The heeling exercises are the same as those in Novice and Open, with hand signals replacing verbal ones. The stand for examination is done while the dog is moving; a hand signal is given to halt the dog in the standing position while the handler continues forward. After four or five paces, the handler halts and turns to face the dog. The judge approaches the dog and touches him lightly on the shoulders, the back, and the hips. Then, at the judge's signal, the dog is recalled and must come in straight and finish competently with either a hand signal or voice command.

Utility also contains a scent discrimination exercise in which the dog must pick out the one leather and one metal article with the handler's scent on it from among a number of unscented articles. He must choose the correct article and bring it to the handler with no instruction other than "Find it!" The dog also retrieves one of three cotton gloves at the direction of his handler and jumps a high jump and a bar jump, taking directions from his handler. No sit-stays or down stays occur in Utility competition. A perfect score is 200, and when your Berner earns three qualifying scores of 170 or above under three different judges, he is entitled to carry the well-deserved letters UD after his name. It is a tremendous accomplishment for both of you.

THE OBEDIENCE TRIAL CHAMPIONSHIP (OTCh)

Pronounced "OTCh" by obedience enthusiasts, the Obedience Trial Championship is the pinnacle of achievement for the obedience handler/dog team. This title represents near-perfect performance and is earned by winning points in competition against other dogs.

The requirments for an OTCh are as follows:

1. You must have completed a Utility title.
2. You must have won a first place in Utility (Utility B, if divided), with at least three dogs in competition.
3. You must have won a first place in Open B, with at least six dogs in competition.
4. You must have won a third place in either Utility or Open B, with at least three and six dogs competing as stated above.
5. The first-place wins above must be earned under three different judges at all-breed obedience trials, whether held separately or in conjunction with an all-breed dog show.
6. You must have accumulated 100 points.

Points in OTCh competition are won, as in conformation competition, by beating a certain number of dogs as listed in the point schedule (see Table 11-1).

Table 11-1
The Current OTCh Point Schedule

OPEN B CLASS

Number Competing	Points for First Place	Points for Second Place
6-10	2	0
11-15	4	1
16-20	6	2
21-25	10	3
31-35	18	5
36-40	22	7
41-45	26	9
46-50	30	11
51-56	34	13

UTILITY CLASS

Number Competing	Points for First Place	Points for Second Place
3-5	2	0
6-9	4	1
10-14	6	2
15-19	10	3
20-24	14	4
25-29	18	5
30-34	22	7
35-39	26	9
40-44	30	11
45-48	34	13

Obedience competition can be very satisfying if you have the desire to do something in partnership with your Berner. Training and competing often deepen the bond that already exists between dog and man, and the Berner Sennenhund has been bred for centuries to work in partnership with people. But watch out — obedience competition is fun, yet it is also serious, tough, and contagious. Once you start, it's hard to stop, and you'll mystify your nondoggy friends with references to "NQs" (nonqualifying scores) and your Berner's "second leg!"

Showing your Berner is a hobby that you can pursue as long as you like and as little or as much as you like. The friends that you make often last a lifetime, and working with a Berner at your side makes it special.

However, remember these points if you want to go the distance. If you win, congratulations! If you lose, you have paid for that judge's opinion of your dog on that day. Each judge has an opinion, and opinions don't often differ; be a good loser. Good sportsmanship should be the hallmark of the veteran exhibitor, and sportsmanship is generally evident at dog shows. Strive to be a good winner as well as a good loser; have a smile for everyone.

Undivided attention. Ch. Nordstaaten's Emma CDX waits to retrieve the dumbbell.

OBEDIENCE COMPETITION IN CANADA

If you are ambitious and have a good obedience Berner, you may want to earn a title in both the United States and Canada. Requirements are similar. You must apply to the Canadian Kennel Club (CKC) for a Canadian registration prior to entering, so start several months ahead of any planned trip.

In obedience, the only difference in the Novice class exercise occurs in the stand for examination, which is performed on-lead in Canada. The Open exercises are the same. In Canada, all breeds are required to jump the dog's height at the withers. The CKC utility scent discrimination exercise uses *three* sets of articles — leather, wood, and metal. The seek back is used in Utility. The handler drops any color of glove except white while heeling the dog, then sends the dog back to find it.

Left to right: OTCh Tanja v. Grünenmatt UD AM CD, first Canadian Utility Bernese October 1983; Ch. Sennenhof Heimat; BIS AM/CAN Ch. Gitana de Braye, AM/CAN CD OFA; and Ch. Sennenhof Kuno de Braye.

Ch. Santera Harmony v. Cresta and owner/breeder Sandra Novocin are a well-dressed pair with the dog nicely stacked.

TWELVE

Showing Your Berner in Conformation

A professional handler once said that you need egotistical and exhibitionist tendencies to show dogs. While that may not be strictly true, you do need to have the attitude that you and your dog are the best team in the ring.

Showing does not begin when you enter the ring. In fact, it begins months before you send in your entry and intensifies as the time nears for you to enter the ring. When the judge's eyes are on your dog, you and he must know that you look and are performing at your very best.

Feeding and Conditioning

The key to having a showy dog in blooming condition is to keep him parasite-free, provide proper nutrition and exercise, and groom him regularly. Feeding the Berner on the show circuit is not very different from feeding the backyard pet if you are already feeding a ration that meets all of your dog's nutritional requirements. A vitamin supplement may be necessary for the dog exposed to the intensive stress of travel and exhibition. Usually no special diet is required, however.

The show dog must also be kept in good hard physical condition by regular exercise. In the show ring, he will be called upon to trot around a large ring several times. Several dogs housed together will keep each other exercised by running and playing together. However, many owners prefer to supervise their show dog's exercise program. There are several methods.

Start slowly and work up gradually. Your Berner should be worked at an easy, even trot. Let common sense and observation be your guide to your Berner's exercise tolerance. Excessive panting, limping, or distress are reasons to stop at once. Of course, neither you nor your dog should work out heavily in extreme heat. With consistent exercise, your Berner will soon be able to trot smoothly and easily without fatigue.

Handlers use many methods to work their dogs: jogging with the dog, leading the dog beside a bicycle, motorbike, or ATV, or working the dog on a treadmill designed for show-dog conditioning. Your Berner must be trained to keep his place beside you and to not try to cross over in front of you. Remember that if you are going to handle

your dog in the ring, *you* will have to be in good condition, too.

One way *not* to exercise your dog is to ask him to trot behind a car with someone holding the lead. Your Berner would breathe in the exhaust fumes, which are dangerous to his health. In addition, pavement soon abrades the leather of a dog's pads, making him footsore. It is much better to exercise him on dirt, grass, or small gravel.

A pretty face can catch a judge's attention.

Conformation Training

In addition to proper conditioning, you need to teach your Berner a few simple exercises. The most basic prerequisites are that he move freely on-lead at your left side, turn smoothly, and know how to move in a straight line on either your right or left side. However, he will also have to stack, bait, and gait. These three terms, although they sound like an advertising jingle in a foreign language, refer to posing the dog for the judge, keeping the dog's attention with food or a toy, and following one of three standard patterns for moving in the show ring.

STACKING

To teach your Berner to stack, you will first teach him to stand. Tell him to stand in a quiet, firm voice, and run the back of your hand underneath his belly to prevent his sitting. Your dog may react ticklishly, but a gentle pat on the tummy is often sufficient to accustom him to being touched there. In conformation showing, the Berner must be on the handler's left side, and in stacking, he faces to the handler's right; therefore, accustom your Berner now to standing that way. When he will stand competently, you may begin teaching him to stack, which is to pose standing foursquare with the legs even.

With your Berner standing at your left side, reach over his shoulders with your left hand and gently but firmly grasp the left foreleg at the elbow. Lift it slightly and place it so that the leg falls underneath the shoulder, perpendicular to the ground. The toe should point straight ahead. Repeat the process with the other foreleg.

To stack the dog's rear, you may reach over the hindquarters or underneath them with your left hand to set the rear legs by gently grasping the hock joint. Place the leg with the hock perpendicular to the ground. The toes should point straight forward. Teach your Berner to hold this stacked position for approximately two minutes.

BAITING

Once your dog is stacked, he is ready to bait. Bait is a bit of food or a toy used to focus your dog's attention. Probably the most common food used as bait is liver that has been boiled with garlic powder until done and then baked in a slow oven (250 degrees) until it is dry. However, you may use any food treat that your dog likes. The purpose of using bait is to get your Berner to put his ears forward and to look interested and excited.

There are two basic ways to use bait. Some handlers like to use a large piece and just let the dog nibble it from time to time, while others prefer to feed small chunks or pieces. The time to bait your dog is when the judge is looking at him from a distance, comparing him with the other dogs in the class. Hold the food inobtrusively in front of your dog with your right hand, catching his attention and focusing it on the bait. Squeaky toys and balls are used similarly. It is good to teach your dog the command "Watch Me."

Some Berners will not bait for food or toys, and many handlers do not bait Berners. If you decide to bait your dog, however, there are a few courtesies to observe. Don't throw food bait around on the floor to distract the other dogs in the ring, and if you use a squeaky toy, try to sound it as unobtrusively as possible so as not to agitate the other dogs.

GAITING

Gaiting refers to the dog's movement as he gaits around the ring. In the conformation ring, your Berner will be shown at an easy trot at your left side. You will want him to be able to move freely beside you on a loose lead. As in obedience work, he must be attentive to your moves and must not cross in front of or behind you. He must be prepared to make large circles and turn corners smartly.

The most common gaiting pattern used in the conformation show ring is the triangle. This means that you and your dog will make a triangle starting with the judge as one point and using the rest of the ring space to trace a three-sided pattern, ending up again in front of the judge. However, also train your dog to trot in a straight line. Many, if not most, judges have dogs gaited straight away and back in order to double-check the trueness of front and rear motion.

Basic training for gaiting consists mainly of leash breaking. Practice moving fast enough so that your Berner moves beside you at a slow trot, making circles and corners with him on the inside. When he can move at an easy working trot on a straight line, around a corner, and in a circle, he is capable of gaiting in the show ring.

Find your Berner's best speed. The point of conformation showing is to show your dog to his advantage, and that is done by letting him move at the trotting speed that suits him best. Most Berners

Ch. Shersan Chip Off The Block, owned by Robert Kinley, Best Puppy in Sweepstakes and Winner's Dog at the 1986 National Specialty. Shown by Bobbi Kinley.

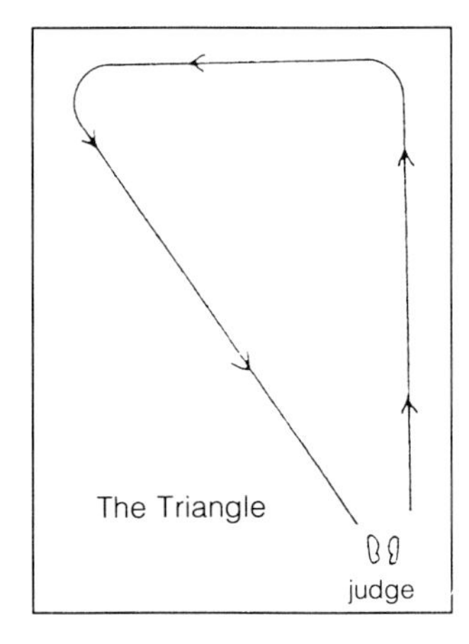

Figure 12-1

have a range of speed from slow to a flying trot, but a pace that is too slow or too fast may make your dog appear to have a structural flaw, or fault, that he does not actually have. You will want to move your Berner at the speed that lets him present his best movement.

When your Berner is moving freely beside you on a loose lead and is making circles and corners smoothly, have a knowledgeable person observe his gait to help you decide whether that speed is showing his gait to advantage. You may find a conformation handling class in your locality. As with puppy kindergarten and obedience classes, local kennel clubs often offer classes to teach you and your dog how to prepare for conformation showing.

Gaiting, baiting, and stacking combine to present your Berner in his best light — as near as possible to the ideal set forth in the Standard. Despite your love for him and your view of him as the perfect Berner, he may not win great prizes. However, when you watch a Berner and his favorite person hamming it up together in the show ring, you know that, win or not, something just as special as a blue ribbon will leave the ring with them.

Veteran Class Winner Ch. Deerpark Iner v. Buttonwillow, 1986 BMDC Specialty.

Grooming for the Show Ring

Show grooming can be as elaborate as you like. In Berners, as in most coated breeds, puffing, fluffing, and coat sculpting do go on. The depth of your involvement in grooming depends on your own desires and possibly with the amount of grooming done in your area. The AKC Standard for the Bernese Mountain Dog states, however, "The Bernese Mountain Dog is shown in natural coat and undue trimming is to be discouraged."

You will need a few more tools in addition to the basic ones listed earlier in this book. Include in your grooming kit the following:

- a small pair of scissors with rounded tips
- a thinning shears
- a portable dryer
- a waterless (rinseless) shampoo in a spray bottle
- plenty of towels

All bathing and clipping should be done a day or two before the show. Start with a thorough brushing to rid the coat of mats and deep-seated dirt. Then, bathe the dog with a mild pet shampoo. Towel the dog damp dry, and gently squeeze the excess water out of the dog's feet with the towel. At this point, have the dog up on a grooming table or any waist-high, sturdy table to make grooming more convenient and easier on your back.

While the coat is still damp, brush the entire coat forward from the tail tip to the head using the slicker brush. This separates the hairs and dries and fluffs the coat. For quicker drying, you can use a dryer such as the Metro Air Force dryer as you brush. The coat should be entirely dry at the end of this process.

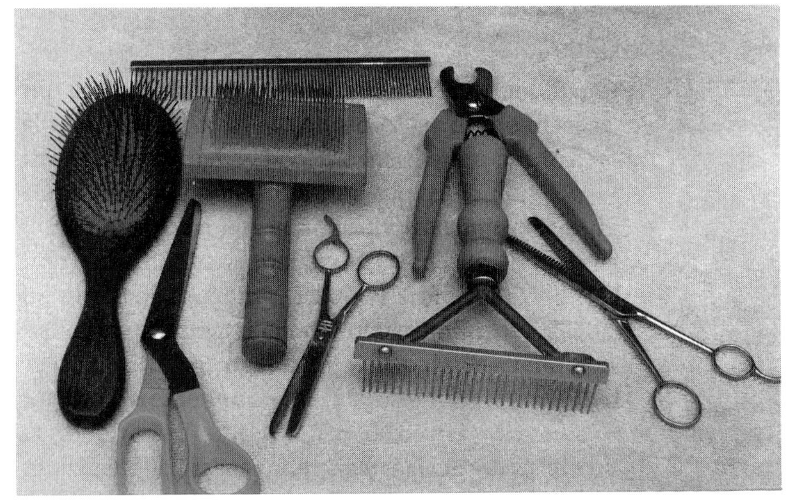

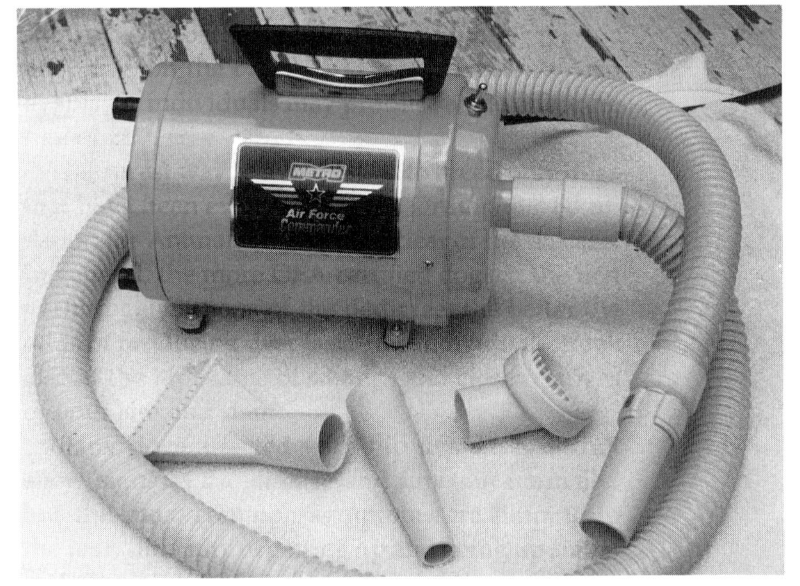

Above left: Additional tools for show grooming: Greyhound comb, scissors, thinning shears, and portable dryer.

Above right: A tack box holds leads, brushes, bottles, and everything else you can get into it.

Left: A commonly used two-speed, high-velocity blow dryer.

Below left: When you take all the equipment, it can get to be a lot: dryer, grooming table, ice chest, extension cords, and chairs.

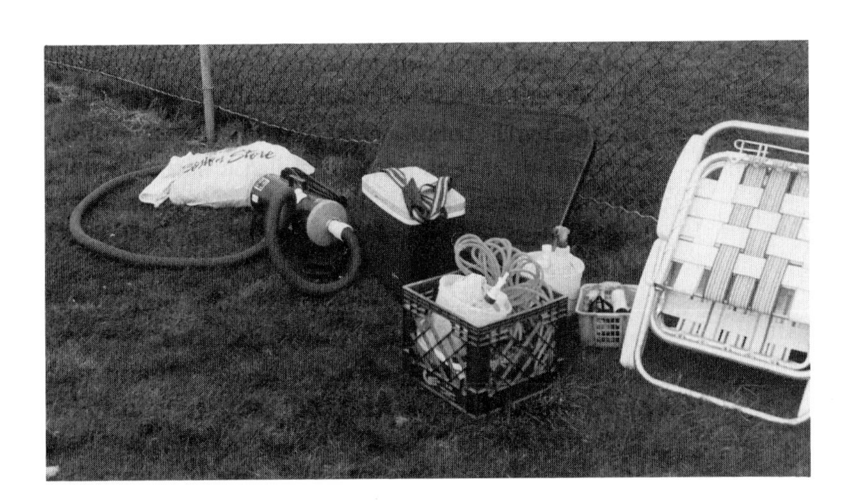

Right: Carefully cut tufts of hair even with the pad.

Below, right: Brush the entire coat forward. O-o-ooo, that feels so good!

Below: Brush the hair on the hocks upward.

Bottom, right: You may remove eyebrow hair and whiskers or not; it is up to you.

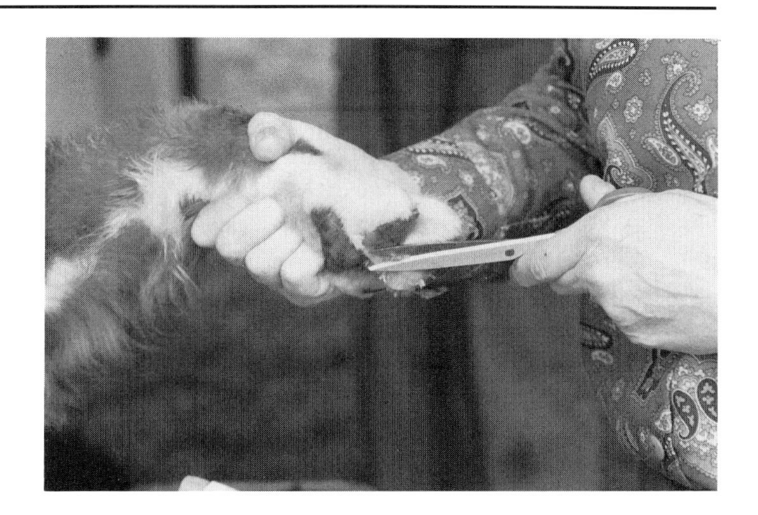

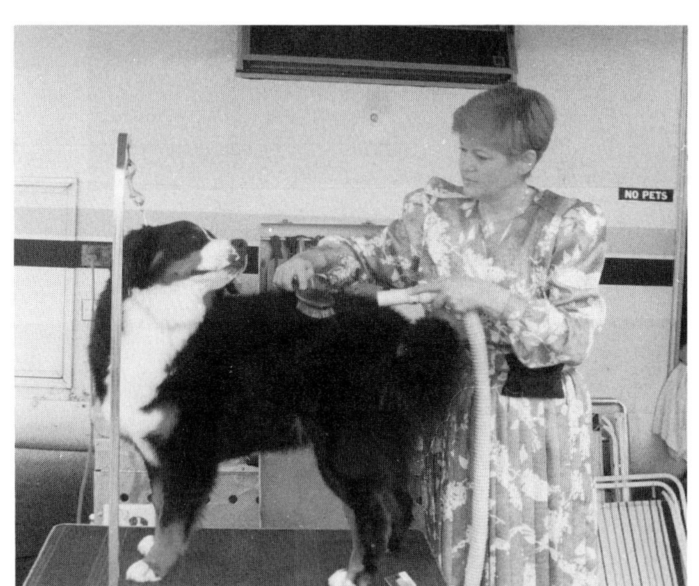

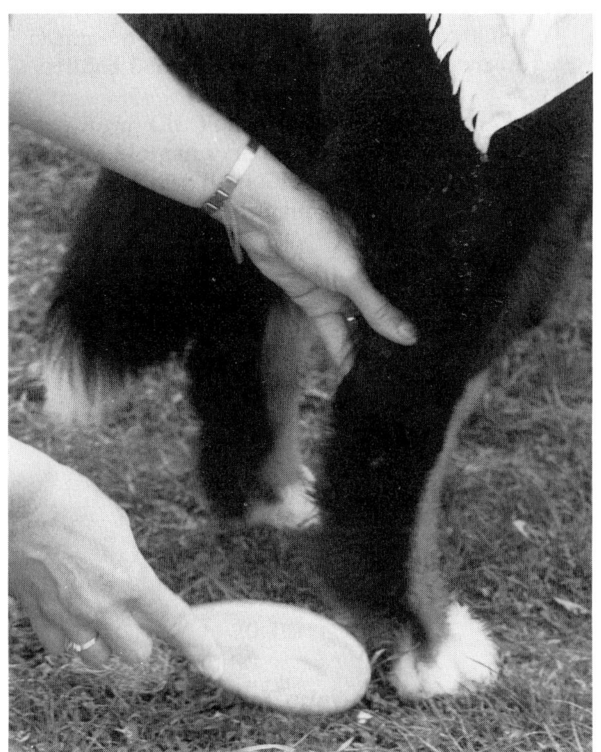

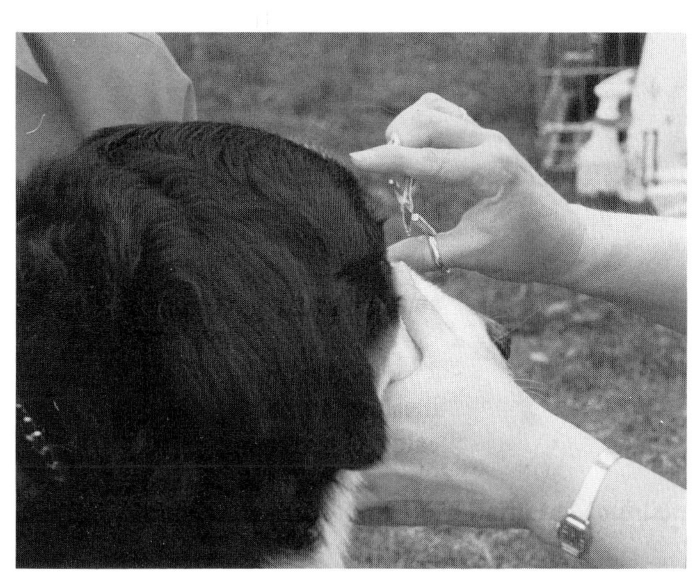

Next, use the scissors to cut the hair that grows between the pads on the bottoms of the feet. Cut these tufts of hair even with the pads, being careful not to cut the pad, so that the bottoms of the feet present a neat appearance. Then trim the long hairs that grow in front of the toes to create a compact, rounded look to the foot.

Use thinning shears to remove excess hair on the insides of the back legs, where the double dewclaws were removed. Blend the remaining hair with the rest of the hair in that area to neaten the appearance of the legs.

Next, brush the hair on the hocks up from the pad to the point of the hock using a slicker brush. When the hair is all brushed up, brush it straight back until it comes to a point in a line running along the midline of the back of the hock. Trim off any stray hairs along the ridge of hair, being careful to cut as little hair as possible. Also, on the inside of the hindlegs there may be a clump of hair where the hind dewclaws were removed. With thinning shears, neaten and blend this hair into the shorter leg hair.

Trimming whiskers is an optional procedure. Some people trim them, and some do not; however, the Standard does call for a "natural coat," which would seem to preclude trimming the dog's face. No further trimming is needed on the Berner's coat; however, if an area of coat detracts markedly from the overall appearance and quality of your dog, you may want to blend it into the rest of the coat to improve balance and proportion in the dog's appearance.

The next step in show grooming involves wetting your Berner. If running water is available, wet him to the skin; if not, use water in a spray bottle to thoroughly wet the coat. Next, while using a high-pressure dryer, blow and brush the coat backward from tail to head. When the coat is just barely damp, stop blowing and leave it as is. This should be done just as shortly before going into the ring as possible. To keep the coat's fluffed appearance, you may want to carry a small spray bottle of water to ringside to spray and fluff the coat if there's a long wait. Do not, however, take a wet dog into the ring.

On the day of the show, a fabric softener sheet (Bounce® or Snuggle®, etc.) can be rubbed over the coat to eliminate the static charge that attracts dust and stray hairs. If you do groom at the show site, please leave your area clean afterward; everyone will appreciate it. Just before you go into the ring, a quick brush forward through the coat will lift the coat attractively, and you're off and running!

The Art of Showmanship

If this is the first time that you will be showing your Berner, arrive early at the ring where Berners will be shown. You can observe what the judge expects from exhibitors and pick up your armband with your entry number at this time. Although another breed is in the ring, Berners will most likely be judged by that same judge later in the day. Most judges do not vary their pattern and method of judging from breed to breed.

You will note that the dogs are shown on the handler's left side and that the armband is displayed on the upper left arm. The ring steward, or judge's assistant, will call the dogs in each class into the ring by number. It is a courtesy to the judge to be waiting at ringside for your class to begin.

When gaiting, the dogs move counterclockwise around the ring at an easy trot. Individual gaiting patterns are at the judge's discretion — usually triangular, L-shaped, or straight down and back. Watch the exhibitors carefully to see what they do, and listen to the judge's instructions.

Showing your dog begins ten feet outside the ring as you line up waiting for your class. Now is the time to size up your competition so that you know how your dog compares with the rest of his class.

Once in the ring, present your Berner to the judge by focusing on his good points. Don't waste time trying to hide his faults. Stack your dog as correctly as possible. He should stand evenly on all four legs with his head up, facing to your right so that the judge views the left side of the dog. Berners are stacked with both the front and hind legs perpendicular to the ground. The tail is allowed to hang in repose. With practice, your Berner will learn to stack himself. Until then, you will have to set his legs in position by hand. You may then stand either beside or in front of your dog.

Multiple BIS Ch. Arthos October v. Berndach, owned by Leon Kozikowski and Sharon Smith, taking a Group First.

When your dog is stacked, which must be done quickly, you want to subtly point out his strengths. If he has a beautiful neck and an exceptional topline, catch the judge's eye and smooth your hand along the neck and topline. Similarly, you can indicate other outstanding features, such as smoothing your hand along a well laid-back shoulder.

During the group gaiting, give your Berner a chance to be seen by himself, not clumped together with the dogs ahead and behind him. Slow down before you approach the judge to give the dog in front time to clear the viewing area. When you see that you have the judge's undivided attention, move boldly with your dog at his best speed.

If you have not attended handling classes or matches to become familiar with dog-showing routines, watch the other exhibitors carefully and do as they do. Above all, listen to the judge. If you do not understand what he or she has said, you may ask for clarification.

The individual gaiting pattern is your dog's time to shine. Remember to keep him on the mat and to line him up with the judge as you go away and come back. The judge wants to see your dog — not you. Glance back at the judge once as you go away, and catch his or her eye as you come in. Not only does this help the judge remember you, it helps you keep your dog lined up on the judge so that he or she can see your dog. Stop well away from the judge when you return. No one appreciates being run down by a dog and his handler, and the judge wants room to view your dog.

Next, the judge will wave you around the ring to return to your line in class. When you are in line again, remember to move your dog forward as the line moves up for examination. In a large class, this will mean setting your dog up over and over. However, your dog does not have to remain stacked and baited with quivering excitation all the time that he's in the ring. In a very large class, or if the judge is a little slow, you have the option of letting your dog relax. This does not mean that he can sit, lie down, or socialize with the other dogs, but he can fall out of stance slightly and look around. Watch your judge, though, and be prepared to stack your dog at a moment's notice. You never know when the judge will step back and take a look at the class as a whole while evaluating a single dog. An unposed dog will stick out like a sore thumb, and a moment's lapse can mean the difference between winning or losing your class.

The key to dog showing is one word: Show. You are there for one purpose — to present your dog in his best way to the best of your ability. Superior showmanship can make a champion of a poor specimen, and failure to show a truly good dog can prevent him from achieving the championship that he deserves. Some people make their living

Sara Dombrowski and Grünberg Onalee CD share quiet reflections.

Junior Showman Becky Ohlsen shows how it's done with her Ch. Dooper v. Bernerliebe CD. Becky is breeder, owner, and handler of this fine bitch.

showing other people's dogs; they are known as professional handlers. So far, there are few professional handlers for Bernese Mountain Dogs, and if owner-handlers make the effort, we will not lose the enjoyment of being able to show and win with our own dogs.

Dressing to Show

Being part of a winning team means dressing for the role. Just as your Berner should be properly groomed for the show ring, you should dress in a way that brings attention to you and to your canine partner while not detracting from him or from the overall effect that you make. Men should wear nice slacks with a coordinated shirt and tie and blazer or jacket. Because you will be showing a mostly black dog, wear colors that contrast. Khaki or light-colored slacks are preferable. Even when it is hot or stuffy, it is a good idea to wear a jacket. The judge will be in the ring several hours and will wear his jacket and tie. You will be in the ring perhaps ten minutes. If, however, the judge removes his jacket and/or tie — and most will ask the class's indulgence for this — you may remove yours. Footwear should be comfortable to run in.

Women should wear dresses or skirts, although culottes and tasteful slack suits are permissible. Remember, you will be bending over to stack your dog. Choose dresses and skirts that are long enough to preserve modesty and good taste. The skirt should contrast with the Berner's coat color. Sneakers make good show shoes, as long as they do not detract in color or style from the rest of the outfit. Long hair should be put up neatly and dangling jewelry left at home. Rings with large stones should not be worn. There is always the danger of losing a stone while showing or grooming.

Ch. Gruezi Patty Melt v. Reuben, Am/Can CD (*Dog World* Award 1987), proves that Berners can do both conformation and obedience.

This award-winning photo by Bobbie Hefner reminds us of the Berner's herding heritage.

THIRTEEN

The Berner at Work

Berners were bred to work, which means that, in addition to enjoying your Berner as a companion, in conformation, or in obedience, you have the option of training him for draft work, pulling a cart, or packing a backpack. In fact, some of these activities are so popular that the BMDCA has organized competitions.

Carting

Training your Berner to pull a cart is an easy process, for the Berner has been bred for this for centuries. As always, praise lavishly and avoid harsh corrections. This is the key to a happy working Berner.

EQUIPMENT

Carting equipment can be simple or elaborate. Harnesses are available from mail-order catalogs. The types used by most people is made of heavy nylon with sheepskin padding. Leather harnesses are also available.

The harness buckles under the dog's rib cage, with a padded chest-band in front, across the chest. The cart shafts fasten into loops on the side, and there is a ring on the back strap to which you can snap your leash. The harness should fit snugly but not be restrictive. You should be able to slip your hand comfortably beneath the straps.

Carts come in many sizes and shapes. Most are homemade, but aluminum-frame carts can be purchased, rigged for one or several dogs. The most important factors are sturdiness, balance, and that the cart be the right size to fit your dog. Several types of carts are illustrated here; one is a child's red wagon adapted with shafts.

TRAINING

To train a Berner to pull a cart, first let him wear the harness around the yard, then fasten two ropes to it that he can pull along the ground. This will accustom him to having something behind him. Next, take two long poles (one-inch PVC pipe works well) and attach them to either side of the harness. About two feet behind the dog, bridge these poles with another length of pipe so that the poles won't cross behind and pinch his body. This also teaches your dog to make turns with something between the "shafts." The sound and rigidity will help prepare your dog for the actual cart.

When your dog is comfortable pulling the pipes, substitute the cart. Be sure that your Berner is physically mature, however, before you ask him to pull any weight. The mature dog in top condition can pull fifty to one hundred pounds easily. Remember, though, that if you are asking your dog to pull for very long, he should build up to optimum condition in stamina and endurance by *gradual* exercise. Also, make sure that the cart is balanced, with the weight over the wheels, not on the dog's back.

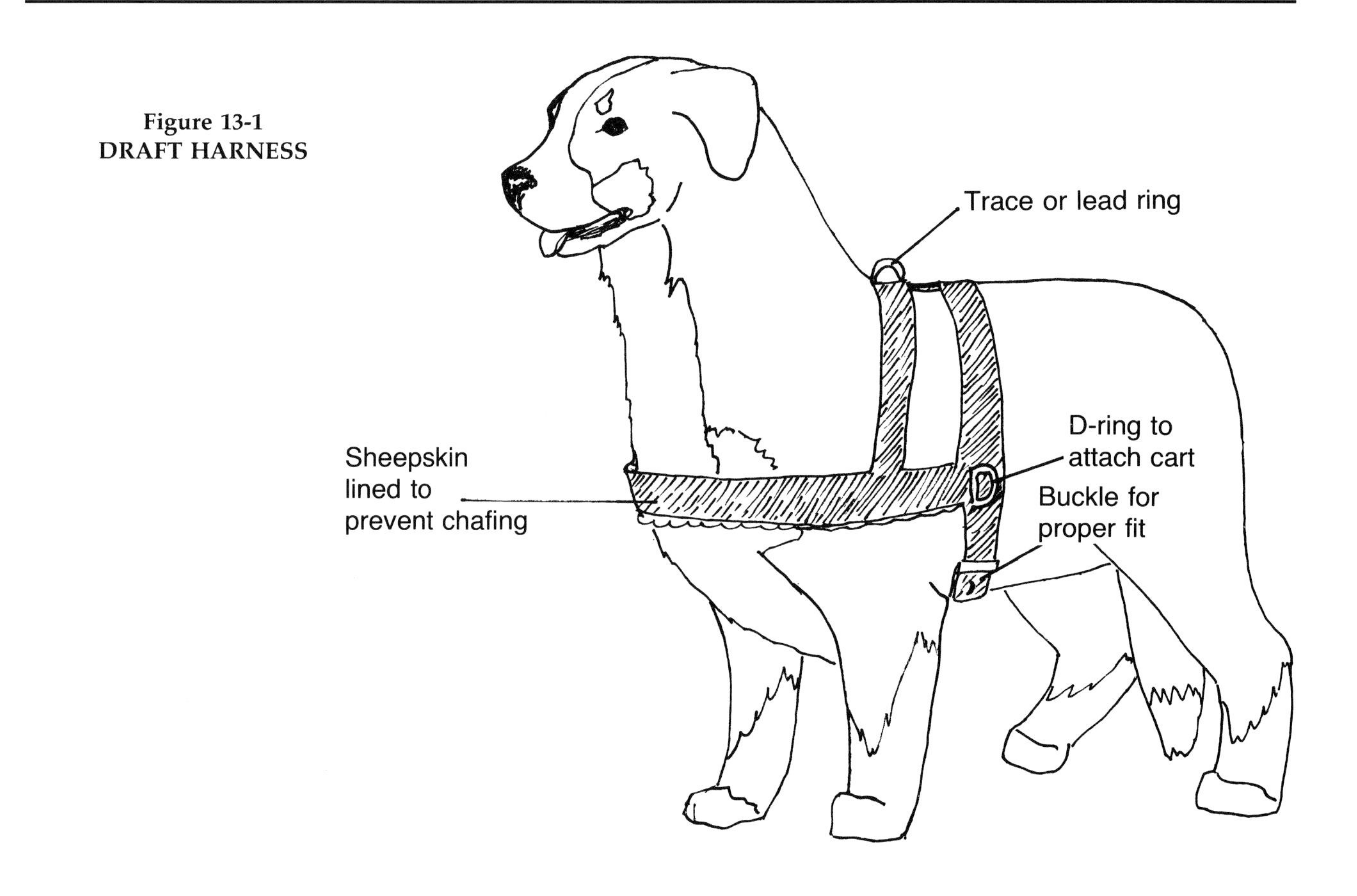

Figure 13-1
DRAFT HARNESS

Left: A tandem team is just right for a leisurely spin around the neighborhood.

Below, left: Ch. Deerpark Irresistible Rambo, owned by Sheila Baxter, with a no-nonsense cart for hauling cargo.

Below, right: This elegant, flower-laden cart is just for looks. Seen at the 1981 National Specialty, this cart displays the Swiss flag in honor of the Bernese Mountain Dog's country of origin.

Even a little red wagon can be used.

The Draft Test

The exercises of the draft test are designed to stimulate the natural and historical working abilities of the Bernese Mountain Dog. Designed by members of the BMDCA, the test is a recognized AKC event, and titles are awarded to dogs that satisfactorily complete it. The abbreviation NDD (Novice Draft Dog) or DD (Draft Dog) after a Berner's name indicates that he is a titled working dog. Dogs must be at least twenty-four months old on the day of the test. A certificate stating the dog's name and weight is required with the entry.

NOVICE DRAFT DOG

The Novice Draft class is for dogs that have not earned the NDD or DD title. All exercises except the recall, harnessing, and group stay are performed on-lead. However, the leash must remain visibly slack. Guiding, jerking, and/or a tight lead will result in a failing score.

A spring-loaded scale is used to calculate the moving weight of the cart and load, which cannot exceed 10 to 15 percent of the dog's weight.

Judging is on a pass/fail basis. A dog must pass all the exercises in a class at one draft test in order to earn the NDD title. The exercises include:

Bartlett's Berners

Used by permission of the artist, Melissa Bartlett.

Draft demonstration at the 1991 Specialty. Chris Cattle and Lupine's Little Tugboat CD.

Basic Control. Each dog/handler team is required to perform a basic obedience routine that includes heeling and a recall before being hitched to the cart. The handler then harnesses the dog, heels him to the cart, and hitches him. The dog should show no resentment or hesitation during this procedure.

Basic Commands. At a single command from the handler, the dog must pull the cart forward, slow down, and stop. The dog must then do a two-minute stay while hitched to the cart. He may stay in either the stand, the sit, or the down position.

Backing. The dog must back the cart a distance of one foot.

Maneuvering. Dog and handler follow a course designated by the judge, and it includes circular turns to the left and right, ninety-degree turns, and moving through a simulated gate, both with and without distractions in the ring.

Distance Freight Haul. Each cart is loaded with "cargo," the weight of which is determined by the type of cart and the weight of the dog. This is a group exercise, and all of the dogs and handlers must walk a one-half-mile course over natural terrain. Handlers may not physically touch or guide the dog or cart except with permission from the judge under unusual trail conditions.

OPEN DRAFT-DOG TEST

The open draft-dog test is for dogs that have already earned the Novice Draft title. Rules are similar to the Novice class, except that all exercises are performed off-lead. The handler must leave the dog on a sit-stay, go to the ring entrance to get the harness, harness the dog, and perform the various tests and the group stay with the dog hitched to the cart. During the freight haul, the Open dog pulls 25 to 35 percent of his weight. As in Novice, all judging is on a pass/fail basis, and a dog must pass all of the exercises in the class in order to qualify and receive the DD title.

Various distractions are arranged at the discretion of the test-giving club and are performed by either the judge or the ring stewards. The purpose of this exercise is to show that a dog has the ability and temperament to do his job without being distracted by activities of daily life around him. For example, one of the stewards may cross in front of the working team with another dog. Or they might

A moment's reflection by the fire. Can/Am Ch. Berndach Bridget CD, International Therapy Dog.

Berners on parade. Can/Am Ch. Gründberg Iridescent Fire displays her babies.

approach and strike a metal pan with a metal spoon several times within ten feet of the working team. Car or bicycle horns might be sounded, food bags crinkled, or a person might ride a bicycle or a horse near the working team.

A booklet giving current regulations for the test is available by writing to the Bernese Mountain Dog Club of America (see Appendices).

THE FIRST DRAFT-DOG TESTS

The first draft match for Berners was held October 22, 1989, by the BMDC of Nashoba Valley in Medfield, Massachusetts. Three teams were entered. Only one team, "Shira," Ch. Olympiana Oracle of Delphi CD TD and Alison Jaskiewicz, qualified.

The first official BMDCA draft test was held two years later on September 22, 1991, in Westford, Massachusetts. The test was a great success, and seven of the twelve Berners entered earned the first BMDCA Novice Draft Dog (NDD) titles. Judges were Beverly Barney from New Hampshire and Mary Alice Eschweiler from Wisconsin.

According to judge Barney, "All twelve dogs passed the harness and hitch, slow, and back. Every team exceeded the required one foot back by a considerable amount. All twelve dogs were unaffected by the distractions. The five dogs that failed did so because of tight leads and/or guiding of the dog, collisions with the ring or equipment, or failure to hold a stay." She prompted future entrants to talk to the dog and to avoid a tight lead.

The seven teams receiving the NDD title were: Bluesky Matt Dillon V Summit CDX and Kathy Heun; Liskarn America Bound Jerry and Alison Jaskiewicz; Ch. Nordstaaten's Emma CDX and Ruth Ballmer; Olympians Helen of Troy CD and Lisa Allen; Ch. Sandusky's Promise Promises CD and Beth Zipsie; and Sudan Neuchatell V Halidom CD and Sue Sanvido.

Berner Power.

Having a working draft dog comes in handy. Harriet Gehorsham and coworker deliver hay.

A moment's reflection by the fire. Can/Am Ch. Berndach Bridget CD, International Therapy Dog.

FOURTEEN

Inherited Conditions of the Bernese Mountain Dog

Berners are susceptible to some diseases and illnesses common to all dogs and to some that are specific to the breed itself. These are not reasons to avoid owning a Berner, because many Berners are not affected. However, it is only fair to the novice Berner owner to mention them. It is important to realize that each breed of dog has its own set of characteristic genetic problems and susceptibilities.

The only way to eradicate these genetic and semigenetic diseases in the Bernese Mountain Dog is to keep accurate records and to be honest when any heritable disease crops up. This does not mean culling every dog except those free of all defects, but it *does* call for careful breeding practices and accurate record keeping.

Hip Dysplasia

Hip dysplasia (HD) occurs when the head of the femur (the upper bone of the dog's hind leg) does not fit snugly into the acetabulum (the hip socket). In this case, the femur may sublux, or slip out of joint. In advanced cases of the disease, the acetabulum may become misshapen due to constant slippage when the dog moves.

Hip dysplasia is a genetically transmitted condition, which means that an affected dog should *not* be used for breeding. Puppies from that dog will have a much greater chance of becoming dysplastic. A dog with hip dysplasia will pass the tendency for the disease much more strongly than one that is not affected. Often referred to as a polygenic or multigenetic disease, hip dysplasia is very difficult to eliminate because its occurrence is controlled by many genes and its expression is influenced by a number of environmental factors. Two dogs that show no sign of the disease may produce dysplastic offspring; on the other hand, and perversely, two dysplastic individuals may produce some offspring free of HD.

The surest way to avoid HD is to breed only dogs that have been evaluated by the Orthopedic Foundation for Animals (OFA) to be clear of the disease. In general, the more OFA-certified dogs in the first to third generations of the pedigree, the better the odds of producing dysplasia-free individuals. Look also at the hip status of siblings and close relatives of both sire and dam.

Many dogs affected with hip dysplasia do not show signs of the disease and function normally, but the most common symptoms are limping in the rear, difficulty in getting up and going up stairs, and "bunny-hopping," in which both rear legs are carried forward at the same time. The only way to be sure whether your dog has HD is to have a radiograph (X-ray) made of the dog's hips. After the X-ray is made, it should be sent to the OFA in Columbia, Missouri, to be evaluated. The dogs are then assigned a rating as compared with other X-rays that have been submitted of Bernese Mountain Dogs. Ratings that are eligible for OFA certification are fair, good, and excellent; dysplasia is rated as borderline, mild, moderate, or severe. Although a dog may not receive certification until he is twenty-four months old, any age dog may be evaluated.

Fortunately for the Bernese Mountain Dog, statistics from Dr. E. A. Corley of the OFA indicated a decrease in the frequency of HD in Berners for the fourteen-year period of January 1, 1974, to De-

Figure 14-1
DYSPLASIA

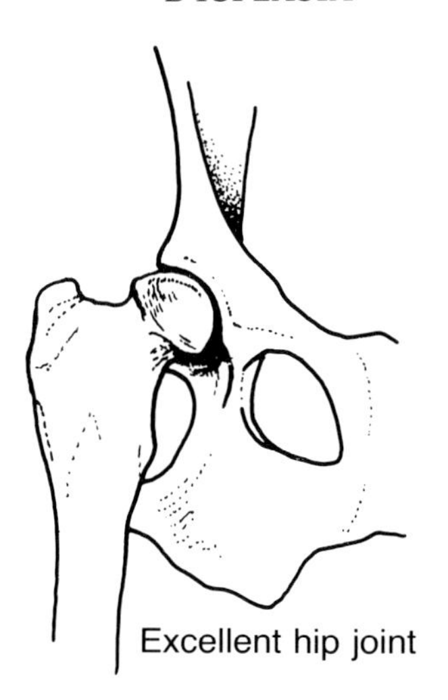

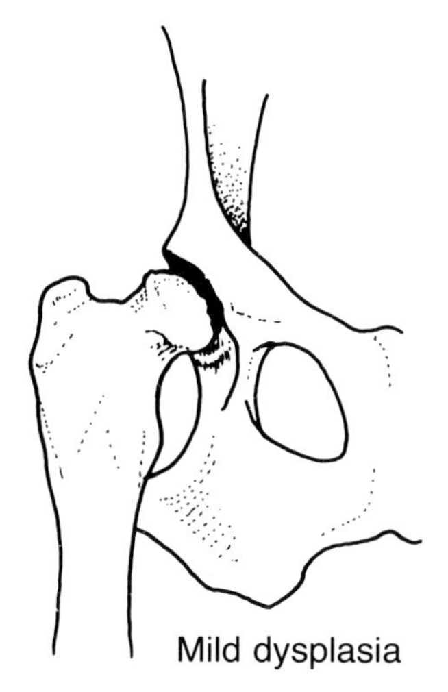

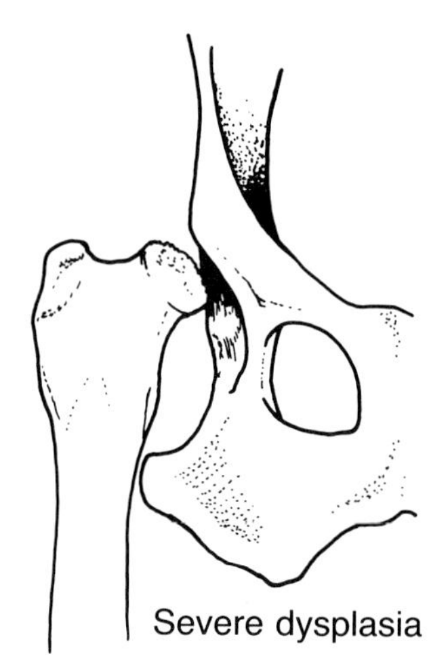

cember 31, 1988 (see Table 14-1). In fact, when those statistics were evaluated year by year beginning with all Berners born in 1984, a dramatic increase occurred in the percentage of normal hips.

Unfortunately, these percentages may represent a biased normal sample, because, according to Dr. Corley, many Berner breeders do not send X-rays to the OFA for evaluation when those dogs are determined at the time of X-raying to be dysplastic. This means that there are actually more dysplastic Berners than show up in OFA's statistics. However, in looking at the percentage of increase of normal hips by birth year, it can be seen that breeders are making an attempt, and are succeeding, at decreasing the amount of dysplasia in Berners. Nevertheless, until every X-ray that is taken is sent to OFA for evaluation, the true extent of progress cannot be known.

Above, right: Ch. Wendy v.d. Grasburg, first champion-producing champion and first OFA certified Berner. Owned by Harold Howison.

Right: Ch. Vollenweider Swiss Harp, Ch. Santera Morgan v. Crest, and Ch. Santera Rio Grando v. Crest, three OFA certified littermates. Beauty and sound structure often go together.

Table 14-1
OFA Hip Ratings for the Bernese Mountain Dog 1/1/74-12/31/88

3.8%	Excellent	1.8%	Borderline
46.1%	Good	12.0%	Mildly Dysplastic
20.1%	Fair	2.1%	Severely Dysplastic

Source: Dr. E. A. Corley of the OFA. The statistics represent the evaluation of 1,678 Bernese Mountain Dogs, all twenty-four months of age or older.

A second type of dysplasia, elbow dysplasia, also occurs in Berners, although not to the extent that hip dysplasia occurs. Elbows may be X-rayed and the film sent to OFA for evaluation as with hip X-rays. For more information on hip and elbow dysplasia, refer to Fred Lanting's excellent text, *Canine Hip Dysplasia and Other Orthopedic Problems*.

Osteochondrosis and Osteochondritis Dessicans

Although anyone who has had Bernese Mountain Dogs for any length of time knows about "OCD" as an ailment that causes pain and limping in the dog, many people do not realize that there are actually two diseases, osteochondrosis (OC) and osteochondritis dessicans (OCD). Both are characterized by disruption of the normal pattern of bone growth. Although osteochondrosis refers to a generalized degeneration of bone and cartilage, the name is misleading because the disease actually affects primarily cartilage.

In order to understand abnormal bone growth, it is necessary to first have some idea of normal bone growth. Ossification, or bone formation from cartilage, does not take place in the fetus until three to four weeks before birth, and at whelping, most of the bones in the puppy's body are at least partially ossified. Bones lengthen from the cartilaginous growth plates at their ends.

In osteochondrosis, the process goes awry as cartilage at the bone ends and at the growth plates becomes unusually thick due to abnormal ossification. As the cartilage continues to grow, it becomes necrotic (dead) at its roots. Cracks and fissures occur, often extending to the surface of the cartilage layer into the joint. These cracks allow synovial fluid from the joint to seep into the deepest layer of the abnormal cartilage and wash debris from the necrotic or dead tissue into the joint.

In osteochondritis dessicans, the above conditions also occur, but, in addition, a piece of the fissured cartilage tears away and forms a flap or loose body of tissue in the joint called a "joint mouse." At this point, inflammation and pain will be apparent as the flap floats freely and irritates the surfaces inside the joint. The usual treatment of choice is surgery and removal of the flap, at which time the AKC show rules disallow the dog from being shown (any surgically altered dog is prohibited from exhibition). However, some evidence indicates that exercise of the affected joint can wear away the diseased cartilage and allow healing and the formation of a tough, fibrous tissue that may allow normal, pain-free movement.

A lovely litter courtesy of Ch. Alphorn's Copyright of Echo and Ch. Franzi v. Nesselacker. *Photo by Bob Abrams.*

Figure 14-2
OSTEOCHONDRITIS DESSICANS

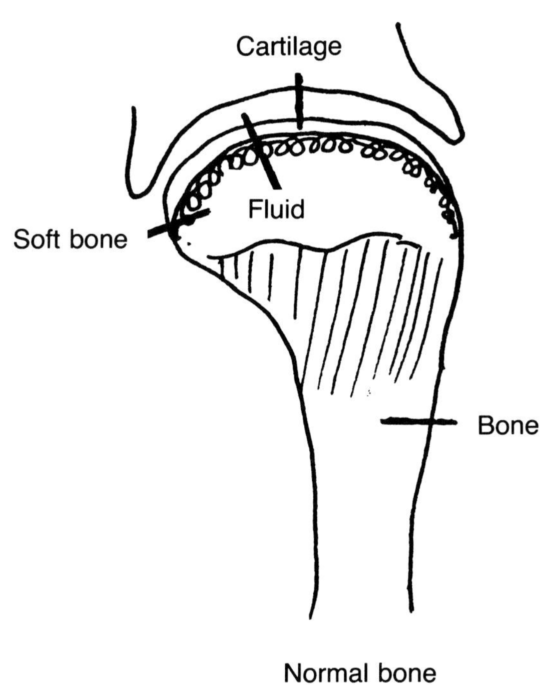

Normal bone

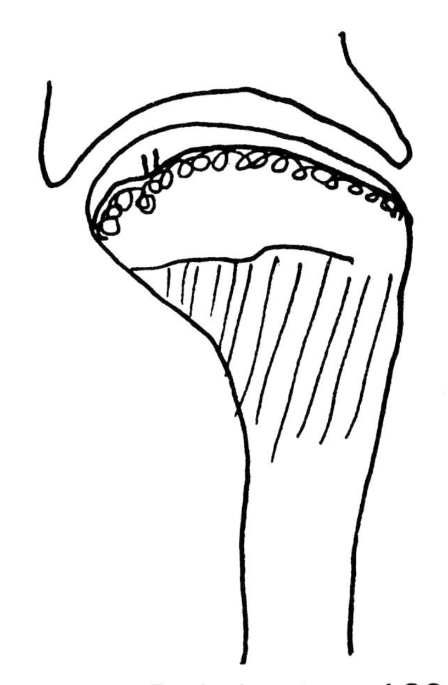

Beginning stage of OC
Thickening cartilage

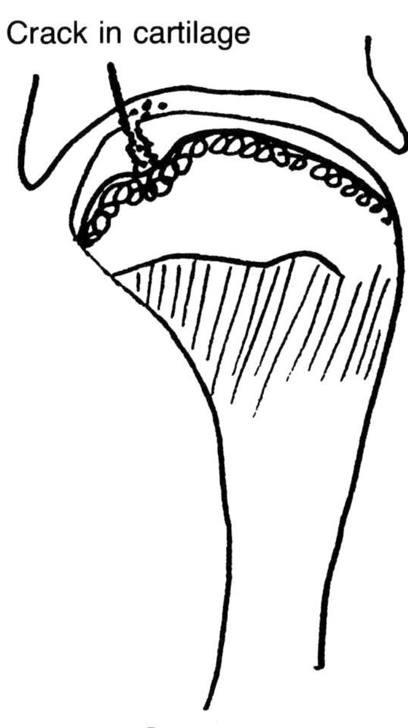

Crack in cartilage
allowing debris to
enter fluid

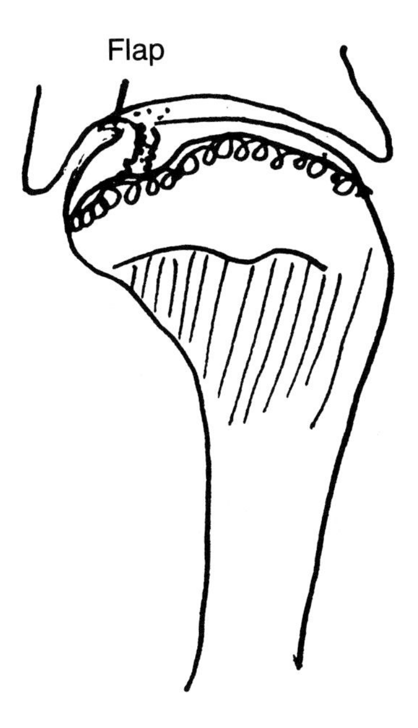

OCD:
Flap has begun to break away

While the causes of OCD are not precisely understood, studies have shown that hereditary and growth/diet factors may be involved. Rapid-growing, large dogs such as the Berner are more prone to OC and OCD than smaller breeds, especially when they are fed a high-protein diet. Puppies from OCD-affected parents are more likely to be affected than those from nonaffected parents. In the Bernese Mountain Dog, a combination of breeding from dogs free from OCD symptoms and feeding a low-protein (24 to 26 percent) diet is very likely to improve the chances of eliminating OCD or its symptoms.

PANOSTEITIS

Panosteitis, a generalized inflammation of the bones, can affect Bernese Mountain Dogs. Five of the long bones in the skeleton are most often affected: the humerus, the radius and ulna of the foreleg, and the femur and tibia of the hind leg. Panosteitis usually occurs between four and twelve months of age and causes pain and limping in the dog. Because of the limping, the condition may be confused with osteochondrosis; however, with panosteitis, the dog limps interchangeably on all legs, with the front legs being the most noticeably affected. There is a typical lameness-recovery cycle of two weeks during which the dog will limp first on one leg, then another.

Panosteitis is not thought to be a genetic disease but simply a related affect of fast growth. Like growing pains in children, panosteitis is simply indicative of rapid growth. Treatment is simple and usually effective — reduce the protein level of the dog's food and keep activity to a minimum. Panosteitis is a self-limiting condition; it will go away whether you treat it or not, but reducing the protein level of your young Berner's diet and giving anti-inflammatory analgesics such as aspirin or ibuprofen for pain while limiting physical activity may make him more comfortable.

Three lovely veteran bitches. *Left to right:* Kati v. Sturmbuhl, nine years old; Ch. Roundtops Abigail, ten years old; and Ch. Halidom Keri CD, eleven years old.

Elbow Dysplasia

Elbow dysplasia includes the following diseases of the elbow joint: ununited anconeal process of the ulna (UAP); fragmented coronoid process of the ulna (FCP); and osteochondritis dessicans of the medical condyle of the humerus. Each of these conditions represents a disturbance of the endochondral ossification process and may be considered to be forms of osteochondrosis. These pathologies are believed to be hereditary, and breeding affected individuals would be a disservice to the breed.

UNUNITED ANCONEAL PROCESS OF THE ULNA (UAO)

Ununited anconeal process is a disease of young, rapid-growing dogs in which the anconeal process of the olecranon of the ulna fails to fuse or only partially fuses to the ulna. Males are more commonly affected than females with a two-to-one ratio of incidence. Although UAP by itself may not constitute elbow dysplasia, it is often present with the other pathologies that make up the disease.

The causes and course of the disease for UAP have not been definitely established, but current evidence strongly supports that it is an inherited

Figure 14-3

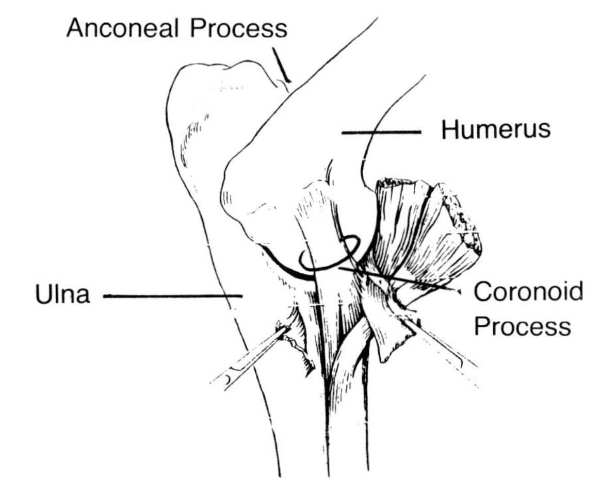

Normal elbow joint showing articulation of humerus with anconeal process and coronoid process.

Figure 14-4

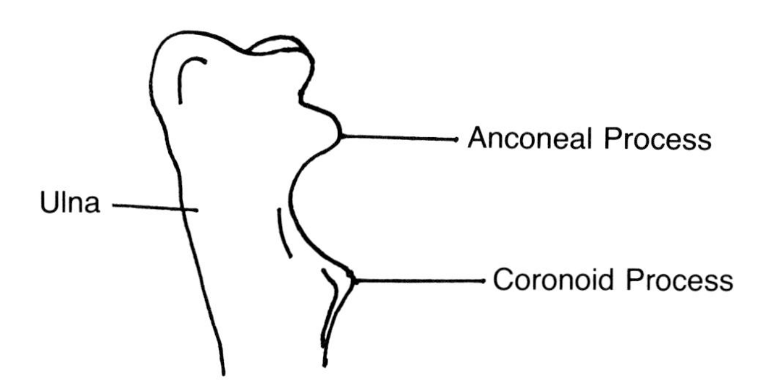

Normal anconeal and coronoid processes.

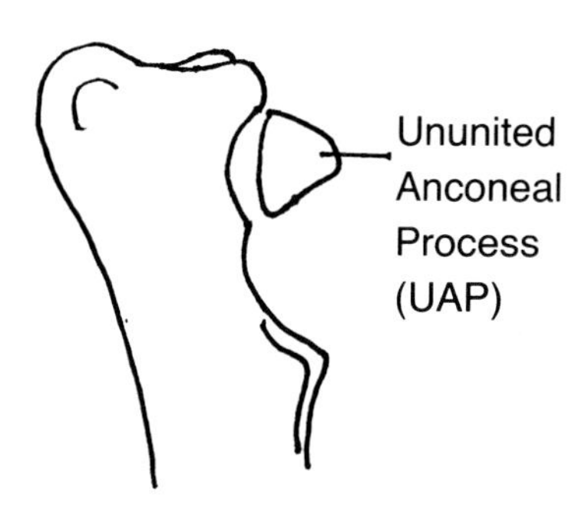

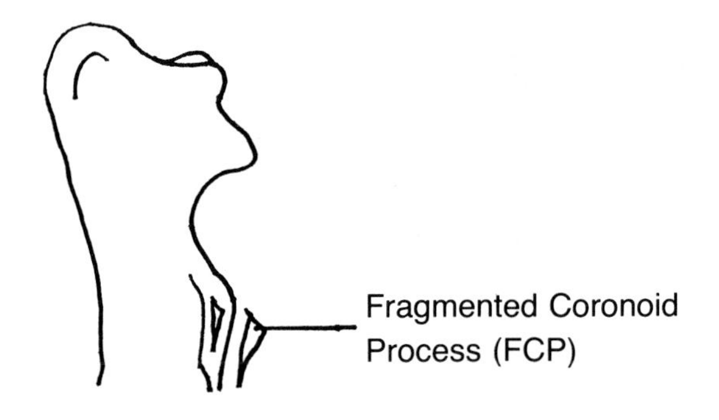

defect in the fusion of the anconeal process to the ulna. Affected dogs are typically brought in for examination between six and nine months of age. Varying degrees of intermittent lameness may have been present for several months prior to examination, but because it may be highly variable and subtle, the owner may not have noticed it at that time.

The condition may affect one or both legs, and one leg may be more severely affected than the other in bilateral cases. Lameness may vary from day to day, with the most affected limb varying as well. At rest, the dog with UAP may stand with less weight on the sorest leg and the toes pointed out in a "wing-out" stance.

UAP is a juvenile orthopedic disease. Ossification in the bones of the elbow jont may not conclude until the dog is four to five months of age; therefore, a diagnosis of UAP should not be made until the dog is four and one-half months old. Treatment consists of surgical removal of the bone fragments of the unfused bone from the joint or reattachment of the anconeal process with pins and screws. Either surgical procedure will make a dog ineligible for exhibition in AKC shows. As in panosteitis and OCD, feeding may be the key to controlling the disease. It is less likely that your Berner will develop orthopedic disease if he is fed moderate protein and allowed to grow slowly without gaining excess weight.

Who says it's a dog's life? A Sandusky Berner enjoys some sack time.

FRAGMENTED CORONOID PROCESS (FCP)

FCP, like UAP, is caused by an ossification failure, in this case, of the coronoid process. The process may ossify as one or two fragments and remain unattached to the ulna at the semilunar notch. This leads to joint laxity and irritation as the head of the humerus has no guide to stabilize its movement. Osteoarthritis is the consequence of both FCP and UAP, with or without treatment. Treatment of FCP is surgical removal of the coronoid fragments, which will relieve the initial pain, but the osteoarthritis will persist.

OSTEOCHONDRITIS DESSICANS OF THE MEDIAL CONDYLE

This disease affecting the medial condyle of the humerus has the same characteristics as previously mentioned.

Cancer

Cancer is a leading cause of canine death in all breeds, and it is a fact of life in the Bernese Mountain Dog. While the disease is not rampant, it is conceivable that you could have a Berner that develops cancer. No one body system seems to be affected more frequently than another, and most tumors are found between two and ten years of age, with a peak incidence between four and six years.

This information comes from a study funded jointly by the Morris Animal Foundation and the Bernese Mountain Dog Club of America. The study, conducted at the University of California at Davis, Michigan State University, and Purdue University, has three objectives: to "determine the age-specific incidence rate of tumors in Bernese Mountain Dogs"; to "determine by analysis of family relationships whether or not there is a genetic predisposition or influence on the occcurrence of tumors in BMDs"; and "to characterize (this) population of BMDs preparatory to a search for specific viral agents, immunologic factors, and/or oncogens that may be involved in the occurrence of cancer."

Previous studies have established that the risk of acquiring cancer (in general, among all breeds of dogs) is related to size, degree of inbreeding, sex, age, and breed, among other factors and in that order. The signs and symptoms of cancer are many and should be verified by tissue sampling. Some signs and symptoms, however, are listed in Table 14-2.

A data bank for information has been set up by Barbara and Martin Packard of Los Altos Hills, California. If anyone has questions about cancer in the Berner or information on cancer in the breed, they may contact the Packards. In Canada, you may contact Ronald F. R. Smith. All information and statistics are confidential.

Hypomyelinogenesis

Hypomyelinogenesis (trembler's disease) affects the production of the myelin sheath that surrounds the nerves of the brain and spinal cord. This sheath acts like the inslulation on electric wiring, preventing arcing and shorting. When the nerves are exposed due to a lack of myelin sheathing, the "short circuit" that occurs is characterized by spasms and jerking of the limbs. In Bernese Mountain Dogs that are affected, the nervous system is defective.

Sometimes the affected individuals are known as "tremblers" due to the uncontrolled, spasmodic movements made by the dog. Symptoms may appear as early as ten to fourteen days of age or may appear later. As the affected puppy learns to stand and walk, the characteristic bobbing motion and trembling become apparent. The trembling is very rapid so that it is not easily seen from a distance, but it can be felt when the puppy is held. Hypomyelinogenesis is not a fatal disease; as the dog grows older, the trembling may remain constant or worsen, but there is no cure.

Table 14-2
Signs of Cancer

Location	Signs
Skin, muscle, connective tissue	Chronic proliferative growth or nonhealing ulcer.
Nasal area, sinuses, and mouth	Persistent bloody or mucous nasal discharge. Noticeable growths or ulcers, reluctance to eat or swallow. Odor is a prominent feature and considerable pain is often seen.
Lung	Coughing, gasping, shortness of breath.
Bone	A common site for cancer in large breeds; characterized by sudden onset, swelling, inflammation, and pain.
Mammary gland	Common in bitches, rare in males, appears as small, hard lump(s) under the skin, often at or near the teat.
Digestive system	Vomiting, rapid weight loss, anorexia, constipation, diarrhea, bloody stools, and palpation of abdominal mass associated with the digestive system.
Pancreas	Weight loss, pain, jaundice, digestive disorders, palpation of abdominal mass.
Endocrine system	Swelling in the region of the thyroids, usually painful to touch and unilateral.

CANCER IN BERNESE MOUNTAIN DOGS

Bernese Mountain Dog Club members are providing a service to all dogs through their sponsorship of a breed-based cancer study. Bernese mountain dogs appear to be extremely prone to cancer, including a very rare form, malignant histiocytosis. About one Berner in ten gets cancer.

The club is collecting statistics and urging owners and their veterinarians to submit samples of cancer tumors to help learn why these dogs have a high cancer rate. The knowledge will help other breeds as well.

Bruce R. Madewell, V.M.D., of the University of California, Davis, a cancer specialist; George A. Padgett, D.V.M., of Michigan State University, a geneticist; and Lawrence Glickman, V.M.D., Ph.D., of Purdue University, an epidemiologist, are coinvestigators on the project, which is jointly sponsored by the Bernese Mountain Dog Club of America and Morris Animal Foundation.

"Bernese mountain dogs are the ideal breed for this study," Dr. Madewell said. "They are a rare breed, only about 5,000 dogs in the country, so their owners have gone to considerable effort to procure one. That means they are pretty dedicated to their dogs. Those which get sick get veterinary attention."

"The owners are instrumental in this study. They have taken the cancer survey forms to their veterinarians. Now the veterinary involvement is growing."

Originally the club set up computer programs to help breed out orthopedic problems, but logged information on other diseases as well. Perusal of the data revealed the high cancer rate and the study was launched.

Malignant histiocytosis appears to be the most common form of cancer seen in Berners, followed by lymphosarcoma. Dr. Madewell receives specimens from each dog in the program, then returns the biopsy report to the referring veterinarian. Because he is doing a concurrent study of ras genes in cancer, he has also examined some of these for ras gene mutations. So far, he has not found evidence to link N-ras mutations with malignant histiocytosis in Bernese mountain dogs.

"It is suspected that genetic factors do play a role in the occurrence of cancer in Berners. Many of the dogs are inbred, tumors often develop at a young age, and many of the tumors are unusual. All of this suggests genetic risk factors, and we hope to be able to identify those genetic factors," Dr. Madewell said.

—From Morris Animal Foundation Newsletter

Hypomyelinogenesis is thought to be heritable. Although cases have not yet been documented in America, the disease is known to exist in Great Britain, where it is said to be a simple recessive trait. In Britain, Duntiblae Nalle, a Swedish import, seems to be the carrier for the disease. As with any heritable disease, it is advisable to avoid breeding affected individuals or known carriers to prevent spread of the trait.

Bloat

Although the exact causes of bloat are not known, the symptoms are well known in the Bernese Mountain Dog, as well as in several other large breeds, and they are dramatic and life-threatening. One physical characteristic, a large, deep chest, is often cited as a hallmark of a dog's potential for bloat. What is fed, how often, and how it is fed are other possible causes of bloat.

A dog with bloat may show little sign at first, or he may immediately roll and writhe in agony. In simplest terms, bloat occurs when gas forms in the stomach of the dog and is unable to escape due to the partial or complete torsion that occurs with the buildup of gas. Torsion is a turning or twisting of the stomach at the pyloric and cardiac sphincters that serve as the entrance and exit from the stomach.

When torsion occurs, the dog may show signs of obvious pain. He may pant heavily, have a staring appearance, and may whine nervously. He may vomit small amounts of white foam. The dog with bloat cannot lie down comfortably; he will pace and try to lie down, only to get up again and pace. The dog's sides may feel hard and tight, like an inflated ball.

In cases of partial torsion, tubing may be passed from the mouth into the stomach to vent the excess gas, and antiflatulents such as Maalox® or Mylanta® may be given to break up the gas bubbles and relieve the condition. If complete torsion has occurred, surgery is the only treatment to relieve pain and save the dog's life.

Something from the vegetable group. A Berner's diet should be varied, right? That's what young Priska vom Dürrbach thinks.

Can't, can't, can't. Well, what CAN I do?

Bloat is a medical emergency. If you even *suspect* that your Berner is suffering from bloat, don't wait for the development of clearly recognizable symptoms. *Go immediately to the veterinarian.* Many dogs have died because the more subtle signs went unnoticed until complete torsion occurred.

The causes of bloat remain a mystery. Diet is thought to be a major factor, along with emotional stress or heavy exercise after a large meal. To avoid bloat in your Berner, divide his daily ration into two or three meals, allow him quiet time after meals, and avoid preventable emotional stress. Be especially careful with Berners five years of age and older, because they are at higher risk for bloat than younger dogs.

Ectropia and Entropia

Ectropia and entropia refer to the turning out or in, respectively, of one or both lower eyelids. When the eyelid turns in (entropia), the lashes irritate the eye, bringing on inflalmmation and infection. When turned out (ectropia), the loose skin forms a tiny pocket that catches dust and debris, fostering inflammation and infection.

This condition is fairly common to varying degrees in the Berner. Surgery is available to correct the problem, but the dog then becomes ineligible for conformation showing under AKC regulations. Management, though not a cure, is simple. Application of antibiotic ointment and/or drops resolves the infection and often the inflammation. A Berner with this condition should be seen by a veterinarian to determine a treatment routine, and a breeder should consider whether to use this individual in a breeding program. Certainly, severely affected individuals should not be used for danger of setting and perpetuating the trait in the breed.

Coat and Skin Problems

Berners have no higher incidence of skin or coat problems than any other breed. Two common conditions that may affect skin and coat are flea allergies and hot spots, and they seem to occur according to the area of the country where the dog lives. Warm, moist climates foster both conditions more than hot, dry climates or cold ones.

If a dog is allergic to fleas, it takes only one fleabite to set him scratching wildly. The effect is often not isolated to the bite area, and the dog may scratch and bite all over his body. If the condition becomes severe enough, the dog will chew and scratch until the coat is gone and he develops sores. The only way to prevent and treat flea allergies is to keep the dog and his surrounding environment free of fleas. Medication such as Prednisilone® may be given to ease the pruritus or itching until the dog and his environment are flea free. Frequent shampooing with flea shampoos, and treatment with flea sprays or dips, can help keep your Berner flea free. Spraying the kennel and yard will kill fleas that might reinfest him.

Hot spots are weeping sores that seem to appear overnight. In actuality, the dog begins licking and chewing some irritation, and over a day or two, the constant moisture and chewing contribute to a typical round, hairless area that is inflamed and exuding clear, sticky fluid. Although they can appear anywhere on the body and may also be the

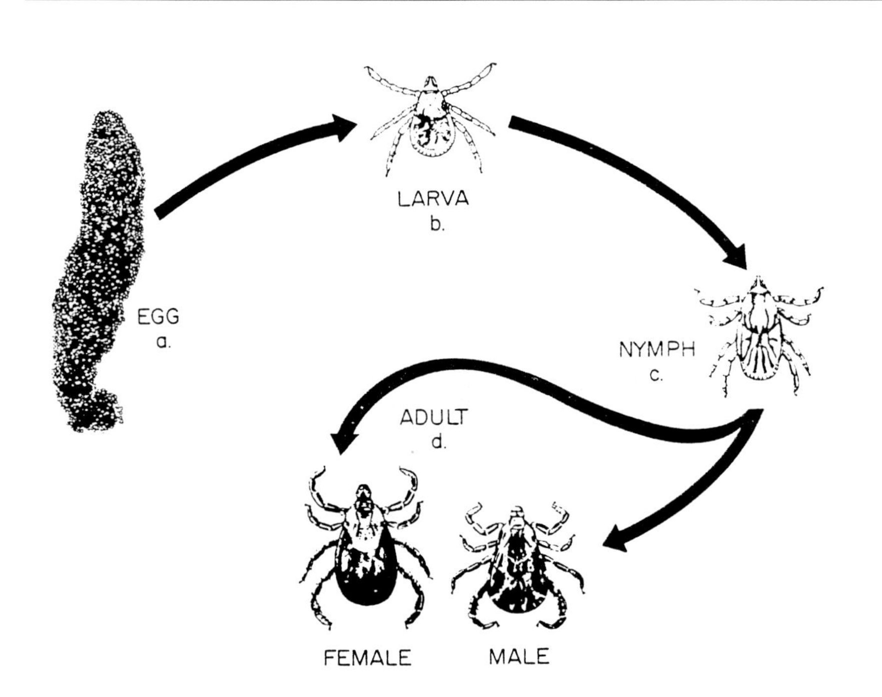

Figure 14-5
DEVELOPMENTAL STAGES OF THE AMERICAN DOG TICK

result of scratching as well as the chewing/licking combination, the most common site for hot spots is anywhere the dog can reach with his mouth. Treatment is washing with mild shampoo and applying a drying agent.

A problem that is breed-specific to Berners (and to any breed with pendulous ears) is hematoma of the ear leather. The leather of the ear is the portion that hangs beside the face. If there is an irritation inside the ear canal (ear mites or infection), the dog may respond by shaking his head violently. The small capillaries in the ear leather rupture and bleed under the skin, forming a hematoma. The bottom half of the ear will apear swollen, although there usually is no indication of pain. If left untreated, the condition may progress to affect the entire ear, because the presence of any hematoma makes the ear heavier and any shaking at that point increases the internal bleeding. With early treatment, the accumulated blood and fluid may be drawn off with a syringe, but later treatment may require opening the skin to remove clotted blood. This is a veterinary procedure.

Hi, my name is Trenton! Want to play?

Five-week-old Berners are ready to be weaned — and Mom's ready, too.

F I F T E E N

Breeding Your Bernese Mountain Dog

Before You Breed

Several important points need to be considered before you breed your dog or bitch.

Everyone who purposefully breeds a dog to a bitch to produce a litter of puppies should take on a responsibility to improve the breed. Breeding for profit or so that the kids can see puppies born are two of the most irresponsible reasons to breed a litter. Yes, most breeders hope to recoup some of the expense of feeding, showing, and caring for the dogs, but the truth of the matter is, few people actually make a profit on the sale of puppies. The only valid reason for breeding is to improve or maintain quality in a breed. There are already millions of unwanted puppies flooding humane-society shelters.

Every poorly planned or unwanted litter of puppies has tremendous impact on the entire breed — often deleterious. The spaying or neutering of a pet-quality Bernese Mountain Dog is a great service to the breed now and for the generations to come, and life with the spayed or neutered Berner is no less full and rich than with his entire counterpart.

As you consider breeding your Bernese Mountain Dog, you will also want to bear in mind that the breed, as a whole, is not tremendously prolific. There are fertility and whelping problems, and sometimes a breeding cannot take place due to lack of interest on the male's part. And the important consideration is that it is not unusual for the Berner bitch to need a caesarean-section to whelp. Perhaps these are the very qualities that help keep the Berner from overpopularity. None of these qualities alone is a reason to not breed a good representative of the breed. Each should be treated as an undesirable characteristic — just as deviations from the ideal set forth in the Standard are treated.

If you intend to produce a litter of quality Bernese puppies, start with a good-quality bitch and choose a dog that will strengthen her good points and improve her faults. The first step toward a breeding program that will produce dogs of quality through the years is to be aware of your bitch's weaknesses and to *be honest with yourself.* No dog is perfect, but there can be no improvement if imperfections are not recognized and corrected by breeding for improvement. Study the Standard and get a picture in your mind of the ideal Berner, then breed for it!

Remember, however, that breeding is a give-and-take business; you may have to take a little less perfection in one area to improve in another. If one line of Berners is noted for a tendency to need caesarean-section for delivery, but also produces superb movement, you might still consider using individuals from that line to improve movement.

Long before you breed your bitch, you should be looking for the right male for her. You will want to choose a stud dog by two criteria: by how well he typifies the Standard, and by his pedigree. A dog's pedigree is his family tree. You should also use a pedigree to learn about the individuals in your bitch's background. You may want to go and see as many of the living dogs in that pedigree as you can. Otherwise, try to see pictures of as many as possible, and talk to people who have seen them in person. The pedigree is a guide to the traits that your dog can produce when he or she is bred, and you can use it to preserve desirable traits and weed out undesirable ones. Desirable traits are charac-

It's a mother's duty, I know, but when can they send out for pizza!

teristics that the standard identifies as being correct for the breed; undesirable traits are faults, or deviations from the standard.

Breeding Programs

If you are breeding your Bernese Mountain Dog, you are probably going to want to produce puppies that will grow up to look like your dog. After all, you chose this dog for its appearance as well as for its personality, and you hope to continue the tradition. Luckily, breeding to preserve the type, personality, movement, and other traits that you like in your dog need not be a "shot-in-the-dark" situation. There are planned breeding systems that make it possible for you to reproduce your preferences.

In breeding purebred dogs, three systems are used. The most common types are linebreeding, based upon the breeding of individuals whose pedigrees have one or more ancestors in common within the first two to three generations, and outcrossing, which is the mating of unrelated individuals within a given breed. A third type of breeding program, which must be used very carefully, is

AN EXAMPLE OF LINE BREEDING

Sire 1 **GALAN v SENSEBODEN** **(litter brother to Ginger)**	**Sultan v. Dursrutti** *Sire (3)*	Bari vd Taubenfluh *Sire (7)*	**Alex v Baurnheim** *Sire (15)*
			Eve vd Kolsteralp *Dam (16)*
		Kindi v Dursrutti *Dam (8)*	Beny v Dursrutti *Sire (17)*
			Cundi v Dursrutti *Dam (18)*
	Diana v. Moosseedorf *Dam (4)*	Galen v Mattenhof *Sire (9)*	York v Fluhwald *Sire (19)*
			Cita v Balmhof *Dam (20)*
		Kaya v Moosseedorf *Dam (10)*	**Alex v Baurnheim** *Sire (21)*
			Cilla v Ranfluh *Dam (22)*
Dam (2) DULT DAPHNE v YODLERHOF	Grand Yodler of Teton Valley *Sire (5)*	Hektor v Nesselacker *Sire (11)*	Kilian v Eggistein *Sire (23)*
			Flora v Nesselacker *Dam (24)*
		Bella's Clara *Dam (12)*	Arno vd Grasburg *Sire (25)*
			Bella's Albertine *Dam (26)*
	Ginger v Senseboden ***(Dam (6)*** **(litter sister to Galan)**	**Sultan v Dursrutti** *Sire (13)*	Bari vd Taubenfluh *Sire (27)*
			Kindi v Dursrutti *Dam (28)*
		Diana v Moosseedorf *Dam (14)*	Galen v Mattenhof *Sire (29)*
			Kaya v Moosseedorf *Dam (30)*

inbreeding, or the mating of very closely related individuals.

Linebreeding may also be thought of as "family breeding," because you breed dogs that are related to each other — cousins, aunts and uncles, nephews and nieces. The purpose of linebreeding is to "set" traits so that they can be consistently preserved for coming generations. The most important point to remember about linebreeding is that it intensifies good traits carried by the common ancestors just as certainly as it intensifies the bad ones. You are doubling up on all of the traits possessed by dogs whose names appear more than once in the pedigree. In order to produce the highest quality, you must not only be familiar with the pedigrees of the dogs that you intend to breed, you must also know the individuals themselves. What are their faults and their outstanding features? Once you separate the undesirable traits from the desirable ones, linebreeding is the most reliable way to produce consistent results. A word of caution, however — if the dogs that you choose to linebreed are exceptional specimens, they may produce exceptional offspring. If they are poor or mediocre, their offspring will most likely be poor or mediocre. The old adage about making a silk purse from a sow's ear is really applicable to breeding dogs.

AN EXAMPLE OF OUTCROSSING

Sire 1 PIKE'S HARPO J ANDREW	Pike's Siegfried v Edo *Sire (3)*	Edo v Moosseedorf *Sire (7)*	Galen v Mattenhof *Sire (15)*
			Kaya v Moosseedorf *Dam (16)*
		Christine vd Speichergasse *Dam (8)*	Bruno v Barenhof *Sire (17)*
			Bella v Barenhof *Dam (18)*
	Bella's Albertins Faymie *Dam (4)*	Arno vd Grasburg *Sire (9)*	Wachter v Konradshaus *Sire (19)*
			Rita vd Grasburg *Dam (20)*
		Bella's Albertine *Dam (10)*	Bobi v Bauerheim *Sire (21)*
			Bella v Moosboden *Dam (22)*
Dam (2) ALPENWEIDE'S ALPHA HEIDI	Valleyvu's Beorn Baron Adalwin *Sire (5)*	Valleyvu's Bytown Barnabus *Sire (11)*	Sir Bruno Vombreiterweg *Sire (23)*
			Valleyvu's Heidi v Gartenhugel *Dam (24)*
		Liesel de Chavannes *Dam (12)*	Baron de la Baumaz *Sire (25)*
			Gittane de Chavannes *Dam (26)*
	Vombreiterwegs Lady Elsa *Dam (6)*	Sablemate Basco Vom *Sire (13)*	Sablemate Machs Na *Sire (27)*
			Sablemate Impossible Dream *Dam (28)*
		Debonhof's Bischen Gidget *Dam (14)*	Noel's von Raulph *Sire (29)*
			Heidi's Gidget Vombreiterweg *Dam (30)*

Outcrossing used as the sole breeding program does not intensify the gene pool for specific traits. In fact, it brings together so many unrelated individuals that it may be difficult to obtain consistent results. Remarkable individuals can be produced by outcrossing; however, the next generation produced by those individuals may not manifest the same quality. The benefit of outcrossing is to bring in traits that are lacking in a breeding program, then to breed back into one of the lines represented on the pedigree. In this way, outcrossing and linebreeding complement each other.

The third breeding program, which should be used very sparingly, is inbreeding, as in a father-to-daughter, mother-to-son, brother-to-sister, or half-brother-to-half-sister mating. This kind of breeding intensifies all traits and can produce well or disastrously. The advantage of inbreeding is that it is the most powerful and surest way to set traits. When superior individuals are used, superior traits are established in a line; otherwise, terrible faults and genetic weaknesses may be intensified. In fact, planned inbreeding is often used as a test to locate genetic defects in the bloodlines. It is not recommended for the novice breeder. For the knowledgeable breeder, however, inbreeding can be valuable in quickly establishing traits without needing several breedings of unrelated or near-related individuals.

AN EXAMPLE OF INBREEDING

Sire 1 **DEERPARK HEARTLIGHT**	Ashley v Bernerliebe *Sire (3)*	Galen v Senseboden *Sire (7)*	Sulton v Dursrutti *Sire (15)*
			Diana v Moosseedorf *Dam (16)*
		Dult Daphne v Yodlerhof *Dam (8)*	Grand Yodler of Teton Valley *Sire (17)*
			Ginger v Senseboden *Dam (18)*
	Deerpark Daisy *Dam (4)*	Gunter von Vogel *Sire (9)*	Holidom Davos v Yodlerhof *Sire (19)*
			Teton's Rocky Mountain Tundra *Dam (20)*
		Deerpark Belesprit D'Azca *Dam (10)*	Bari de la Truche *Sire (21)*
			Deerpark Iner v Buttonwillow *Dam (22)*
Dam (2) DEERPARK DOUBLE PLAY	**Deerpark Heartlight** *Sire (5)*	Ashley v Bernerliebe *Sire (11)*	Galen v Senseboden *Sire (23)*
			Dult Daphne v Yodlerhof *Dam (24)*
		Deerpark Daisy *Dam (12)*	Gunter von Vogel *Sire (25)*
			Deerpark Belesprit D'Azca *Dam (26)*
	Deerpark Ferkin v Buttonwillow *Dam (6)*	Klause v Buchsischlossli *Sire (13)*	York v Bernetta *Sire (27)*
			Diana v Buchsischlossli *Dam (28)*
		Deerpark Brta v Buttonwillow *Dam (14)*	Bari de la Truche *Sire (29)*
			Deerpark Iner v Buttonwillow *Dam (30)*

As you compare pedigrees and consider a breeding system, choose a male to offset your bitch's weak points and complement her pedigree. Then select an alternate dog in the event the first-choice male is ill, uninterested, or unavailable. The preferred system of breeding Berners in the United States and Canada is linebreeding, and there are several lines of excellent dogs from which to choose. Many Swiss dogs are the product of outcrossing and must be used carefully with knowledge of the dogs in the pedigree. Otherwise, consistency may be hard to achieve.

Making Arrangements for a Stud

Contact the owners of the stud dogs and find out the stud fees and health requirements for bitches coming to be bred to their male. In most cases, the bitch is taken or shipped to the stud, but occasionally a bitch refuses to be bred away from her home territory. In these cases, the stud owner may consider sending the male to the bitch.

Nearly all breeders require a negative brucellosis test for the bitch before they will allow her to be mated to their stud. You will also wish to see proof that the stud has a current negative brucellosis test. This is important, because brucellosis, a canine venereal disease, can cause infertility in both sexes, stillborn puppies, and massive uterine infection that necessitates spaying the bitch. The brucellosis screening is an inexpensive, simple blood test that any vet can perform. The blood may have to be sent to another lab, but the results are usually available within a week to ten days and are well worth the effort. The test may be done a few weeks before the bitch comes in season, or during the first days of proestrus.

Other important vital statistics to request about the stud dog include his registration number, whether he has been X-rayed for hip dysplasia and whether he has an OFA certification number. If you are breeding a bitch that is not two years of age, or if the stud is not yet two years of age, the dogs should still be X-rayed and those radiographs screened by a competent veterinarian for hip-joint abnormalities.

If you are the owner of a stud dog, be as honest about your male's weaknesses as you are about his good qualities. The stud-dog owner has a special responsibility to the breed, because one stud can produce hundreds of puppies. People coming to you for stud service need to know his weaknesses as well as his desirable traits so that he will complement the bitch. Your honesty will only improve your reputation, while the results of dishonesty will turn up in the puppies for everyone to see.

Your Berner bitch should be current in all vaccinations before she is bred, because *none should be given during the pregnancy.* She should also be on a high-quality, nutritious diet that will support her as well as the growth of the unborn puppies. She should be in good, firm condition and not be overly fat.

Payment of the stud fee is usually expected at the time of breeding. Sometimes a breeder will accept partial payment at the time of breeding and the remainder when the litter application is signed, or will take a pick puppy in lieu of a stud fee. Such arrangements should be spelled out in a stud service agreement (see Figure 15-1).

Good morning world! This youngster is nearly ready to leave the whelping box.

Figure 15-1
SAMPLE CONTRACT FOR STUD SERVICES

KENNEL STUD SERVICE CONTRACT

The ______________ stud dog, ______________
BREED NAME

Registration # ______________ owned by ______________ kennels

was bred on ______________ to the bitch ______________

owned by ______________ of ______________.

______________ kennels guarantees two living puppies to the age of eight weeks.

If less than that number result the owners of the bitch are entitled to a free return service to a male owned by ______________

______________ kennels subject to the availability of the dog requested. Stud fees are payable at the time of service and will not be refunded. A culture may be required at the owner's expense to protect both dogs if an infection is suspected.

The owner of the bitch agrees that no puppies from the resultant litter will be sold to pet shops or other wholesale outlets.

Stud fee for this animal: $______________. Paid in full ☐ yes ☐ no

Special Provisions:

Signed ______________
owner of bitch

Signed ______________
owner of stud

Address ______________

The Heat Cycle

In order to breed a bitch, you need to be aware of her heat cycle. Most Bernese bitches come in heat for the first time at eight to ten months of age, with many as late as a year of age. After their first heat, they will usually cycle every six months. Rarely should the Bernese Mountain Dog bitch be bred until her second birthday. By this time, she will be physically and emotionally mature and can have OFA certification of hips and elbows.

You will know that your bitch is coming into heat by the first external signs. The heat cycle is a four-week process, and the first signs are often nearly invisible. The first "silent" part of the heat cycle is signaled by frequent urination by the bitch as she leaves her "calling card" for all males smelling the pheromones in her urine. At this time, there will also be a slight swelling of the external genitalia (vulva) and a small amount of mucus discharge; however, most bitches will clean themselves so scrupulously that you may not notice this discharge. Excess cleaning of the vulva may be a sign of the bitch coming into heat. (Or it could be a symptom of vaginitis or a urinary infection.) This stage usually lasts from seven to fourteen days.

The second stage of the heat cycle is the one that most people recognize and count as the beginning

METHODS OF PINPOINTING THE OPTIMUM BREEDING DATE

Most bitches have a fairly normal season in which the outward signs of heat and acceptance correspond with what is going on inside their reproductive tract, hence the success of breeding when nature says "breed." However, it is not unusual to find a bitch who will accept a male on the first or second day of heat and throughout her season. Conversely, some will never want to accept at all and may have to be restrained, even muzzled and forcibly held for breeding. Still others have "silent" heats and show almost no visible swelling or other outward signs. For these bitches, and for estimating the time of ovulation and fertilization within the cycle, vaginal smears are helpful.

As estrogen levels rise, the vaginal epithelium (lining) increases in thickness. Cells are sloughed off the surface of this lining and carried away by the discharge. Variation of the appearance of these epithelial cells under the influence of estrogen gives an accurate reading on the estrogen influence the bitch is undergoing.

Three kinds of cells are present in the vagina: red blood cells, white blood cells, and epithelial cells. During the early stages of a normal season the microscope will reveal numerous red blood cells.

You will also see white blood cells, which are larger than the red ones and stain dark blue. (If an infection is present the white blood cells will completely obliterate the other types. However, any time you see a large number of white cells it would be a good idea to have your veterinarian culture the bitch before breeding.)

The third type of cell, the epithelial, is still larger and resembles a fried egg in appearance. These cells have a nucleus (the yolk of the egg) which the stain will have turned a deep blue, surrounded by a wide transluecent rim.

As the season progresses the slides will show fewer and fewer red and white blood cells, and a gradual progression in the changing shape of the epithelial cells from the more regular egg shape to an irregular shape closely resembling a potato chip or a taco. The edges begin to turn up so that the cell looks like a deep "U" and the nucleus is almost, if not completely, invisible. Such cells are referred to as cornified.

Pinpointing Ovulation

The appearance of nearly 100 percent "cornified" cells in the vaginal smear marks the beginning of true estrus, even though the bitch may or may not stand for the dog at this point. The cells will remain fully cornified for between 10 and 14 days.

Occasionally bitches will ovulate only one or two days after the onset of any visible signs of heat, or conversely, very late in their season. If the epithelial cells are cornified, breed regardless of the outward signs. If you know the day that cornified cells first predominate, you will also know that ovulation will occur about six days later, and that is the time to breed. Counting backward from the first day of diestrus, you can calculate that fertilization took place in the bitch three days previously and if she was bred within seven days before this date the chances of fertilization are good. (Remember, the spermatozoa survive eight days.)

If you do not know whether a bitch is in the early or late stage of her season, vaginal smears taken over a period of three days should tell you. If she is in proestrus you will see a progression toward the cornified cells. If she is in diestrus the progression will be in the other direction. If a bitch comes in heat but no cornified cells appear at any stage of the season you can be sure that no ovulation has occurred; therefore, the bitch cannot conceive.

Another method of determining the time a bitch will ovulate is by having a veterinarian run a progesterone blood level. Progesterone levels in the bitch rise sharply, peak out about 48 hours before ovulation, and then drop just as rapidly. If progesterone does not increase, the bitch will not ovulate, regardless of the appearance of other signs of estrus. Often veterinarians will combine this test with a series of vaginal smears to determine the optimum time to breed or to pinpoint a problem when a bitch has failed to conceive from a previous breeding.

A bitch will ovulate about 1¼ times as many eggs as she actually produces puppies. Providing that live sperm are present in the oviduct, fertilization takes place as soon as the eggs mature. It takes only a few seconds for ejaculated sperm to find its way up the reproductive tract to the oviduct. If the ova are mature they will be fertilized immediately. If they are immature the sperm will surround them and remain motile (alive and able to move) for several days. The eggs are then fertilized as soon as maturation allows.

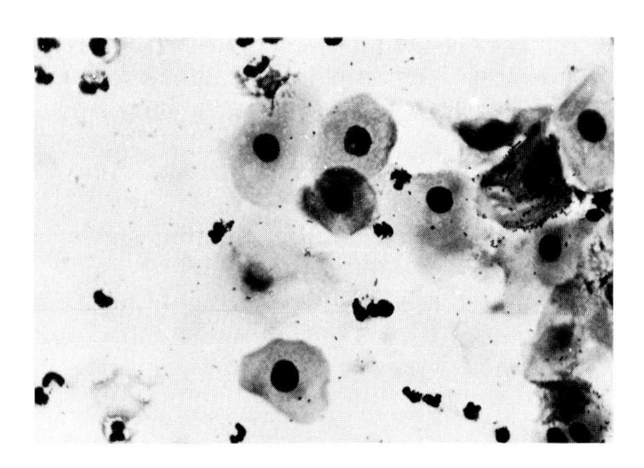

of the heat cycle in the bitch. It is announced by the appearance of a bloody discharge that looks like pure blood. There will be obvious swelling and hardening of the vulva. However, the bitch is not yet ready to breed. She may mount and playfully ride other bitches but will not accept the male. By the end of a week after the bloody discharge begins, the swelling and hardening of the vulva are at their maximum, and the bitch is ready for the next stage of the cycle.

At this time, the discharge becomes less copious and changes to a straw color (light red or tan). The vulva begins to soften, a sign that the bitch is ready to mate. At approximately ten days after the first sign of blood, the bitch is ready to accept the male. Another sign of readiness to mate is the flagging of the tail to one side when the bitch is touched on or near the vulva or on the croup at the base of the tail.

Breeding the Bitch

When the bitch is ready, introduce her to the stud dog. The dogs will play together, and the bitch will present her rump to the male and stand braced, with her tail to one side. At this time, the stud will mount the bitch. When he has penetrated, a bulb at the base of his penis will enlarge while a band of muscle on the outside of the bitch's vulva will contract to hold them together. This is the "tie." The tie is not essential for fertilization to occur, but chances are better if the dogs do tie.

After the tie is made, the male will begin to swing one hind leg over the bitch's rump, and he will turn himself so that they are rump to rump, facing away from each other. There is usually no need to assist the male in turning unless it is very evident that he needs help, which may happen in the case of a large bitch and a small male. Don't rush to

Figure 15-2
THE FEMALE REPRODUCTIVE SYSTEM

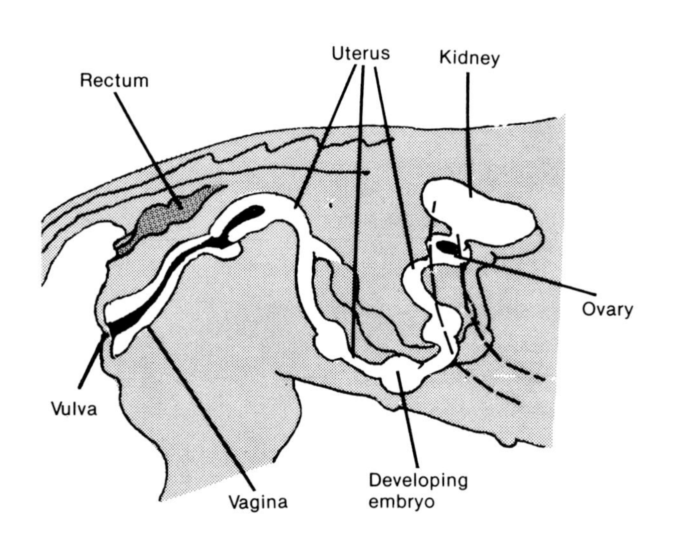

The female reproductive system consists of the ovaries, uterine tubes, uterus, vagina, and vulva, as illustrated.

The ovaries are responsible for egg production, and are also the source of certain hormones. The ovaries of the newborn bitch contain her lifetime supply of eggs—hundreds of thousands.

After ovulation the eggs pass through the tubes into the uterus. Each tube is about the size of a two-inch section of spaghetti. Unlike most mammals, in the dog fertilization takes place in the uterine tubes, and the fertilized eggs remain there for about six days before moving to the uterine horn.

The uterus is "Y" shaped, and during pregnancy the developing fetuses are distributed between the two horns. The uterus is divided into three areas: the horns, the body, and the cervix. The horns lead to the body of the uterus, which is the passageway to the vagina. The cervix, lying at the base of the uterus, is the doorway. On one side of it lies the uterus, the ideal environment for the incubation of the fertilized eggs. On the other side lies the vagina, the opening to the outside.

The vulva is the external genitalia of the female. The lips of the vulva swell and become puffy during estrus.

Figure 15-3
THE MALE REPRODUCTIVE SYSTEM

The male reproductive system of the dog is unique in that the bulbis glandis enlarges after intromission. The swelling of this gland locks the dog and bitch together until ejaculation has taken place. This "tie" may last anywhere from five to thirty minutes or more.

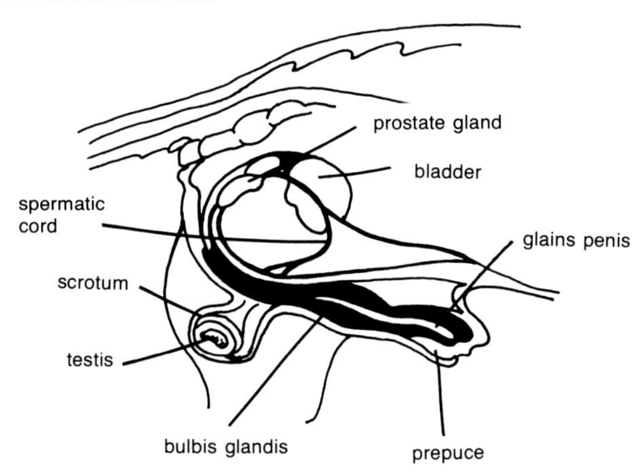

RECORD KEEPING IMPORTANT TO BREEDING MANAGEMENT

In the event that your bitch ever experiences reproductive failure, a serious infection, or other reproductive problems, it is important that you have accurate, detailed records. Knowledge of previous cycles is the foundation for evaluation and treatment. Therefore, each heat season record the following information:

1. Date of first sign of vaginal bleeding.
2. Date bitch would first stand and accept a male.
3. Vaginal cytology or progesterone test results, if available.
4. Breeding dates, if bred.
5. Date of first refusal of male.
6. Any abnormal behavior or symptoms, vaginal discharge, etc.
7. Whelping date or date of false pregnancy if one occurred.
8. Any problems, infections, abortion, etc.

Take this record to the clinic with the bitch when she comes in season. If you have had difficulty getting a litter, any veterinary examinations, diagnoses, and treatment should also be carefully recorded.

help the male turn, because early assistance can abort an incomplete tie and interrupt fertilization. However, when the male does need your assistance, simply lift his leg gently over the bitch's rump.

While the dogs are tied, hold them in place so that they do not pull against each other and possibly cause injury to either of them. The tie will last from a few minutes to half an hour, with fifteen minutes being the usual duration. However, don't panic if the tie lasts longer than expected. When ejaculation is finished, the bulb at the base of the dog's penis will return to normal, and the two will slip free. The usual breeding schedule is two to three breedings one day apart.

When dogs are unable to conceive by natural breeding, artificial insemination may be used. Semen is taken from the stud and placed into the bitch's uterus. Special care must then be taken to ensure that the semen does not dribble out; usually the hindquarters of the bitch must be kept elevated for ten to fifteen minutes. Although artificial insemination is sometimes used in Berners, it is not recommended. When two dogs cannot conceive naturally, it is often an indication that there is some problem with one or both of them. It would not be wise to perpetuate breeding problems by forcing pregnancy on a bitch that may then transmit her or the stud's inability to breed to subsequent generations. Artificial insemination is not widely used in Bernese Mountain Dogs.

After the breeding, remember that the bitch is still in heat and will still accept any male. She should be confined during this last week of her heat cycle to prevent her from being bred by a different male. The signs of heat will begin to diminish during the third week, and the heat cycle will be completed. In some bitches, however, the heat cycle will last longer than usual, and they may breed later in the cycle. This is why some bitches bred during the early part of the cycle, which would seem to be the optimum time for conception, do not ultimately deliver puppies. This is also the reason why a bitch that was thought to be out of heat produces a surprise litter! Watch your bitch carefully and let the size and discharge of her vulva decide when she is allowed to go outside with the males.

Waiting for Puppies

Now begins the part of the bitch's reproductive cycle known as gestation. Gestation is the period from conception to birth, as reckoned from the first successful mating. This time period in dogs can range from fifty-eight to sixty-five days, although the average length is sixty-three days. The actual length varies from bitch to bitch.

The first signs of pregnancy are subtle. The vulva shrinks from its size during heat but remains visibly larger than it was before the bitch came in season. Most Berner bitches do not experience morning sickness, but it happens occasionally, and some may become picky eaters. They may eat grass and vomit it back. Between four and eight weeks on a maiden bitch, the nipples will enlarge, although there is no mammary enlargement at this time. By twenty-one to twenty-eight days, puppies may sometimes be palpated by your veterinarian as walnut-sized swellings in the uterine horns. At the same time, the fetuses can be seen by ultrasound or X-ray, although an X-ray is not recommended if it is not necessary.

From about seven weeks, the bitch will appear pregnant, and at this time you may be able to feel the puppies move. The mammary glands will enlarge and teats or nipples will swell. There also may be signs of a creamy protein and antibody-rich colostrum or "first milk." This is a good time to notify your vet that your bitch is pregnant so that he or she can anticipate a midnight call if problems arise during whelping.

After approximately nine weeks, the bitch will start to get ready for labor. You can recognize the beginning of labor by the bitch's obvious discomfort and heavy, rapid panting. She will lie down and get up repeatedly as if trying to find some comfortable positon. Most will already have exhibited some "nest-making" behavior, such as digging in the yard or in the whelping box. They will shred paper that has been put in the whelping box to make a cozy little nest for themselves and the puppies.

Waiting for puppies. Alpenrose Sunbear v. Harlequin at sixty days into her gestation. Eleven puppies were whelped the day after this photo was taken.

WHELPING CHART

Date bred	Date due to whelp	Date bred	Date due to whelp	Date bred	Date due to whelp	Date bred	Date due to whelp	Date bred	Date due to whelp	Date bred	Date due to whelp	Date bred	Date due to whelp	Date bred	Date due to whelp	Date bred	Date due to whelp	Date bred	Date due to whelp	Date bred	Date due to whelp	Date bred	Date due to whelp
January	March	February	April	March	May	April	June	May	July	June	August	July	September	August	October	September	November	October	December	November	January	December	February
1	5	1	5	1	3	1	3	1	3	1	3	1	2	1	3	1	3	1	3	1	3	1	2
2	6	2	6	2	4	2	4	2	4	2	4	2	3	2	4	2	4	2	4	2	4	2	3
3	7	3	7	3	5	3	5	3	5	3	5	3	4	3	5	3	5	3	5	3	5	3	4
4	8	4	8	4	6	4	6	4	6	4	6	4	5	4	6	4	6	4	6	4	6	4	5
5	9	5	9	5	7	5	7	5	7	5	7	5	6	5	7	5	7	5	7	5	7	5	6
6	10	6	10	6	8	6	8	6	8	6	8	6	7	6	8	6	8	6	8	6	8	6	7
7	11	7	11	7	9	7	9	7	9	7	9	7	8	7	9	7	9	7	9	7	9	7	8
8	12	8	12	8	10	8	10	8	10	8	10	8	9	8	10	8	10	8	10	8	10	8	9
9	13	9	13	9	11	9	11	9	11	9	11	9	10	9	11	9	11	9	11	9	11	9	10
10	14	10	14	10	12	10	12	10	12	10	12	10	11	10	12	10	12	10	12	10	12	10	11
11	15	11	15	11	13	11	13	11	13	11	13	11	12	11	13	11	13	11	13	11	13	11	12
12	16	12	16	12	14	12	14	12	14	12	14	12	13	12	14	12	14	12	14	12	14	12	13
13	17	13	17	13	15	13	15	13	15	13	15	13	14	13	15	13	15	13	15	13	15	13	14
14	18	14	18	14	16	14	16	14	16	14	16	14	15	14	16	14	16	14	16	14	16	14	15
15	19	15	19	15	17	15	17	15	17	15	17	15	16	15	17	15	17	15	17	15	17	15	16
16	20	16	20	16	18	16	18	16	18	16	18	16	17	16	18	16	18	16	18	16	18	16	17
17	21	17	21	17	19	17	19	17	19	17	19	17	18	17	19	17	19	17	19	17	19	17	18
18	22	18	22	18	20	18	20	18	20	18	20	18	19	18	20	18	20	18	20	18	20	18	19
19	23	19	23	19	21	19	21	19	21	19	21	19	20	19	21	19	21	19	21	19	21	19	20
20	24	20	24	20	22	20	22	20	22	20	22	20	21	20	22	20	22	20	22	20	22	20	21
21	25	21	25	21	23	21	23	21	23	21	23	21	22	21	23	21	23	21	23	21	23	21	22
22	26	22	26	22	24	22	24	22	24	22	24	22	23	22	24	22	24	22	24	22	24	22	23
23	27	23	27	23	25	23	25	23	25	23	25	23	24	23	25	23	25	23	25	23	25	23	24
24	28	24	28	24	26	24	26	24	26	24	26	24	25	24	26	24	26	24	26	24	26	24	25
25	29	25	29	25	27	25	27	25	27	25	27	25	26	25	27	25	27	25	27	25	27	25	26
26	30	26	30	26	28	26	28	26	28	26	28	26	27	26	28	26	28	26	28	26	28	26	27
27	31	27	May 1	27	29	27	29	27	29	27	29	27	28	27	29	27	29	27	29	27	29	27	28
28	Apr. 1	28	2	28	30	28	30	28	30	28	30	28	29	28	30	28	30	28	30	28	30	28	Mar. 1
29	2			29	31	29	July 1	29	31	29	31	29	30	29	31	29	Dec. 1	29	31	29	31	29	2
30	3			30	June 1	30	2	30	Aug. 1	30	Sep. 1	30	Oct. 1	30	Nov. 1	30	2	30	Jan. 1	30	Feb. 1	30	3
31	4			31	2			31	2			31	2	31	2			31	2			31	4

Courtesy of Gaines.

One sign of approaching labor is a drop in the bitch's body temperature from her normal temperature of approximately 102 to 99 degrees F. When this happens, you can anticipate whelping within twelve to thirty-six hours. The bitch may refuse food and will become preoccupied with finding a place to whelp and with making a "nest." It is important that someone with whom the bitch is familiar be available to stay with her during this time.

The bitch should be in a safe, enclosed place out of all weather; otherwise, several puppies may die from exposure or from the bitch's stepping on them. The ideal place for the bitch to whelp is in the house, where you can keep an eye on her while carrying out your normal routine. Whelping may last eight to twelve hours. The bitch will most likely want to choose her own spot to whelp, and it is usually not your choice. Therefore, at least two weeks before the puppies are due, have a room picked out that is out of a busy traffic pattern, and have a whelping box ready for her.

The Whelping Box

A whelping box is an open-topped box about five feet square by ten inches high. Many breeders prefer lower sides and an extension, or they move the pups to a pen or other area as they grow. When the sides of the box are too tall, the bitch may injure a puppy as she jumps in or out.

An essential part of a whelping box is the "pig rail." This is a dowel or projecting ledge that is situated about four inches off of the floor of the box. This "rail" extends approximately four inches from the sides of the box and prevents the mother from lying on newborn puppies and suffocating them with her weight. When the puppies are about two weeks old, remove the pig rails so that the pups do not become trapped behind or underneath them and injure or frighten themselves.

If your puppies are born in the winter, or if your house is air-conditioned, you will need to have a heat lamp to keep the puppies warm. Puppies cannot regulate their own body temperature until they are about two weeks old, and a puppy that becomes chilled will die. Follow the manufacturer's recommendations for using the heat lamp, and place it over one corner of the box approximately three feet off of the floor. The floor of the whelping box under the lamp should be kept at 85 degrees F. This system keeps the puppies adequately warmed, while the bitch can be comfortable in the cooler part of the whelping box away from the lamp. The puppies will crawl in and out of the heated area to regulate

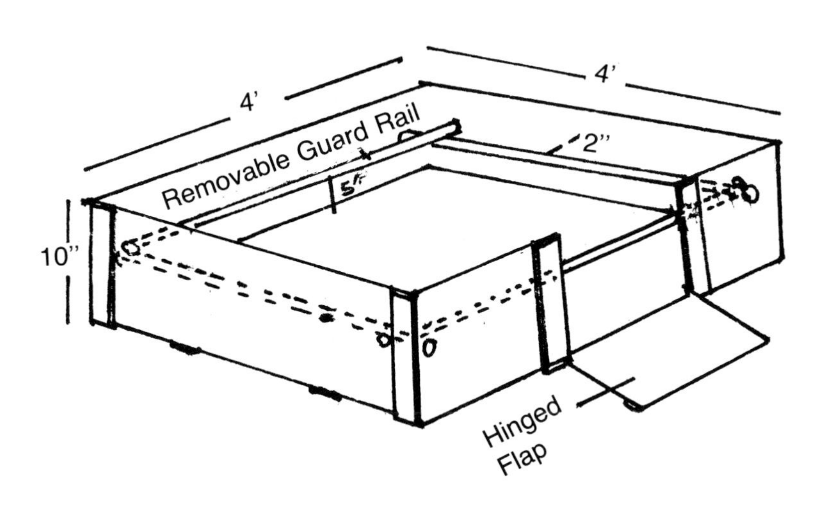

Figure 15-5
WHELPING BOX

Whelping box showing the ledge that prevents the mother from rolling on the puppies.

their temperature, and when they nurse, they will be warmed by contact with their mother. Using a vaporizer to add humidity is desirable in dry climates.

Cover the bottom of the whelping box with an old blanket or flannel sheet for the first two days so that the puppies can get traction to crawl to their dam to nurse. After that, newspaper will be easier to clean up, plus the puppies will be strong enough by that time to get up on their feet a little without sliding on the slick surface. If the bitch is inclined to digging or shredding the bedding, thus "burying" the puppies, a piece of indoor/outdoor carpet may be used. This must be washed and dried in the sun daily.

Introduce the bitch to the box prepared for the whelping, and let her become accustomed to it. A bitch may try to convince you that she prefers using the closet among the shoes for whelping, but gentle perseverance usually will change her mind.

Normal Whelping

Now you are ready for the puppies. A frequent sign of hard labor and imminent delivery of a puppy is the release of a straw-colored fluid from the vulva. The presence of this fluid means that the cervix is open and a puppy has entered the birth canal. If the placenta has broken, a clear, watery, or even greenish discharge may be present. At this stage, the bitch should soon be bearing down in hard labor, and you will be able to see as well as feel the muscular contractions. The presence of greenish discharge *without* subsequent labor and delivery of a puppy is an indication of trouble.

Once the bitch begins bearing down, the *first puppy* is usually born within two hours. The second puppy can come at any time fifteen minutes to two hours later. Subsequent puppies normally arrive within the same time period. If delivery of a puppy *while the bitch is in obvious hard labor* takes longer than one hour, or if you suspect trouble, notify your vet and prepare to take your bitch and any puppies that have already been born to the office. Protect the puppies from inclement weather while you travel and keep them warm. They can ride safely, snuggled together in a small box with a blanket beneath them and a towel covering the box. Wrap a hot-water bottle, or just a plastic bottle filled with hot water, in a towel, and put it next to the puppies.

The maiden bitch may react fearfully with the birth of the first puppy. She may cry out or actually try to run away from the pain. Your calm and reassuring attitude will soothe her. Usually, after the

Beginning of labor; the bitch strains to deliver a puppy.

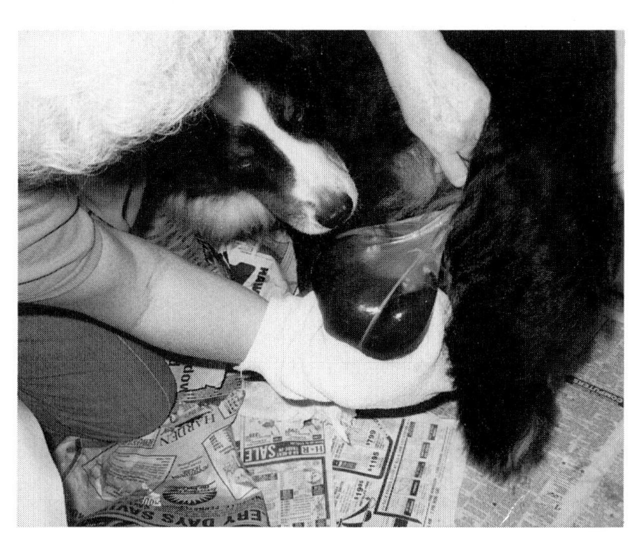

The puppy and placenta are delivered.

Removing the placenta from the puppy's face.

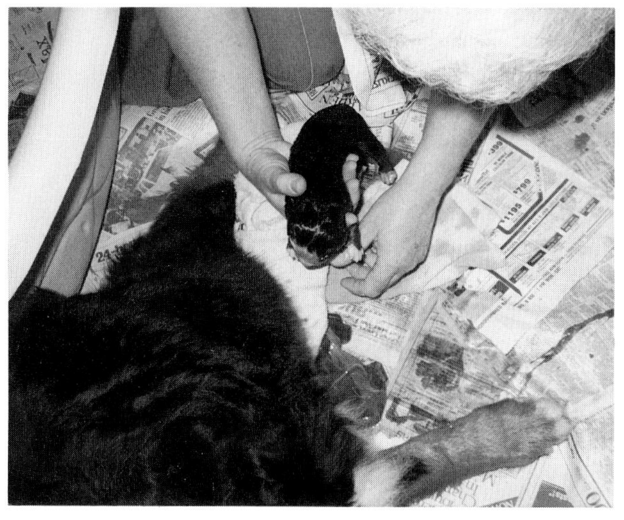

Puppy free of the placenta. Note towel underneath the puppy ready to dry him and stimulate him to breathe.

first puppy, she will setttle down and carry on without further anxiety. Puppies may be born headfirst or breech; either way is entirely normal, and the breech birth usually presents no problem.

The puppy is born in a placenta, a semi-opaque sac, and each puppy has his own placenta. Inside the placenta is clear amniotic fluid; it is vital to break the sac at the puppy's head so that he can breathe. You may or may not want to remove the sac from the rest of his body, but usually the bitch will do it. Nearly all bitches will eat some of the discarded placentas; however, it is not necessary that she eat every one. This is a normal part of the birth process for dogs, and the afterbirth contains hormones that promote the letdown of milk. In any event, the placenta is thin and is broken easily.

Once the sac is removed, the umbilical cord must be severed. This should be done only after the umbilical cord is limp and flat. If the bitch does not chew through the cord herself, you may imitate her chewing motion by shredding it with your fingernails and breaking the cord. Another way is to tie off the cord with a piece of unwaxed dental floss about one-half inch to one inch from the puppy's body. Cut below the floss on the side *away* from the puppy. Otherwise, the puppy may bleed. Leave about two inches of cord. Always use surgical scissors that have been boiled for fifteen minutes to sterilize them, and keep them immersed in isopropyl alcohol between puppies. Do not pull on the umbilical cord during these procedures or allow the bitch to pull or jerk while she bites the cord; too much pressure on the puppy's abdominal wall at this time can cause an umbilical hernia. Within a few days, the stump of the umbilical cord will dry up and slough off.

At this point, use a rough towel to gently rub and stimulate the puppy to breathe. Usually he will blow any remaining amniotic fluid out of his respiratory passages with a tiny sneeze, after which he will squeak indignantly. Note the bright pink nose after the newborn has begun to breathe well. This is normal, and the nose will begin to acquire its black coloration within days. When his coat is mostly dry, put him with his mother to nurse. The colostrum (first milk) is rich in calories, vitamins, and antibodies that are necessary for the newborn puppy.

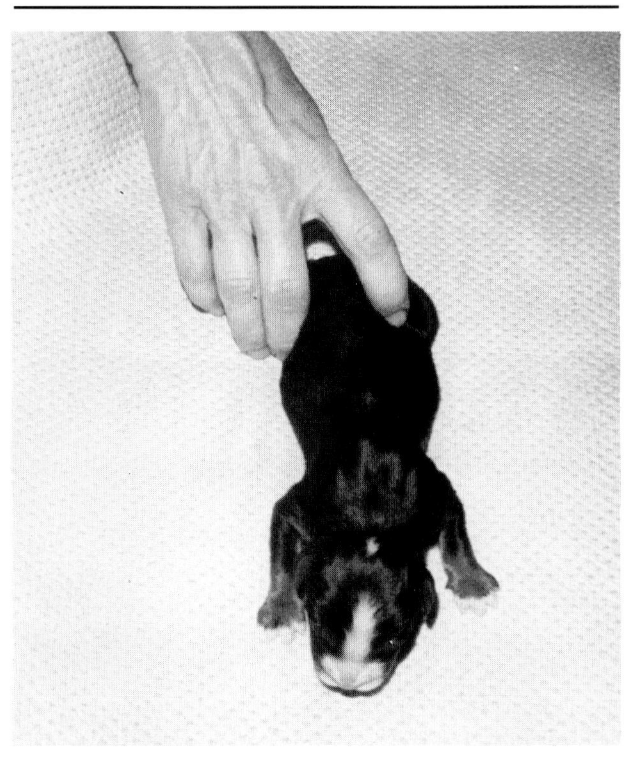

A newborn Berner. This puppy has a small white spot that will disappear as he grows.

If the puppy does not breathe right away, cup his body in your hands and swing him in a big arc with his head down to clear the passages; be sure to support his head. To allow excess fluid to drain, open the puppy's mouth slightly. Artificial respiration can be given by covering the nose and mouth with your mouth and blowing *gently*. Open the puppy's mouth and clear any fluid or mucus. Blow only enough to feel the chest rise as if in a normal respiration. In this fashion, give the puppy ten to twelve breaths per minute. The method of choice is swinging the puppy several times; artificial respiration should be the last resort, because it is likely to damage the alveolar sacs in the puppy's lungs. If the puppy begins to breathe, he will usually do so with a gasp and with much choking and gagging. Continue rubbing and stimulating the puppy until he is breathing normally and complains vehemently. Now he can be put with his mother to nurse.

After nursing, the puppies can be moved a very short distance away to lie beneath the heat lamp or on a blanket-covered heating pad while the rest of the litter is born. Remember to return those puppies to nurse periodically. When labor is complete, replace all of the puppies with the bitch. In Berners, litter size ranges routinely from two to ten puppies, but litters of one to fourteen are not unheard of. The average number is six.

Abnormal Labor and Whelping

If your bitch has her litter without complications, congratulations. Unfortunately, this does not always happen. If you suspect anything out of the ordinary while your bitch is whelping, call your veterinarian immediately and prepare to take your bitch to the clinic. The most common difficulties associated with whelping in Berners are overextended labor and stillborn puppies. Many Berners are slow whelpers, and it is not unusual for a Berner bitch to need a caesarean-section to deliver a litter. However, bitches needing a C-section with one litter may whelp normally the next time, and vice versa.

If the bitch seems anxious and hasn't produced a puppy despite straining to do so for two hours, consult your vet. Once the first puppy is born, the interval between births can be fifteen minutes to two hours. Signs of trouble are excess straining without the delivery of a puppy, exhaustion, or cessation of labor while more puppies obviously remain in the womb. It is usual for a bitch to rest between puppies, she may even lie flat on the floor. However, the resting bitch will lift her head in response to your voice, whereas the exhausted bitch may be unable to move.

A corollary to overextended labor is uterine inertia, in which the uterine muscle is unable to expel the puppies. The bitch may fail to go into hard labor at all, or may stop having contractions before all of the puppies are delivered. Any time you suspect problems, call your vet. If puppies are not delivered within a normal time frame, they may suffocate in the birth canal. Your vet may recommend one or two injections of the hormone oxytocin to induce and speed labor, but the drug should

Mother and newborn litter. One idea for a whelping box — a child's large wading pool may also be used.

be used with caution. If given when there is a stricture, obstruction, or other problem that prevents normal delivery, the injection could cause rupture of the uterine wall. Use of oxytocin can also cause early separation of the placenta, leading to stillborn puppies and uterine fatigue. This will make subsequent injections of the drug useless, because the uterine muscle will not be able to respond to expel the fetuses.

Stillbirth is commonly a result of the puppy being too long in the birth canal but also may be caused by the placenta's early separation from the uterus. A puppy receives oxygenated blood through the umbilical cord attached to the placenta. Should the placenta break away from the uterus too soon before birth, or if the puppy remains in the birth canal too long, he suffocates and is born dead. Some of these puppies can be resuscitated by artificial respiration, but it is not always successful.

The Newborn Berner and Care of the Nursing Bitch

At this point, you may wish to weigh the puppies; the normal weight for a newborn Berner puppy is one to one and one-half pounds. Some puppies may weigh less, but if they are breathing and nursing well, there is no cause for alarm. They are not runts, and they will reach full normal size.

Make sure that the smaller puppies have the same access to the teats as their older siblings, or supplement mother's milk with a commercial bitch's milk replacer such as Esbilac®. Do not take the puppy away from the bitch. It is important that he receive antibodies from her milk, yet supplementing will ensure that he gets adequate calories. Most so-called "runts" turn out to be normal size for their breed, and usually it is not even necessary to supplement unless the litter is abnormally large or the bitch loses her milk.

One reason for a loss of milk in nursing bitches in one or more teats is mastitis. Check the bitch's teats often, and note if there is one teat from which the puppies do not nurse. If it is just a full teat that has been overlooked, guide a puppy to it. If the teat is hard and hot to the touch or is ulcerated, mastitis is the most likely cause. This will require prompt attention from your veterinarian, because it is an infection and an inflammation of the mammary tissues. If not treated promptly, mastitis will damage the teat until there is a loss of function.

Another potential health problem related to the nursing bitch is puerperal tetany, or eclampsia, due to calcium deficiency. Signs include weakness, difficulty standing, and mild to violent trembling. The condition, though rare in Berners, constitutes a veterinary emergency; rush the bitch to the clinic for treatment.

If the litter is whelped without difficulty, notify your vet's office as a courtesy, because the vet was on call just before the litter was whelped. Also, schedule a checkup for the bitch and litter within twenty-four hours. At this time, your vet may recommend a "clean-out" shot of oxytocin for the bitch. The bitch's temperature should return to a normal 102 degrees F. after whelping. If her temperature is above normal or there is a bad-smelling, puss-like discharge, see your vet immediately, because either is a sign of infection. It is normal for the bitch to have dark, tarry stools for a few days from eating the placentas. Also, she will have a small quantity of dark-red vaginal discharge changing to a pinkish color for several weeks after whelping. A more profuse bright-red discharge can indicate hemorrhage, and the bitch should be taken to the clinic immediately.

This baby's nose will soon "color in" and assume its normal black pigment.

Dewclaw Removal

Removing the front dewclaws, while not mandatory, gives a cleaner appearance to the front legs and avoids the possibility that a dewclaw may later be torn by accident. Front dewclaws may be removed at home, but removal of rear dewclaws in the Berner is a minor surgical procedure and should only be done by your veterinarian. In the rear, the dewclaws are attached to a thick cartilage that must also be removed, and a stitch must be taken to prevent bleeding and infection.

Physical Abnormalities in Berner Puppies

Abnormalities in Berner puppies are rare, but they may sometimes cause death or may necessitate euthanasia. With the exception of split-nose, which may be a throwback to an earlier characteristic of the breed that has long been selected against, abnormalities that occur in the Bernese Mountain Dog are the same as those that occur in other breeds. The ones that you are likely to see are cleft palate and clubfoot. Split-nose does not affect the puppy's ability to grow and develop, but it is unsightly and is suspected to be related to cleft palate. Cleft palate is a defect caused by incomplete closure of the hard palate; you will notice that a puppy with this abnormality will nurse poorly, and most of the milk will bubble back out of his nose. If you open the puppy's mouth, you can often see an open slit in the roof of the mouth. If you are unsure, have the puppy checked by a veterinarian. These puppies are poor candidates for survival, becuase they cannot get an adequate amount of milk to support growth and development. It is kinder to them to have them put to sleep as soon as possible.

Clubfoot in puppies is a condition where a foot or feet are turned under so that the puppy walks on his ankle with that foot. He will never be able to move naturally or run, and it is best to have him put to sleep. These occurrences are rare.

Breeding Ethics

It would be wonderful if everyone who wanted to breed Bernese Mountain Dogs would have only perfect litters without complications, but statistics prove otherwise. Perhaps what separates the true breeder from the opportunist seeking a fast profit is a willingness to take the emotional and financial losses of the whelpings and litters that were not perfect. Ethical breeders of Berners keep the breed Standard in their heads and the future of the breed in their hearts.

Mother and newborn litter of ten. Though not an unusually large litter, larger ones are rare.

Canadian Ch. Valleyvu's Heidi v. Gartenhugl, owned by Ron Smith, bred by Grace Borgh.

SIXTEEN

The Art of Puppy Rearing

Eyes

At ten to fourteen days of age, the puppies' eyes will open. The grand event begins as a tiny crack in the sealed eyelid, and one day you'll be surprised to see a tiny glint as a Berner puppy first begins to survey his world. The eyes open gradually, and the eyesight is poor at first. The puppy's eyes will be smoky blue in color but will gradually darken to the proper dark brown within four weeks after opening. Occasionally, a Berner will be born with a lighter blue eye, and it usually happens to just one eye. It won't be apparent that the eye is going to remain blue for a week or more after the eyes open, at which time the blue eye will definitely appear lighter in color. A blue eye is not a reason to put a puppy down; the dog *will not be blind,* nor will his vision be affected. However, a blue eye is a disqualification for showing in conformation. These dogs should be neutered or spayed to avoid perpetuating the unwanted trait in the breed, but they are showable in obedience competition and have all of the other wonderful traits that make a Berner a joy to own.

Ears

At fourteen to twenty days, the puppies' ears start to open. Often the first indication is a startled yip from the whelping box when you drop a pan in the kitchen: "What! What was that?" Soon, there will be choruses of tiny barks and growls resounding from the box, and there's always the one that barks for the first time and surprises himself: "Oh! Was that me?"

Exploring the Environment

At about three weeks of age, the puppies begin to explore and expand their horizons. It will be hard for you to keep them in the whelping box, and to do so will retard their natural development. A large puppy pen or a "puppy-proofed" area such as a utility room or porch will suffice. If you live in a mild climate, the puppies can be put out for part of the day in a secure pen or yard as long as the weather is moderately warm and not rainy. Introduce your litter to the great outdoors gradually, and stay with them to make sure that they don't meet anything that they can't handle. This is a good time to give their mother a break from nursery duty. Weather permitting, gradually lengthen the puppies' stay outside to three or four hours. If you are comfortable that there is nothing that will harm them, you need not spend the entire time out with them — but it is a good idea to check on them often.

If your puppies cannot be put outside due to inclement weather, you can build a puppy "recreation area" inside. Use a garage, spare room, or basement. Select a ten-by-ten-foot area and fence it with lightweight wire that can be clamped or tied together. You can put vinyl flooring under the pen to prevent damage to the floor underneath. Make the fence at least three feet high; you can probably just step over it without making a gate. Cover the

At ten to fourteen days, the puppy's eyes begin to open. Eyelids are now visible.

A canine Christopher Columbus sets out to explore the new world.

This spot will shrink, but will remain visible on the adult.

A small, portable pen acts as a transition between whelping box and outdoor home for puppies.

floor of the puppy pen with papers, and shred more on top of this layer. When you see which part of the pen the puppies have chosen for a bathroom area, take up the shredded paper except for that area. This way, your Berner puppies can have a safe place to grow and explore.

Help the puppies to grow and develop psychologically by giving them toys to play with. Empty plastic milk jugs with popcorn kernels inside provide an irresistible rattling noise for inquisitive puppies, and thick, knotted ropes lead to furious romps that develop muscles and reflexes. Vinyl balls too large for the young Berners to chew are also fascinating, and the puppies will bunt and shove them.

By the time the puppies are five weeks old, they can safely be put outside with their mother in mild weather. A well-sheltered area should be provided, one that is securely fenced and not subject to extremes in temperature. Bedding in the sleeping area can be clean wheat straw or wooden flooring, such as a pallet, to keep the puppies off the ground or concrete. Never use cedar chips, especially with young puppies. Cedar contains a resin that, although toxic to fleas, is also toxic to young puppies. Extended exposure will result in symptoms of poisoning, such as staggering, drooling, and possible paralysis, and may result in death.

Worming and Vaccination

When the puppies are three weeks old, they can be wormed for the first time. One symptom of worm infestation is a bloated appearance to the puppy's stomach; however, puppies can harbor roundworms that take a substantial portion of the nutrition meant for them, yet show no signs. Your veterinarian can recommend a safe wormer that you can give. When you talk to your vet about worming the puppies, set up a vaccination

Breakfast in the breakfast nook. Dark Sky Finor feeds the masses.

Suggested Immunization Schedule

Age	Interval	Type of Vaccine
6 to 6 1/2 weeks	first shots	Distemper Measles vaccine (effective regardless of maternal antibodies present in puppy's system). Killed Parvovirus vaccine (given separately or in combination).
10 to 12 weeks	4 weeks	DA2PL+CPV+CV (Distemper, Hepatitis (Adenovirus Type II), Parainfluenza, Leptospirosis, Canine Parvovirus, Corona Virus (These are given in various combinations or all in one. Follow recommendation of your veterinarian.) Bordatella. Lyme disease when available in your state.
14 to 16 weeks	4 weeks	Booster shot of all above DA2PL+CPV+CV, bordatella, lyme disease. First Rabies Shot.
1 year	8 months	Booster all vaccines.
Annually as adult	1 year	Booster Distemper, Hepatitis, Lepto, Parainfluenza, Parvo and Corona Virus, Bordatella vaccines.
1 year	1 to 3 years	Rabies booster (Varies according to state and local laws. Vaccine is good for 3 years after initial booster at I year).

schedule. The most important vaccinations are for distemper and parvovirus, and the puppies will need two to three booster shots.

Weaning

Another important stage of a Berner puppy's life is weaning. If you are feeding a litter of puppies, the following schedule can be used. At about three to four weeks of age, Berner puppies can begin to eat a dry puppy food that, according to the manufacturer's label, may be moistened. The packets of soft-moistened food that are prepared by some dog-food manufacturers are not recommended. Add hot water to the dry food in a small plastic bowl, then cover the bowl with a tightly sealed lid. In about ten minutes, mash the food with a fork. If the consistency is too dry, add warm water. Stir in Esbilac® to make a gruel. Once the puppies are finished with this mixture, feed the remainder to the mother. Offer this mixture to the puppies five or six times a day, and have fresh, clean water available to the puppies in a low-sided container at all times. The type of crockery bowl used for rabbits is excellent. It does not turn over easily and is low enough to be safe for the puppies.

Once the puppies have eaten, be sure to clean them gently with a dampened washcloth unless the mother has cleaned them adequately. Towel-dry the puppies to prevent them from getting chilled.

The amount of liquid that the puppies will be getting from their mother will be decreasing steadily. Gradually decrease the amount of liquid added to the food, until at about five weeks the food is soft but only slightly mushy with liquid. By the time the puppies are six or seven weeks old, they will have a respectable set of "milk teeth" and will be able to chew dry kibble fairly well. Dry food can be used as a snack and for chewing exercise, but continue feeding food that has been softened, because the puppies will be teething and their gums may be tender.

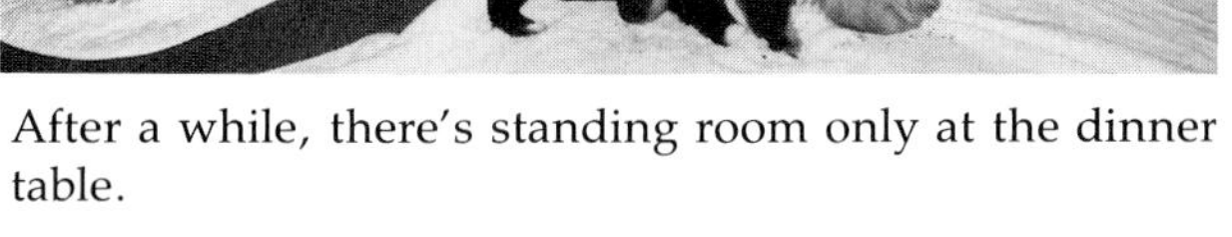

After a while, there's standing room only at the dinner table.

A good fence keeps these puppies safely enclosed while they meet visitors.

Older littermates share the feeding dish.

Clean up the dish, then clean up your brother.

Socialization

What is socialization and why is it important? Socialization refers to the mingling of individuals with the members of their society. For dogs, that means being comfortable and competent at interacting with members of their own species and with humans, as well as with the environment in general. In order to be psychologically stable, dogs must be socialized with other dogs and with people. The orphan puppy that grows up only in the company of humans will have great difficulty relating to other dogs. A dog that grows up without human contact will be shy and fearful of people. Dogs that never travel away from their own yards will be uncertain and easily frightened in unfamiliar locales. These are very important concepts to remember for the Bernese Mountain Dog. He is very happy to stay at home with just his family, but he must be socialized so that he can travel and meet people without being fearful.

Socialization begins at birth. While you help with delivery, you are accustoming the puppies to their new world. Even before their eyes open, your puppies are aware of their environment through touch and scent. You can develop the puppies' sense of self-confidence and level of socialization by gently handling them and letting them get to know the scent of the humans in the family. Touch each puppy all over, including his face, tail, and feet, gently massaging him. Cuddle him close to you so that he feels safely supported. Even though his eyes and ears are not open, he will soon learn your scent. This is the beginning of trust in humans for a puppy.

Although the whelping box is out of the heavy traffic pattern, your home routine goes on as usual. When their ears open, the puppies become accustomed to peoples' voices, to the television and radio playing, to doors slamming, and to children playing. Continue to socialize your puppies until they go to their new homes. Touch them all over, cuddle them, and talk to them in a reasonable tone of voice. It is important, too, to separate each puppy from the litter and take it to a different location. This gives each puppy an opportunity to develop its personality away from the group influence of the litter, where more-dominant littermates may overwhelm less-dominant siblings.

By the time your Berner puppies are five or six weeks old, they are eating well on their own and are starting to notice the world beyond their own territory. Expose them to a variety of sights, sounds, and people so that they do not become shy of the world outside their home environment. Provide toys that can be mouthed and make noise, and invite friends over to meet the puppies so that the pups become accustomed to strangers. Although puppies may not have had their vaccinations at this age, maternal antibodies circulating in their blood and normal hygiene precautions, such as clean clothes and hand washing for visitors, prevent exposure to disease while providing much-needed socialization.

At this age, puppies can benefit from enrichment in their environment as well. Obstacles such as tunnels and climbing platforms teach coordination and balance while providing an interesting landscape. An old bath towel hooked into a swing provides a safe swing and exposes a puppy to vestibular stimulation. Early stimulation of the inner ear in familiar surroundings may decrease the incidence or severity of motion sickness.

Ready for a stroll, four puppies await an opportunity for enrichment and socialization.

Playtime! Hope nobody needed that towel.

DEVELOPMENTAL STAGES OF A PUPPY

Age	Basic Needs	Behavior and Training
1-14 days (1st & 2nd week)	Warmth • Food Sleep • Mother	Not responsive to humans • Sleeps 90% of time Needs stimulation for urination & defecation
15-21 days (3rd & 4th week)	Warmth • Food Sleep • Mother	Eyes open • Begins to walk Should be handled carefully • Needs mother and littermates • First worming
22-35 days (4th & 5th week)	Socialization with canines and humans • Rest • Play	Begins to eat, bark, and play • Begins to respond to human voice Needs play and socialization outside the puppy pen
36-49 days (6th & 7th week)	Weaning • Separation from littermates • Human socialization	Strong dominant/subordinate relationships are developing • Motor skills improved • Temporary immunizations given • Capable of learning simple commands and being leash broken • May go to new home during seventh week
49-56 days (8th week)	Security • Love	Often termed the "fear period" • Puppy should not be frightened or unnecessarily stressed during this period
50-63 days (9-12 weeks)	Bonds to human • Learns to accept human as pack leader Socialization	Totally removed from dam and littermates • Capable of learning Come-Sit-Stay Needs confidence instilled • Begin housebreaking • Exposure to variety of environments important
64-112 days (12-16 weeks)	Security • Discipline Socialization • Attention	Learns by association • Goes through "avoidance period" Needs continued low-key socialization and exposure
113-168 days (16-24 weeks)	Socialization • Love • Consistent Discipline • Basic Training	Fully developed mentally; needs experience • Will attempt to establish dominance • Adapts a negative or positive attitude toward training at this time Praise lavishly for correct behavior
25-32 weeks (6-8 months)	Basic Training • Consistent discipline • Continued attention and socialization	Ready for beginning show or obedience classes • Attention span is lengthening • Needs continuing exposure to new situations • Males begin to assert dominance
33-56 weeks (8-12 months)	Continued socialization, reassurance and training • Affection and reassurance necessary	Show pups often in "puppy bloom" but should not be pushed too fast • Teething period ends • Puberty (period of sexual maturation) begins • May go through a second avoidance period • Neutering can be performed.
12-18 months (1-1½ years)	More disciplined and structured training • Love	Bernese Mountain Dogs take a soft hand and easy temper • Training can be more intense

As you allow your Berner puppies to explore their surroundings, prevent them from jumping off of porches or steps or anything taller than themselves.

Going to a New Home

Now that you have whelped, weaned, and socialized your puppies, they are ready to leave you. Berner puppies are ready to go to their new homes by the time they are seven to eight weeks old. Many Berner breeders prefer to wait until the eighth week. However, recent behavioral studies indicate that seven weeks, the beginning of the socialization period, may be better. Some studies show that at eight weeks, puppies enter a fearful stage lasting two to three weeks when change is perceived as more traumatic.

Raising a litter entails a great deal of responsibility, both to the breed and to potential puppy buyers, but there is also tremendous joy and satisfaction. Watching the puppies grow and develop into individuals each with his or her own personality is fascinating and fulfilling. But once you have bred and whelped your own litter, beware! One woman carries around her puppy photos in a tiny scrapbook labeled "Let Me Show You My Grandchildren!"

Bathtime can be pleasant if you are gentle and patient.

Dry the puppy thoroughly and gently.

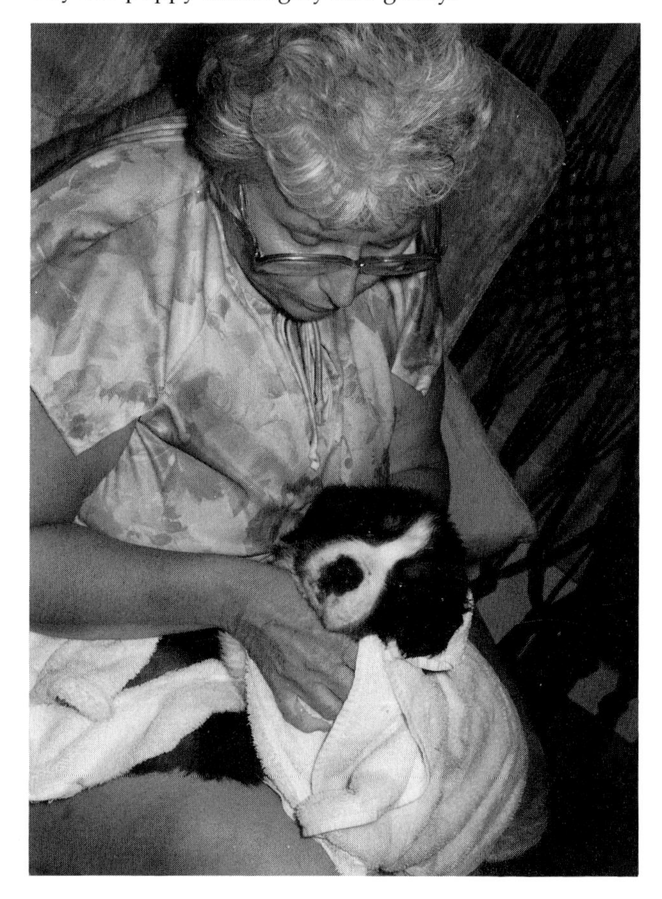

Be sure to register your litter within the first week or two after birth so that the litter registrations are back before you sell any puppies. A sales agreement and an AKC "blue slip" should accompany each puppy you sell. If a puppy dies or is put down, you must return the blue litter registration slip to the AKC with an explanation.

Marketing Your Berner Puppies

The best way to sell the puppies that you produce so carefully is by word of mouth. Many Berner breeders do not use the classified ads to merchandise puppies. Dog shows, local kennel-club activities, and training classes present opportunities to show off the breed and assess potential owners. The Bernese Mountain Dog Club of America maintains a registry for breeders and keeps an ad in major dog magazines. When someone interested in purchasing a Bernese Mountain Dog calls the

Ch. Gruezi Heidi, owned by M.C. Chismar, takes Winner's Bitch.

Below: Sample blue slip for AKC. The reverse side of the form shows the sire and dam, sex, date of birth, breeder's name. Breeder must mark the dog's color, if applicable, and breeder or owner must select a registered name for the pup. Registration papers must be filed with the AKC before the pup is one year of age.

INSTRUCTIONS: PLEASE TYPE — OR USE **PEN. NO PENCIL.** Erasures or Corrections may cause return of application for an explanation.

SEC. A. TO BE COMPLETED IN FULL AND SIGNED BY OWNER OF LITTER (AND CO-OWNERS, IF ANY)

Check one and only one box

1 ☐ I (we) still own this dog, and I (we) apply for a LIMITED REGISTRATION—OFFSPRING WILL NOT BE ELIGIBLE FOR REGISTRATION and to have ownership recorded in my (our) name(s).

2 ☐ I (we) still own this dog, and I (we) apply for full registration and to have ownership recorded in my (our) name(s).

3 ☐ I (we) certify that this dog was transferred DIRECTLY TO THE FOLLOWING PERSON(S) ON ______ mo. day year

MUST be filled in by owner(s) of Litter

PRINT NAME(S) OF PERSON(S) TO WHOM DOG WAS DIRECTLY TRANSFERRED ______

ADDRESS ______

I CERTIFY, BY MY SIGNATURE, THAT I AM IN GOOD STANDING WITH THE AMERICAN KENNEL CLUB.

Signature ______ OWNER OF LITTER AT BIRTH

Signature ______ CO-OWNER (IF ANY) OF LITTER AT BIRTH

SEC. B. TO BE COMPLETED and SIGNED BY THE PERSON(S) NAMED IN SEC. A ABOVE, PROVIDED the person(s) owns the dog at the time this application is submitted to the A.K.C. If the person(s) named in SEC. A has transferred the dog to some other person(s), obtain a Supplemental Transfer Statement form from the A.K.C. Instructions for its completion and use are on the form.

I apply to The American Kennel Club to have Registration Certificate for this dog issued in my/our name(s), and certify that I/we acquired it on the date set forth above DIRECTLY from the person(s) who Signed Sec. A above, and that I/we still own this dog. I agree to abide by American Kennel Club rules and regulations.

New Owner's Signature ______

New Co-Owner's Signature ______

New owner must complete this Section PRINT Name ______ Address ______ City ______ State ______ Zip ______

Complete only if co-owner is named in Section A PRINT Name ______ Address ______ City ______ State ______ Zip ______

Fees must accompany application. See top left corner of the reverse side for the required fees. Make checks payable to the American Kennel Club — DO NOT SEND CASH. Application becomes the property of the American Kennel Club when submitted.

SALES CONTRACT FOR SHOW OR BREEDING QUALITY DOGS

On ______________________ , __________________________________ kennels agrees to sell
date name

to __________________________________ of __________________________________
name address

the following __________________________________ for the sum of $ __________
breed

Name: ______________________ Whelped ______________________

Sire: ______________________ Color: ______________________

Dam: ______________________ Sex: ______________________

Reg. #: ______________________

This animal is guaranteed to be free from all hereditary defects affecting its suitability for breeding, and is guaranteed to be free of disqualifying and serious faults of a structural or temperamental nature. Health is guaranteed for 48 hrs. and it is recommended that the buyer have the animal examined by a reputable veterinarian during that time.

A replacement or credit for the amount of purchase will be given for any animal sold for $ __________ or more if the dog matures at less than the represented quality at 18 mos. of age, unless it is mutually agreed to determine this at another date.

Special Provisions of sale:

Signed: ______________________
buyer

Signed: ______________________
seller

Address: ______________________

CONTRACT FOR CO-OWNERSHIP OF A DOG

On ______________________ , __________________________________ kennels agrees to sell
date name

co-ownership in the following ______________________ to ______________________
breed name

of __________________________________ for the sum of $ __________
address

Name: ______________________ Color: ______________________

Sire: ______________________ Whelped: ______________________

Dam: ______________________ Sex: ______________________

Registration # ______________________

The buyer agrees to be responsible for adequate maintenance and promotion (i.e., training, showing, and advertising) of this animal except as specified below or when the dog is in the possession of ______________ kennels.

Co-ownership entitles ______________ kennels in the case of a male to ½ of all outside stud fees earned by the dog (both co-owners may use the dog free) and in the case of a bitch to use her for every other litter when she is not being shown.

Special Provisions:

In the event of sale of this dog, the remaining co-owner will have first chance to purchase the dog.

Signed: ______________________
buyer

Signed: ______________________
seller

Address: ______________________

club, they are given a list of breeders in their area that they may contact to buy a puppy. Individual breeders also often put ads in dog magazines such as *Dog World*.

Members of the BMDCA sign an agreement upon joining the club stating that they will not sell any puppies to pet shops, puppy mills, or irresponsible parties. It is also wise to investigate the buyer that comes to you for a puppy. Does he or she have a fenced yard, other dogs, small children? Have they had a dog before? Responsible breeders will explain the pros and cons of owning a Bernese Mountain Dog to the potential buyer and will keep in contact with anyone who buys a puppy from them.

will explain the pros and cons of owning a Bernese Mountain Dog to the potential buyer and will keep in contact with anyone who buys a puppy from them.

Producing a litter of Berners is time consuming and not inexpensive. Stud fees, transport of the bitch, and veterinary care of the puppies all contribute to the cost of breeding, but choosing responsible owners and maintaining a relationship with them and the dog that you sold them can be satisfying and provide you friendships that last a lifetime.

Eight-week-old "Ted" learns to come.

A day at the beach makes a good socializing experience.

Learning house manners is important for a Berner.

With practice, even a young Berner can stack like a pro.

Appendix A
PUPPY APTITUDE TEST SCORESHEET

Test and Purpose	Score	Comments
1: SOCIAL ATTRACTION **Purpose:** Degree of attraction to people. **Method:** Place pup in testing area 4 feet from tester, who coaxes puppy to her/him.	Comes readily, tail up, jumps, bites at hands .... 1 Comes readily, tail up, paws, licks at hands .... 2 Comes readily, tail up .... 3 Comes readily, tail down .... 4 Comes hesitantly, tail down .... 5 Does not come at all 6	
2: FOLLOWING **Purpose:** Degree of willingness to follow human leadership. **Method:** Stand up and walk away from puppy, encouraging him verbally.	Follows readily, tail up, gets underfoot, bites at feet .... 1 Follows readily, tail up, gets underfoot .... 2 Follows readily, tail up .... 3 Follows readily, tail down .... 4 Follows hesitantly, tail down .... 5 No follow or went away 6	
3: RESTRAINT **Purpose:** Degree of dominance or submission. Response to social/physical dominance. **Method:** Gently roll the pup on his back and hold him for 30 seconds.	Struggles fiercely, flails, bites .... 1 Struggles fiercely, flails .... 2 Settles, struggles, settles with eye contact .... 3 Slight struggle, then settles .... 4 No struggle, tail tucked .... 5 No struggle, strains to avoid eye contact 6	
4: SOCIAL DOMINANCE **Purpose:** Degree of acceptance of human social dominance. How "forgiving" the pup is. **Method:** Pup sits facing tester at a 45°angle. Tester strokes pup and puts his/her face close to pup.	Jumps, paws, bites, growls .... 1 Jumps, paws, licks .... 2 Cuddles up to tester, tries to lick face .... 3 Sits quietly, accepts petting, nudges/licks hands .... 4 Rolls over, no eye contact .... 5 Goes away and stays away 6	
5: ELEVATION DOMINANCE **Purpose:** Degree of accepting dominance while in position of no control. **Method:** Cradle pup under his belly, fingers interlaced, and elevate just off ground for 30 sec.	Struggles fiercely, bites .... 1 Struggles .... 2 No struggle, relaxed, tail wags .... 3 No struggle, relaxed .... 4 No struggle .... 5 No struggle, froze, tail/rear legs tense 6	
6: RETRIEVING **(Obedience & Aptitude)** **Purpose:** Degree of willingness to work with humans. High correlation between ability to retrieve and successful guide dogs, obedience dogs, and field trial dogs.	Chases object, picks it up and runs away .... 1 Chases object, stands over it, does not return .... 2 Chases object, picks it up and returns to tester .... 3 Chases object, returns without object to tester 4	

Test and Purpose	Score	Comments
Method: Attract pup's attention with crumpled paper ball. When he is watching, toss paper 4 feet away. When pup goes after it, back up 2 feet and encourage him to come back.	Starts to chase, loses interest .... 5 Does not chase 6	
7: TOUCH SENSITIVITY **Purpose:** Degree of sensitivity to touch. **Method:** Take webbing of one front foot and press between finger and thumb lightly, gradually increasing pressure on a scale from 1-10. Stop as soon as pup shows discomfort.	9-10 counts before response .... 1 7-8 counts before response2 5-6 counts before response .... 3 3-4 counts before response .... 4 1-2 counts before response 5	
8: SOUND SENSITIVITY **Purpose:** Degree of sensitivity to sound. **Method:** Place pup in center of area and make a sharp noise a few feet away. A large metal spoon struck sharply on a metal pan twice works well.	Locates the sound, walks toward it .... 1 Locates sound, barks .... 2 Locates sound, shows curiosity, walks toward it .... 3 Locates the sound .... 4 Cringes, backs off, hides .... 5 Ignores sound, shows no curiosity 6	
9: CHASE INSTINCT **Purpose:** Degree of response to moving object; chase instinct. **Method:** Tie a string around a towel and drag it in front of pup from left to right.	Looks, attacks, bites .... 1 Looks, barks, tail up .... 2 Looks curiously, attempts to investigate .... 3 Looks, does not go forward, tail down .... 4 Runs away, hides .... 5 Ignores, shows no curiosity 6	
10: STABILITY **Purpose:** Degree of intelligent response to strange object. **Method:** Place pup in center of testing area. Closed umbrella is held 4 feet away and pointed perpendicular to direction the pup faces. Umbrella is opened and set down so pup can investigate.	Walks forward, tail up, bites .... 1 Walks forward, tail up, mouths .... 2 Walks forward, attempts to investigate .... 3 Looks curiously, stays put .... 4 Goes away, tail down, hides .... 5 Ignores, shows no curiosity 6	Note: Puppies frequently startle upon seeing the umbrella open. Score pup's response after umbrella is set down.
11: ENERGY LEVEL **Purpose:** Degree of physical energy. **Method:** Observe pup on other subtests and score according to most frequent activity observed. Check with breeder for confirmation.	Continually runs, pounces, wiggles, paws .... High Mostly trots, occasionally runs, pounces, wiggles .... Medium Walks slowly, sits quietly, remains in position usually ...... Low Stands rigidly, eyes roll, tail down, ears back .... Stress	

SELECTED REFERENCES

BOOKS/PAMPHLETS

American Kennel Club. *The Complete Dog Book.* New York: Howell Book House, 1986.

American Kennel Club. "Dog Show Classifications: Rules Applying to Registration and Dog Shows." January 1988, pp. 23-24.

Bernese Mountain Dog Club of America. "Draft Test Regulations." April 1991.

Brackett, Lloyd C. "Planned Breeding." Westchester, Ill.: *Dog World Magazine,"* 1961.

Cochrane, Diana. *The Bernese Mountain Dog.* Stratford-on-Avon, Warwickeshire, England. 1982.

Dawson, Mary R. "50th Anniversary of Bernese Mountain Dogs in America 1937 to 1987." *The Alpenhorn.* February 1987, pp. 1-12.

Ettinger, Stephen J., DVM. *Textbook of Veterinary Internal Medicine: Diseases of the Dog and Cat.* W.B. Saunders and Company, 1975.

Evans, Howard E., Ph.D., and Christensen, George C., DVM, MS, Ph.D. *Miller's Anatomy of the Dog* (2nd edition). W.B. Saunders and Company, 1979.

Fisher, Clarence M. (ed.) *The Merck Veterinary Manual* (6th edition). Rahway, N.J.: Merck and Company, Inc., 1986.

Fisher, Gail Tamases, and Volhard, Wendy. "Puppy Personality Profile." New York: Pure-Bred Dogs/*The American Kennel Gazette.* March 1985, pp. 36-42.

Forsyth, Robert and Jane. *The Forsyth Guide to Successful Dog Showing.* New York: Howell Book House, Inc., 1976.

Frankling, Eleanor. *Practical Dog Breeding and Genetics.* New York: Arco Publishing Company, Inc., 1977.

Hill's Pet Products. *Hill's Atlas of Veterinary Clinical Anatomy.* Veterinary Medicine Publishing Company, Inc., 1989, pp. 48-49.

Lanting, Fred L. *Canine Hip Dysplasia and Other Orthopedic Problems.* Loveland, Colo.: Alpine Publications, Inc., 1981.

Rutherford, Clarice, and Neil, David H., MRCVS. *How to Raise a Puppy You Can Live With.* Loveland, Colo.: Alpine Publications, Inc., 1981.

Schweizerischer Klub fur Berner Sennenhunde. Der Berner Sennenhund. Schweizerischer Klub fur Berner Sennenhunde, 1967.

Shadow, Glen. "Bernese Mountain Dogs Take Rapidly to South." San Francisco: *Western Kennel World,* January 1938, p. 4.

Shadow, Hale [brother of Glen Shadow]. "Deer story," received in phone conversation, April 1989.

Simmonds, Jude. *The Complete Bernese Mountain Dog.* New York: Howell Book House, Inc., 1990.

Sinibaldi, Kenneth R. "Ununited Anconeal Process." *Current Techniques in Small Animal Surgery* (2nd edition). Joseph M. Bojrab, DVM, MS, Ph.D., editor. Philadelphia: Lea and Febinger, 1983, pp. 719-720.

Slater, Margaret R., DVM, "Researching Osteochondrosis." New York: *Purebred Dogs/American Kennel Gazette* , December 1988, pp. 66-69.

Sweeney, Sheila (editor). "Is My Puppy Sick?" New York: *Pure-Bred Dogs/American Kennel Gazette,* July 1986, p. 26.

Swiss Club for Bernese Mountain Dogs. Der Berner Sennenhund (English translation by Esther Mueller and Margaret Wilson). The Swiss Club for Bernerse Mountain Dogs, 1971.

Vanderlip, Sharon Lynn. *The Collie: A Veterinary Reference for the Professional Breeder.* Cardiff-by-the-Sea, Cal.: Biotechnical Consultants, 1984, pp. 239-257.

MAGAZINES

The Alpenhorn, Publication of the BMDCA, 1825 Grant Street, Downers Grove, IL 60515

Dog World, Maclean Hunter Publishing, 29 N. Wacker Drive, Chicago, IL 60606-3298

Purebred Dogs, The American Kennel Gazette, 51 Madison Avenue, New York, NY 10010

Dog Fancy, Subscription Department, P.O. Box 53264, Boulder, CO 80322-3264

CLUBS AND ORGANIZATIONS

The American Kennel Club, 51 Madison Avenue, New York, NY 10010

Bernese Mountain Dog Club of America, Ruth Reynolds, 211 E. Fort Road, Greenwood, FL 32443

Bernese Mountain Dog Club of Canada, c/o Tracy Ricard, Secretary, Box 12, Site 9, RR #3, Tofield, Alberta, Canada TOB 4J0

Bernese Club of England, c/o Brenda Griffiths, Marlfield, Redditch, Worchester, England.

REGIONAL BMDC REPRESENTATIVES

Regional Club Council Coordinator
Deborah J. Wilkins, 20560 Huntington Way, Prior Lake, MN 55372, (612) 440-5040 or 440-5041

Chattahoochee Valley BMDC
Ruth Reynolds, P.O. Box 86, Greenwood, FL 32443, (904) 544-1002

BMDC of the Finger Lakes
Joan La Mendola, 6365 E. Bethany Rd., Stafford, NY 14143, (716) 768-4282

Grand Canyon BMDC
Marcia Zuger, 5425 E. Grandview Rd., Scottsdale, AZ 85254

BMDC of Greater Seattle
Suzanne Hostetter, P.O. Box 717, Rochester, WA 98579

BMDC of the Greater Twin Cities
(was Minnesota Boundary Waters Berners) Nancy Mayer, 6333 Hwy. 14 East, Rochester, MN 55904

Heartland BMDC
Opal Newell, 1500 9th Avenue NE, Miami, OK 74354, (918) 542-7761

BMDC of Nashoba Valley
Amy Cohen, 1 Essex Road, Medfield, MA 02052, (508) 359-7030

North Coast BMDC
Larry Plants, 955 Eastlawn Drive, Highland Heights, OH 44143

Pacific Northwest BMDF
Jim and Cheryl Dickson, 8250 Highway 47, Carlton, OR 97111

Potomac Valley BMDC
Kathy Donohew, 16560 Sioux Lane, Gaithersburg, MD 20878

BMDC of the Rockies
Valerie Horney, 11561 E. Dakota Avenue, Aurora, CO 80012, (303) 367-5059 or 534-4160 days

San Francisco Bay Berners
Barbara Packard, 12640 LaCresta Drive, Los Altos Hills, CA 94022

Sierra West BMDC
Michael Rosenbaum, 14 Madona Box 1104, Ross, CA 94957

BMDC of Southeastern Wisconsin
Elizabeth Pearson, 1825 Grant Street, Downers Grove, IL 60515, (708) 852-8850

BMDC of Southern California
Roni Leighty, P.O. Box 52, Newbury Park, CA 91319

Three Rivers BMDC
Debra J. McGuire, 1632 Chislett Street, Pittsburg, PA 15206-1313

NATIONAL CLUBS

BMDC of America
Lori Jodar, President, U.S. 31 North 505, Charlevoix, MI 49720

BMDC of Canada
David Denis, RR 3, Ladysmith BC VOR 2E0, Canada

ABOUT THE AUTHORS

Diane Russ has been a prominent breeder of Bernese Mountain Dogs for more than twenty years. During this time, she has owned or produced under her Buttonwillow Kennel name nearly thirty champions, including four top producers.

She first started her interest in dogs at the age of ten, when she won her first benched show with a Staffordshire Terrier named Bo's Flashing Fawn. She later became a breeder of Labrador Retrievers, until in 1969 she became enamored with Bernese Mountain Dogs at a show in Hemet, California. Her first Berner — and the love of her life — was Zodiac's Fancy v. Sablemate, who came from a litter bred by Harold and Sylvia Howison.

Diane Russ now resides in Athens, Alabama, with her husband, and together they continue the outstanding tradition of Buttonwillow Kennels.

Although new to Bernese Mountain Dogs, Shirle Rogers has for the past fifteen years been an exhibitor of Australian Shepherds in both obedience and breed and has taught obedience for the past five years.

Her interest in Berners covers all areas of their capabilities: conformation, obedience, drafting, and even herding. She currently owns a Berner bitch, Deerpark Kameo, and three Aussies at her home in Alabama.

Author Diane Russ.

INDEX